LONDON
CRIME, DEATH
& DEBAUCHERY

Gin Lane, *probably Hogarth's most famous allegorical image of the excesses of eighteenth-century London.*

LONDON
CRIME, DEATH & DEBAUCHERY

NEIL R. STOREY

SUTTON PUBLISHING

First published in the United Kingdom in 2007 by
Sutton Publishing, an imprint of NPI Media Group Limited
Cirencester Road · Chalford · Stroud · Gloucestershire · GL6 8PE

British Library Cataloguing in Publication Data
A catalogue record for this book is available from the British Library.

ISBN 978-0-7509-4624-7

For Jenny and Andy

Typeset in 10.5/12.5pt Galliard.
Typesetting and origination by
NPI Media Group Limited.
Printed and bound in England.

CONTENTS

Life, Trial, Sentence, and
EXECUTION
Of R. COOPER, for the Murder of Annie Barnham, at Isleworth.

COPY OF VERSES.

Tune, Wife's Dream.

Oh, what is this fate of my poor soul,
As I'm Newgate lay,
To-morrow there now shall I seem meet
The fatal judgment day.
My reason will condemn me,
A slave to die with dread,
Oh, pray for me poor criminal,
When I stand at God's right hand

Robert Cooper is my name,
At his watch did dwell,
Once I stood the same,
And was supported well
I loved my sweetest Annie,
And well I was to blame,
Through all my lot too dearly
Has brought me to the shame.

Oh, my Lord & own Creator,
And be in ...
Before ...
I loved ...
For ...
It is time ...
That I ...
Oh, Robert Cooper, and thy love,
Annie proved false to thee,
You murdered her devoid of thought,
And met with pain ...
...

THE EXECUTION.

Newgate, Monday Morning.

Robert Cooper was executed at 8 o'clock. Great excitement was occasioned amongst all classes by the melancholy event. People generally sympathised with Robert Cooper and evidently quite anticipated the reprieve of Gardner, the city sweep. The evidence against the man was by all believed to have been too slight and circumstantial to demand his death, at any rate, there was a doubt about the case, and people believed that Gardner, in common with others tried for murder, should have had the benefit of that doubt.

It is many years since such excitement existed round the old gallows at Newgate. At midnight thousands had taken their places for the sight. Coarse songs and brutal jokes were freely indulged in. While the morbid crowd indulged themselves after their own fashion outside the dreary prison walls, the minister of religion was with the wretch of culprit—consoling him, and holding out to his troubled spirit the olive branch of peace and hope, fortifying his mind for the long mysterious journey it was doomed so soon & sadly to commence. The Sheriffs having arrived, and Calcraft having finished pinioning the unhappy man, the mournful cavalcade, at eight o'clock, proceeded to the gallows, where Calcraft having adjusted the rope, he was launched into eternity with but few struggles.

THE ISLEWORTH TRAGEDY.

At the Central Criminal Court Robert Cooper was charged with the wilful murder of Anne Barnham.

The learned counsel for the prosecution addressed the jury in a very temperate speech, and the following letter, which was found upon the prisoner, was then put in and read.

"Isleworth, Wednesday Evening.

"I am wretched indeed. I love my dear Annie. Oh, how can I see her night after night with another man, when she bids me she does not go with another man. When I met her at six o'clock on Tuesday morning arm in arm with another, and the little she wore for liquor, and when I accosted her and she did not scarcely notice me, my blood at the moment curdled, my brains were hot with passion, and it was that placed like a raving lion, seeking whom he may devour, I am in virtue, and may the lord have mercy. Oh, I would bear to live home my dearest Annie, that I love better than my own life. I have fallen among headed knees while the tears fell from mine eyes like drops of rain. I've begged time after time for her to be true to me, but she has deserted me, and how can I live when she has trifled with me when she once loved, and who can't on his knees and prayed to his God from his heart to guard her life through her confinement. Dear Annie my heart bleeds for you. I feel you have deceived me, as I once wretched. When I come from the country on Monday and brought you 10s., I asked you to forgive me. You said it was well, that you were glad to see me, and you also kissed me. The remainder of that day we spent together...

... "When I asked you to stop with me till Monday, you said you could not, and I found out you wanted to meet another, and so was the one that you were with on Monday night between twelve and one o'clock. Oh, Annie, my dearest Annie, my sweet Annie, how I love you! and that very day in Brentford park you and I walked affectionately together with our lovely babe in your dear arms. I gave you a sovereign and we were to have visited the Crystal Palace together on Tuesday. Your grandmother told me to come home and have some supper with you, and you told me in the park you would go to bed early, and you promised me a week you would come back to your poor dear Robert, but when I came to supper you told your grandmother to say that you were gone to Twickenham Green, but I myself thought different, soon sudden change came over me, and still the that you were with another, and my steps were directed to Hounslow, and it was there I saw you arm in arm with another, and your wicked mother-in-law, had I not wanted to be true to you. Many a time I had done and done words to you, and my dear, dear Annie, it is her who shall pen Peace too, but of decent from the 5th chapter of Proverbs. I was driven to commit the first deed, and, oh, what an awful thing it is to commit manslaughter but for a Salvation do all you can, and your mother-in-law is the cause of our separation. I have endured for her, and had her come to her. God help, poor Annie! Oh, that I could be in your grave with you, that we would be buried together, but I shall be wretched. I have watched and gazed upon my heart has been breaking to you a long time. I have the world a wretched abort, a way the Lord have to see me, and though the blood. Jesu I have not me.

The reading of this document, which was not signed, closed the case for the prosecution.

It will be remembered that the prisoner has confessed he shot the unfortunate woman at Isleworth, consequently, but little evidence was wanting to prove the fact.

Mr. Best then proceeded to address the jury on behalf of the prisoner. He said he did not wish to say a word against the dead, but on this case he felt he might say that the unfortunate young woman had not been true to the prisoner who certainly regarded her as his wife. He loved her to madness, and but she been true to him, as she professed she was, it would have been well for them both. The learned counsel concluded a very able and feeling address by urging upon the jury the fact that one life had already been sacrificed, and, expressing his conviction that if the jury could do so consistently, they would willingly return a verdict that would have the effect of presenting the fearful spectacle of the sacrifice of the life of the wretched prisoner upon the scaffold.

Baron Martin having summed up the jury, without leaving the box, deliberated for a few minutes, and they then returned a verdict of Guilty of Wilful Murder.

Baron Martin, having put on the black cap most feelingly addressed the prisoner, and then passed sentence of death in the usual form.

The prisoner did not seem at all affected at the result of the trial.

THE CITY TRAGEDY.

Gardner was reprieved on Saturday ...

Samuel Gardner, aged 34, ... at a sweep was sentenced to death at the Central Criminal Court for the murder of his wife, at their residence in Northumberland Court, in the City.

It appears that the condemned man had his wide have led a very unhappy life of late, owing to his having kept a young woman in the house on whom he bestowed his attentions. This young woman had formed an acquaintance with Gardner when her was but fifteen years of age. Her name was then Clarke, but she married a painter named Humbles. She had not been married many months but by she left her husband and returned to Gardner, who installed her into his own house as mistress. Of course continual and some contention existed between Mrs. Gardner and Mrs. Humbles who is now only nineteen years of age. On the morning of the murder he was seen by many persons following his avocations in the usual way. The learning of his wife's death he at once accused Humbles of the murder, she is then accused him. Both were charged with the crime, but by the advice of the Judge who tried this case, Humbles was admitted as a witness against Gardner. Many witnesses were examined, and the result having addressed the jury he was found guilty and sentenced to death. The evidence was slight, and he strongly asserts his innocence.

INTRODUCTION

Here malice, rapine, accident conspire,
And now a rabble rages, now a fire;
Their ambush here relentless ruffians lay,
And here the fell attorney prowls for prey;
Here falling houses thunder on your head,
And here a female atheist talks you dead.

How, when Competitors like these contend,
Can surly Virtue hope to fix a Friend?
Slaves that with serious Impudence beguile,
And lye without a Blush, without a Smile;
Exalt each Trifle, ev'ry Vice adore,
Your Taste in Snuff, your Judgment in a Whore;
Can Balbo's Eloquence applaud, and swear
He gropes his Breeches with a Monarch's Air.

London! The needy villain's gen'ral home
The common sewer of Paris and of Rome;
With eager thirst, by folly or by fate,
Sucks in the dregs of each corrupted state.

From *London: A Poem* by Dr Samuel Johnson (1709–84)

London, our capital, has a universal face as the seat of monarchy, governance, law, fashion and taste; a veritable mirror which reflects the status and power of the greatest modern empire the world had ever seen. It can be truly said that all human life has, in its time, been found in this beating heart of the country; some, curious to the eye by desire, misfortune or affliction have drawn the scrutiny of the populace, others have been received at court or society, while most live or visit invisibly – or do they? Dare we pass though the looking glass to the world hidden behind the grand frontages, high-walled gardens, rookeries, slums or the city after dark, for here may be found crime and debauchery enjoyed, indulged in, designed and created from and for all strata of society?

It has been argued that Jack the Ripper gave birth to the twentieth century; his crimes and the ensuing public fear and panic were broadcast across the country through the burgeoning gutter press and public conversational concern during the Autumn of Terror in 1888. Many eyes were opened for the first time by this media fury to the depravity and depredation suffered by individuals and families in the abyss of London's most poverty stricken areas, but there were wider concerns. Rumours have always abounded of some conspiracy in the Ripper crimes involving the authorities, indeed even 'the highest in the land', but I would suggest it is far more likely the fear was of exposure and damage to members of 'the establishment' who had nothing to do with the murders, but with the media spotlight cast upon the criminal and immoral netherworld which had remained invisible for so long, many of those who had descended from their rich and powerful portals to take a 'walk on the wild side' feared exposure of their penchant for the male or female brothels, unorthodox sexual acts, gambling dens or any one of a host of debauched entertainments.

It is true to say an exhaustive and detailed study of crime, death and debauchery within the capital would require several considerable volumes, so in the spirit of the saucy almanac and list compilers and the writers of the more marginal, grotesque, esoteric and downright horrible accounts of misdeeds, misfortune and misdemeanours I have chosen a cornucopia of salutary tales to illustrate the many faces and forms of crime, death and debauchery in the metropolis up to the 1880s, selecting many from what I consider the heyday of excess in the eighteenth and early nineteenth century when Thief Takers were corrupt and only a small band of law enforcement officers such as the 'Charlies' of the Watch, Thames Water Police and Bow Street Runners attempted to maintain some order in the city, while artists such as Hogarth, Gilray and Rowlandson captured and satirised the excess, debauchery, addiction and human consequences.

Stephen Macdaniel, one of the lesser-known eighteenth-century 'Thief Takers' of London. Just as corrupt as all the others, he died in Newgate Gaol.

Here is another London; a city of coffee shops whose pungent aromas were mingled with displays of curiosities from the human and animal world, some misunderstood, some skilful fakes, some plain rip-offs, some downright weird. A city rife with disease, some epidemic, much of it venereal or caused by unsanitary conditions where the only treatment was to be found in surgery or medicine which frequently walked a thin line between ignorance, quackery and deceit. Here was a darker city where gentleman and ruffian may jostle and gamble together and suffer the same sprays and gobbets of blood at the bear pits, dog or cock fights, but a wrong word, fault in protocol or manners among polite society could result in a challenge to gain satisfaction in a duel.

We meet people who would have remained invisible, and probably wish they had remained so, if they had not gained notoriety through being caught and punished for their misdeeds, or untimely or unusual demise. Here is a London with the most infamous prisons and punishments for those who transgressed the laws of the land that, in the early nineteenth century, saw over 200 offences punishable by death. Of course, unless you were particularly notorious, your death would not have been alone; ten, fifteen or twenty people at a time could be seen regularly on the 'triple tree', all swinging 'gallows apples' dancing the 'piss hornpipe' as the knot grew tight around their necks and their lives slipped away – if they were lucky the hangman would swing on their legs to hasten them on their way. Thousands would mass around Tyburn and later Newgate to watch the executions, with plenty of food and drink on offer the occasion of public execution was described as 'one of the greatest entertainments of London.' But in a city of hospitals and medical schools, whether you met your end on the scaffold or not, death and burial was often far from your final rest.

Join me in this volume to walk some of those dank, dark pathways buried in the polite history of the past, scratch the surface and squeeze out some of the corruption and, if you dare, peek through the keyhole at the London of crime, death and debauchery but be wary and perhaps take with you this prayer oft quoted in the sermons of the City:

From lightning and tempest; from plague, pestilence and famine;
From battle and murder, and from sudden death:
Good Lord, deliver us.
(The Book of Common Prayer)

Neil R. Storey
2007

ONE

THE NOTORIOUS & NEFARIOUS

THE CATHEDRAL OF SIN

In 1553 St Paul's Cathedral was treated like an exchange by and for the lower echelons of society in London. The Common Council of London found it necessary to pass an Act whereby horses and mules were prohibited from being led through the cathedral and Queen Elizabeth I had to pass another law forbidding swords to be drawn within the sacred walls. The walls were plastered with advertising posters and acted as a hiring place for all manner of servants. In 1628 Bishop Earle lashed out;

> Paul's Walk is the land's epitome . . . the noise is like that of bees . . . a kind of still roar. It is the general mint of all famous lies . . . It is the thieves' sanctuary, who rob more safely in the crowd than a wilderness, whilst every searcher is a bush to hide them. It is the other expense of the day, after plays, tavern and a bawdy-house; and men still have some oaths left to swear here.

SCHOOL FOR SCOUNDRELS

In 1585 Stow recorded the story of a man named Wotton who 'kept an academy for the education and perfection of pickpockets and cut purses' set up in an alehouse at Smart's Quay near Billingsgate. Here he trained groups of young boys in the art of one two devices, a pocket and a purse hung about with hawk's bells with a little sacring bell over the top. The purse had silver in it, the pocket counter. Once boys had been trained and mastered the art of quickly removing the contents without causing the bells to make any noise, they were adjudged a judicial 'nypper' (a cut purse).

MOLL CUTPURSE

Probably the most notorious of the London 'nyppers' was Mary Markham, alias Frith, and better known to history as Moll Cutpurse. Born in 1585 she began at an early age working the old street thief standard scheme with two others, one called 'bulk' created an obstruction, Moll the 'file' cut the purse and handed it to a third named the 'rub' who would run off with it. She wore male attire for the first time as a bet in 1612 but was brought before an ecclesiastical court for this 'offence' and was ordered to do penance at the door of St Paul's Cathedral. Having atoned for the offence she decided to wear male clothes ever after. She became an adept swordswoman and bold rider, ideal skills for her next criminal adventures in the guise of highwayman, during which her most notable robbery was the time she relieved the parliamentary general Thomas Fairfax of 200 gold jacobuses on Hounslow Heath. Moll was often in and out of the city compters, Bridewell and Newgate, and was branded on the hand as a thief on four occasions. Having had a brush with the gallows Moll set herself up in

See here the Prefideſſe o'th pilfring Trade
Mercuryes ſecond;Venus's onely Mayd
Doublet and breeches in a Uniform dreſſe
The FemaleHumurriſt a Kickſhaw meſſe
Heres no attraction that your fancy greets
But if her FEATURES pleaſe not read her FEATS..

*Mary Markham, alias Frith –
better known as Moll Cutpurse,
the most notorious London
'nypper'.*

business on Fleet Street as a negotiator between thieves and the public to enable the recovery, at a price, of stolen items. In later life she earned a fairly honest trade training and exhibiting a variety of exotic animals, and was said to have been the first English woman to smoke tobacco; an illustration of her in male attire puffing away on her pipe appears in Middleton's play *Roaring Girl*, in which Moll figures as the principal character. It was said in her lifetime she had amassed and spent a fortune. Moll died of dropsy in 1659.

YULETIDE THIEVERY

On Christmas Day in 1611 as King James, Queen Anne, the Duke of York and several nobility were receiving the sacrament in the Chapel Royal at Whitehall a Mr Dubbleday spotted a stranger in their midst. Observing the man hovering suspiciously near a Mr Barrie and then moving to leave, Dubbleday went to Barrie and enquired if he had lost anything. Barrie said he had not, but instinctively feeling for his purse which contained some 40*s*, discovered it was gone. The two men quickly caught up with the stranger and arrested him. Upon searching the man the very same purse was found secreted about his person. The man gave his name as John Selman, upon enquires being made it was discovered he was a notorious 'nypper and foyster' (a nypper was a cut purse and a foyster was a pickpocket). Selman paid for his audacity, he was found guilty of his crimes and was executed between Charing Cross and the Court Gate on 7 January 1612.

Selman the cutpurse.

MULL'D SACK

John Cottington had been a petty criminal and pickpocket since about the age of about thirteen when he ran away from being bound an apprentice and climbing boy to a chimneysweep. He became notorious after the English Civil War when he and a number of others who fought for the Royalist cause took to the road as highwaymen. He claimed he was continuing the fight by attacking wealthy Parliamentarians. A successful criminal, he was nicknamed Mull'd Sack after the drink he favoured. When he was in funds, he was said to have stolen goods 'almost enough to have built St Paul's Cathedral.' One of his most notorious exploits was the robbery of Lady Fairfax, wife of the General. As she arrived at St Martin's Church, Ludgate members of his gang swiftly and discreetly removed the axle pin of her carriage causing it to collapse. Dressed as a gentleman, Cottington stepped forward, apparently to help her ladyship but in the process he cut her watchchain and made off with a gold watch set with diamonds. After numerous narrow escapes his luck ran out when he killed a man in the course of a robbery and fled to the continent. Instead of joining the Royalists there he could not resist the theft of £1,500 of plate and made his way back to England, where he was arrested and hanged at Smithfield Rounds in 1656.

Mull'd Sack.

THE GENTLEMAN OF THE ROAD

One character beyond all others helped create the image of 'the gentleman of the road', his name was Claude Duval. Born in Normandy, he was an ardent Royalist and travelled to London at the Restoration of Charles II in 1660. Tiring of this lifestyle, he sought the adventure of life as a highwaymen, particularly favouring Blackheath and Hounslow Heath. He was always mannered and well dressed as he presented his pistol and demanded the occupants of the coach to 'stand and deliver.' His most notorious exploit was when he led his gang to hold up a coach which they knew to be carrying booty of £400. In the coach was a 'a knight, his lady and only one serving maid.' To show she was not afraid, the lady took a Flageolet out of her pocket and played, Duval played also. The coachman and the occupants knew the purpose of these men and fearing for their lives knew they had better stop and attempt to humour the highwaymen. Then Duval gentlemanly assisted the lady out and they danced the Coranto most elegantly under the circumstances. Afterwards he relieved the passengers of their money and valuables.

Duval was finally captured while drunk at the Hole-in-the-Wall tavern in Chandos Street, near Covent Garden, and was hanged on 21 January 1670. His body was displayed surrounded with suitable funeral impedimenta at the Tangier Tavern, St Giles. Many of the fashionable ladies of the day came to see the rugged highwayman; they wore masks but is was said tears could be seen upon their cheeks. His funeral was held at St Paul's Church, Covent Garden, where he was buried under the epitaph,

> Here lies Duval. Reader, if Male thou art,
> Look to thy purse: if female to your heart.
> Much havoc has he made of both, for all
> Men he made stand, and women he made fall.
> The second Conqueror of the Norman race,
> Knights to his arms did yield, and Ladies to his face.
> Old Tyburn's Glory: England's illustrious thief,
> Duval, the Ladies' joy; the Ladies' grief.

WANTED!

Some of the earliest public appeals for wanted criminals date back to the first newspapers and periodicals of the seventeenth century. This one dates from 1680:

> Whereas one John Stuart, of a tall stature, black brows, a wart upon his cheek, in a black periwig, and a tawny or black suit, and campaign coat, has been lately intrusted to sell several pieces of black worstead, crapes, hair chamblets, black philemot, and sky-coloured mohairs, watered and unwatered; with which goods he is run away, and cannot yet be heard of. Whoever gives notice of the man and goods (who, it is thought, is gone towards Ireland) to Mr Howard, Milk Street Market shall have 40s reward.

DICK TURPIN

The one name still associated with highwaymen is, of course, Dick Turpin. In reality he was a merciless and desperate criminal, far removed from the image of folk hero attached to him since his death. In 1737, Turpin shot dead a man who attempted to

Stand and deliver!

capture him at Epping Forest, a reward was offered and the Secretary of State made this proclamation:

> It having been represented to the king that Richard Turpin did, on Wednesday 4 May last, barbarously murdered Thomas Morris, servant of Henry Thompson, one of the keepers of Epping Forest, and commit other notorious felonies and robberies near London, his majesty is pleased to promise his most gracious pardon to any of his accomplices, and a reward of two hundred pounds to any person or persons, that shall discover him, so that he may be apprehended and convicted. Turpin was born at Thaxted in Essex, is about thirty, by trade a butcher, about five feet nine inches high, very much marked with small-pox, his cheek-bones broad, his face thinner towards the bottom, his visage short, pretty upright, and broad about the shoulders.

TYPES OF RIVER CRIMINALS

River criminals in the seventeenth, eighteenth and nineteenth centuries could be divided into distinctive gangs each with their own methods. 'River Pirates' were always heavily armed with sword, pistol and dagger. They specialised in cutting lighters adrift at night and plundering them when they ran aground. 'Heavy Horsemen' were dishonest porters and labourers who handled ships cargoes. They would throw goods overboard at high tide for the 'Mud Larks' to collect at low tide. Criminally inclined watermen were 'Night Plunderers' who either robbed their passengers while on the river or dropped the unsuspecting visitor to London at a dock where their confederates ashore, known as 'Scuffle Hunters', laid in wait to rob the poor soul. At their height in the late eighteenth and early nineteenth centuries such criminal activity cost the merchants and Government as much as £800,000 a year.

THAMES RIVER PIRATES

The *Annual Register* dated 6 June 1770 recorded that 'Between 11 and 12 o'clock at night three gentlemen and two ladies returning from Vauxhall by water, were boarded by six men who had their faces covered with black crape about 200 yards above Westminster Bridge who demanded their money without any hesitation or they would throw them overboard. They took from the company near £20 besides two watches, and immediately rowed up the river.'

WHO GOES HOME?

At the conclusion of every sitting of Parliament the door-keepers throw open the doors and the cry goes up 'Who goes Home?'. Now a signal for adjournment, this call harks back to when the streets of London were not policed by a formal force but rather watchmen or 'Charlies.' Every pedestrian was vulnerable to attack on the streets of London so many MPs were not inclined to travel home alone and set forth in groups attended by men bearing torches. On similar lines a bell was rung nightly in Kensington Gardens to warn homeward bound promenaders to gather together in large parties to defy attacks from footpads.

THE THIEF-TAKER GENERAL

Jonathan Wild is first recorded as having been thrown into the Wood Street Compter for debt in the early eighteenth century. It was here he formed a relationship with Mary Molyneaux, a prostitute and pickpocket. He also learned much about the criminal underworld of London. When released he found work with Charles Hitchen, an Under Marshal in the City of London. They soon found they could earn well from taking bribes from criminals, prostitutes' brothels and tavern keepers to turn a blind eye when necessary but by far their most successful scam was to meet with criminal gangs and fence stolen goods. Wild also 'kept his hand in' as a thief in his own right and even established a school for pickpockets. He set up an office in Cock Alley where those who had been robbed could come to see if Wild and his team could trace their stolen goods. Of course he knew the criminal gangs and could pay a far greater price for the goods than they would have ever received on the street. Wild then earnt his profit in his charges for services locating and returning the goods. Often the thieves would uncover incriminating letters which enabled Wild to conduct a lucrative sideline in blackmail. Wild also protected his suppliers by bribing court officials and prosecution witnesses; if this failed there was always intimidation. Before the days of the police the City authorities turned a blind eye to the conduct of Wild, he was the next best thing to a police force, albeit a corrupt one. Business was brisk and he moved to larger premises at the King's Head, ironically, in Old Bailey. Not only did be become the Thief-Taker General but to be honest he was the Thief General too, any thief who crossed him would simply be served up to the authorities on a plate, and most ended up on the gallows. His hold over London was not to last forever and

Invitation to the execution of
Jonathan Wild, Thief-Taker General,
24 May 1725.

tolerance of his behaviour waned with time. His demise began after a quarrel between Wild, a thief named Edwards and Roger Johnson, a highwayman. Wild took the side of Johnson so Edwards informed on them both by telling the authorities of how Wild had assisted Johnson escape from a constable. Wild was sent to Newgate; this sent a shockwave through the underworld, many feared for their own skin, many wanted to kick the powerful Wild when he was down and the accusations and information against him poured in to the authorities. Acquitted at his first trial, Wild was finally caught out over a deal with a Mrs Stetham where he had said he would recover a piece of lace worth 10 guineas which had been stolen from her. At his first trial it was made apparent he knew Kelly and Murphy, the men who had stolen the lace from Mrs Stetham, but had not taken any action nor did he give evidence against them. Under the 1719 Act he should not have taken the 'reward' and was thus convicted of the crime and sentenced to death.

On the night before his execution Wild tried to take his own life in the condemned cell by swallowing laudanum, it did not kill him and he was still stupefied when he was carted to Tyburn on 24 May 1725. It was said no greater concourse of people ever lined the route nor packed the stalls and ground around the gallows as to observe the hanging of the Thief-Taker General, they were said to number in their tens of thousands. Some cheered him but most shouted abuse and pelted his cart like a pillory as Wild passed. After he had been swung Wild's wife managed to obtain possession of the body and it was buried quietly in St Pancras churchyard. But the location of the grave was betrayed to a surgeon who paid for the information and had the body removed. Flayed of its skin and muscle (these were dumped in the Thames) the bones were removed and kept in a private collection. These bones were rediscovered in 1847 and were presented to the Royal College of Surgeons.

SLIPPERY JACK SHEPPARD

One of the legendary figures of London's criminal past, John Sheppard was born in Spitalfields in 1702. Trained as a carpenter, Sheppard frequented the Black Lion tavern on Drury Lane, a notorious hostelry of harlots and criminals. He soon fell in with a crowd of prostitutes, especially Elizabeth Lyon, a girl known to most as Edgeworth Bess. She persuaded the agile 5ft 4ins Sheppard that he could be far more adept at being a house burglar and he was soon co-opted into one of Jonathan Wild's 'tame' gangs. It was at this time Bess had been thrown into St Giles roundhouse for stealing a gold ring. Sheppard went to visit her but was denied admission by the beadle. Without another thought Sheppard knocked him to the ground, broke open the door and carried off Bess. This was to be the first of Jack's legendary gaol breaks. On the run from the authorities they joined with Jack's brother, Thomas, and carried out more robberies from houses, they were also joined in their gang by Charles Grace and Anthony Lamb. After the arrest and transportation of Lamb and Jack's brother Thomas, they worked with Joseph 'Blueskin' Blake and added highway robbery to their criminal cannon. Over the ensuing years Sheppard was caught on a number of occasions, each time he escaped, including a return visit to St Giles' Round House where he got out through the roof. When in Clerkenwell Prison, Sheppard was in the same cell as Bess, he filed off his leg irons, broke a hole in the wall and having fabricated a rope by tieing their sheets and blankets together, they descended the 25ft into the yard of the adjoining Bridewell, climbed the 22ft yard wall and escaped.

Most notoriously, Sheppard broke out of Newgate while under sentence of death, on more than one occasion. On 30 August 1724 Bess and one of her confederates, Poll Maggot, visited Jack in Newgate and he broke through the door hatch and ran off to hide in a Finchley alehouse. Someone informed the authorities of his hiding place and Jack was returned again to Newgate. This time he was placed in handcuffs and their heaviest irons, and chained to the floor of the most secure cell, known as 'the castle'. Sheppard found an old nail, fashioned a picklock and let himself out of the handcuffs and fixings to the floor. With his leg irons still on, he climbed up the chimney to the roof, got into the chapel then onto the chapel roof and then descended to free ground by means of a blanket rope. But rather than flee the city, Sheppard became arrogant. He burgled a pawnbrokers and stole the clothes, jewellery and even a sword to affect the air of a gentleman, and walked the streets of London in what he considered a disguise and basked in the tales of his daring escapes. He was, however, recognised and brought back to Newgate and this time they took no chances, weighing him down with cuffs, chains and irons weighing a total of 300lbs. Members of the public flocked to see the legendary Slippery Jack and paid the gaolers handsomely for the privilege. Sheppard's execution was now imminent but he had plans. He secreted a small knife with the intention of cutting the noose but this was detected when he left the prison on the fatal morning of 16 November 1724. But all was not lost, his allies in the crowd were primed to rush forward when he was 'turned off' to dangle on the noose; it would be assumed they were to be coming to swing on his legs to speed his demise, but in fact they would hold him up and cut off the noose. The problem was that Sheppard was a hero. Many came to cheer him and threw flowers rather than dung at the cart which carried him to Tyburn. Such were the numbers who came to witness the execution, Sheppard's supporters (in every way) could not run through the crowd fast enough to save him, but Jack's body was saved from the surgeons. He was taken to the Barley Mow Tavern in Long Acre where a doctor was waiting to attempt to revive him but to no avail. Jack was finally laid to rest in the churchyard of St Martin's in the Fields, he was just twenty-three years old.

'Slippery Jack' Sheppard in the condemned cell, Newgate, 1724.

GAY WORDS FOR LINCOLN FIELDS

For many years Lincoln's Inn Fields had a terrible reputation for all manner of street criminals. In the early eighteenth century Gay wrote:

> Where Lincoln's Inn, wide space is rail'd around,
> Cross not with virtuous step; there is oft step; there oft is found
> The lurking thief, who, while the daylight shone,
> Made the walls echo with his begging tone:
> That critch, which late compassion mov'd, shall wound
> Thy bleeding head, and thee to the ground.
> Though thou art tempted by the linkman's call,
> Yet trust him not along the lonely wall;
> In the mid-way he'll quench the flaming brand,
> And share the booty with the pilfering band.
> Still keep the public streets where oily rays
> Shot from the crystal lamp o'erspread the ways.

THE ST GILES ROOKERY

The most infamous resort of criminals in London was the Rookery otherwise known as the 'Holy Land.' The Rookery, partly demolished to make way for New Oxford Street covered, in total, an area from what is today Great Russell Street, south to Long Acre, with Drury Lane and Charing Cross Road. Most of the buildings in this infamous area were in abysmal condition, truly one of the worst slums of London it was described in 1851 as 'Rows of crumbling houses flanked by courts and alleys . . . squalid children . . . haggard men with long, uncombed hair . . . women without shoes or stockings . . . wolfish looking dogs, decayed vegetables strewing the pavement, low public houses.' Few had an unbroken window pane in them; bent and bowed with age, most of the houses here dated from the seventeenth and eighteenth centuries. When Dickens was escorted around the site with a police officer, he wrote his observations of the people 'men and women, in every variety of scanty and dirty apparel, lounging, scolding, drinking, smoking, squabbling, fighting and swearing. W.A. Miles added the 'population existing in all the filth attendant upon improvidence, crime and profligacy, as if the inhabitants by common consent deem themselves only "tenants at will" until the gallows or the hulks should require them.' Amid this warren of passageways the streets were so narrow in places men would have to turn sideways to pass through. Most of the houses in Buckeridge Street were lodging-houses habitually occupied by thieves, prostitutes and cadgers. The rooms were crowded; fourteen women were often crowded into a single cellar at 3d a night, 4d would be paid for the upper rooms but they were still overcrowded with as many as sixteen people crammed into a 12ft by 6ft room. District Lodging House Inspector Hunt recalled 'Many lay on loose straw littered on the floor, their heads to the wall and their feet to the centre, and decency was entirely unknown among them'. If a man was a stranger to the City or had been picked up when he was drunk and taken there by a prostitute, 'When they had plundered the poor dupe he was ejected without ceremony by the others who resided in the room; often without a coat or hat, sometimes without his trousers, and occasionally left on the staircase as naked as he was born.' This 'lawless kasbah' was riddled with escape routes, hidey-holes and runs that ran from house to house by roof, yard and cellar. In other instances escape routes

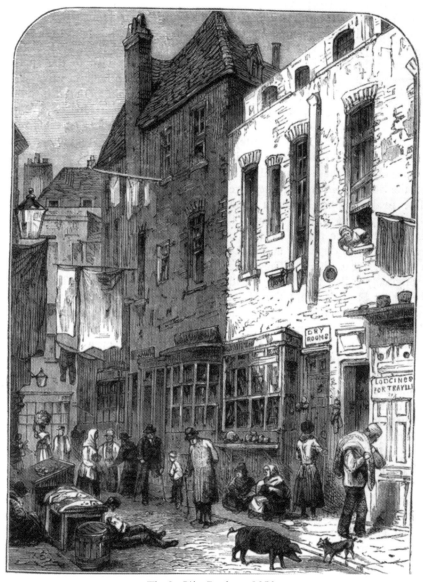

The St Giles Rookery, 1850.

from one back window to another by means of large spiked nails, one row to hold by, and another for the feet to rest on. Traps were set in case a policeman decided to chase after the criminal who fled to the Rookery. Sewage pits were deliberately disguised to trap the unwary, other cellars had holes just two foot square, low in their walls, no policemen would have dared the continue pursuit along these on hands and knees in the dark. If police did need to enter the Rookery to arrest someone they would come in force with reinforcements on stand by. Police officers would be met with a hail of abuse, stones, mud and pots of effluent, then, 'directly a panic is created, men, women and boys my be seen scrambling in all directions through the back yards and over party walls, to affect an escape.'

CRIMINAL TYPES

The experiences of the Newgate Prison schoolmaster published in *Frasers Magazine* in 1832 were accompanied by his *Classification of Rogues* or *Principal Actors in Criminality* which stated their crime and the vulgar street parlance by which the crimnal type would be known viz;

> Housebreakers – Cracksmen, pannymen
> Highwaymen and Footpads – Grand-tobymen or spicemen
> Coiners – Bitmen
> Utterers of base metal – smashers
> Pickpockets – Buzzmen, elyfakers, conveyancers
> Stealers of goods and money from shops etc. – Sneaks
> Snatchers of reticules, watches etc. – Grabbers
> Horse and Cattle Stealers – Prad-chervers
> Women and men who waylay inebriate persons for the purpose of robbery – Ramps
> Receivers of stolen goods – Fences
> Forgers – Fakers
> Embezzlers – Bilkers
> Swindlers of every description, among which are – Macers, duffers and ring-droppers
> Stealing from carts and carriages of all kinds – Dragsmen
> To which my be added, all kinds of plundering on the river and its banks
> On board shipping, barges etc. – Light Housemen, heavy-horsemen, game watermen, do. Lightermen, scuffle-hunters, copemen etc.

AN OBSERVER'S GUIDE TO THE PICKPOCKET

Published in the *Mirror* 1832: 'The qualifications for a pickpocket are a light tread, a delicate sense of touch, combined with firm nerves. These boys may be known by their shoes in the street; they generally wear pumps, or shoes of very light make, having long quarters. There is about their countenance an affected determination of purpose, and they walk forward, as if bent on some object of business: it is a rule with them never to stop in the street. When they want to confer for a moment they drop into some by-court or alley, where they will fix on an object of attack, as the people pass down a main street; when they start off in the same manner, the boy going first, to do what they call 'stunning,' that is to pick the pocket. The first rate hands never, on any occasion, loiter in the streets, unless at a procession or any exhibition, when there is an excuse for so doing. Many have a notion that instruments are used in disencumbering the pockets: this is a false idea; the only instrument they use is a pair of small scissors, and which will always be found on the person of a pickpocket when searched; these they use to cut the pocket and all off when they cannot abstract its contents. To these qualifications they unite a quick sight, and a tact of observing when the attention is engaged, or of devising some means to engage it themselves, until the act is done. They are most busy in foggy weather . . . Pickpockets are the least faithful to each other of all known rogues, and are the most difficult of all biped animals to tame, or make anything of in the way of improvement when caught.'

THE FIRST GREAT TRAIN ROBBERY

On the night of 15 May 1855 three London firms despatched three boxes of gold to the then value of £12,000 via Messrs. Chaplin & Co. Carriers for Paris. Each box was securely made of wood, bound with iron hoops. The route they were to be taken was from London Bridge station (South Eastern Railway), via Folkestone and Boulogne, for Paris. After being weighed and sealed at the carrier's office the boxes were taken to the station where they were placed in iron travelling safes secured with two Chubb patent locks. The keys for the safes were then entrusted to the care of railway staff in London, Folkestone and the Captain of the cross channel steamer, *Lord Warden* that was to take the boxes to France.

When *Lord Warden* docked in Boulogne the boxes were removed from the safes and weighed. There was no sign of any interference on the boxes and no suspicions were aroused. Conveyed to Paris, when the France officials opened the boxes they were found to contain nothing more than lead shot! The Metropolitan, South Eastern Railway and French Police forces launched an extensive investigation into the theft and the embarrassed South Eastern Railway offered a substantial reward. Little progress was made and just as it appeared the trail of any suspects had gone cold an exchange of letters between Edward Agar, a prisoner recently placed in Newgate for cheque fraud and Fanny Kay the mother of his illegitimate child aroused suspicion. The letter had mentioned William Pierce, a former railway employee, had been supposed to pay her £7,000 but she had received none of it. This led to suspicions and soon, Mr Rees, one of the leading investigators on behalf of the South Eastern Railway, met with Fanny Kay and went to visit Agar who was then on the prison hulk at Portland.

Agar told his story of how he met William Pierce, a ticket printer and how they had discussed the viability of stealing gold passing between London and Paris. Pierce set about observing the transport operation to look for criminal chances but concluded it would have been impossible without copies of the safe keys by co-opting train car guard James Burgess and station master William Tester. By a variety of devious means and abuse of trust they had made wax impressions and copied keys. Once these were in their possession all they had to do was wait for a large shipment of gold. Burgess altered the rota of guards to ensure that he was the guard; Agar and Pierce then bought two first class tickets to Dover. They hid the lead shot in carpet bags and saw to it that a porter placed them in the guards van. As soon as the train was moving Agar slipped into the guard's van with Burgess inside. Agar opened the safes and boxes, replaced the gold with the lead, resealed the boxes and locked the safes again. There was nothing untoward seen by railway authorities at Dover as the boxes were moved to the steamer and the thieves recovered the carpet bags from Burgess and discreetly made their way back to London.

In November 1856 Pierce and Burgess were located and arrested in London. Tester had obtained a position as a general manager for Swedish Railways but was arrested when he returned to visit relatives. The robbers were brought to the Old Bailey in January 1857. The main witnesses were Agar and Kay and on 12 January Burgess and Tester were sentenced to fourteen years transportation and Pierce, two years for larceny.

THE REAL FAGIN

Ikey Solomons began his criminal life as a pickpocket who was sentenced to transportation after being caught stealing a pocket book containing £40 from a gentleman in the crowd at an election meeting in Westminster Hall. He was never to

Isaac 'Ikey' Solomons.

face the journey abroad and spent six years on a prison hulk. When he was discharged he was soon working on the wrong side of the law as a receiver of stolen goods and money launderer. His reputation rapidly spread and his house on Ten Bells Lane, Spitalfields was soon 'looked upon as the universal resort of all the thieves of the metropolis.' Ikey managed to evade capture from this house when the police raided it in 1826 only to be arrested in Islington a few months later in 1827. His room was said to contain a 'coachful' of stolen property. He escaped from the hackney coach taking him to trial but the rest of his family were tried and found guilty of handling stolen goods. His wife Ann was sentenced to fourteen years' transportation, Ikey also joined them later. Dickens undoubtedly saw the tall and slender Ikey as an ideal basis of his notorious character, Fagin, in *Oliver Twist*.

CHARLIE PEACE, MASTER CRIMINAL

Peace was the most notorious burglar of his day. Born in Sheffield he was an adept and habitual burglar and a skilled musician. His violin seldom filled his case as he used it to carry his burglar's tools, some of which he made or improvised himself such as his fold-away ladder. Between 1851 and 1872 he spent a total of sixteen years at Her Majesty's Pleasure within such illustrious walls at Millbank, Pentonville, Dartmoor and Portland. In 1876 he shot and killed PC Nicholas Cock when he was disturbed

Charlie Peace hurls himself from a train in a last desperate attempt to escape from the gallows.

during a robbery at Whalley Range, Manchester. Peace was married and settled in his native Sheffield but became obsessed with his neighbour, Mrs Katherine Dyson. She had an affair with Peace but he became persistent and made threats with a firearm. When the Dysons saw a police warrant was issued against him, Peace fled to Hull. The Dysons moved to Banner Cross but Peace turned up on their new doorstep one night. Sent away by Arthur Dyson shortly afterwards Peace waylaid her at gunpoint; Arthur Dyson intervened but the fracas ended up with him being shot by Peace, who then quickly made his escape again. Peace was finally brought to law when he was challenged by PC Edward Robinson while he was burgling a house in Blackheath on 10 October 1878. Peace fired five shots at Robinson, only one hit the constable, but the wound to Robinson's arm did not stop him overpowering the burglar and Peace was in custody but under one of his aliases, John Thompson. Tried and found guilty of the attempted murder of PC Robinson at the Old Bailey, Peace was sent to Pentonville, a prison where his true identity was soon revealed. While under escort aboard a train to Leeds to face trial for the Banner Cross murder, Peace made one last gambit and flung himself out of the window. The warders stopped the train and searched up the tracks for a mile before they found him unconscious, having landed on his head. Tried at Leeds, it took the jury just twelve minutes to find Peace guilty. While in the condemned cell he turned to God and spent a long while in prayer with the chaplain, to whom he confessed to the murder of PC Cock. Peace was hanged at Armley Gaol on 25 February 1879.

TWO

THE CRIMINALS OF LONDON

In the 1790s Patrick Colquhoun, twice Lord Provost of Glasgow and the leading magistrate of the Worship Street Office compiled his controversial *Treatise on the Police of the Metropolis* in which he presented his arguments with an impressive array of statistics, commentary and analysis. In the volume are the Estimates of Persons who are supposed to support themselves in and near the Metropolis by pursuits either criminal-illegal-or immoral.

1. Professed Thieves, Burglars, Highway Robbers, Pick-pockets and River Pirates, who are completely corrupted – many of whom have finished their education in the Hulks, and some at Botany Bay:

NB: There will be a considerable increase of this class on the return of Peace, now estimated at about: 2,000

2. Professed and known Receivers of Stolen Goods (of who eight or ten are opulent):
                                                                                                                                              60

3. Coiners, Colourers, Dealers, Venders, Buyers, and Utterers of base Money, including counterfeit Foreign and East India Coin: 3,000

4. Thieves, Pilferers, and Embezzlers who live partly by depradation, and partly by their occasional labour: 8,000

5. River Pilferers, viz Fraudulent Lumpers, Scuffle-hunters, Mudlarks, Lightermen, Riggers, Articifers and Labourers in the Docks and Arsenals: 2,500

6. Itinerant Jews, wandering from street to street, holding out temptations to pilfer and steal, and Jew Boys crying Bad Shillings, who purchase articles stolen by Servants, Stable Boys, etc: generally paying in bad money: 2,000

7. Receivers of stolen goods, from petty pilferers, at Old Iron Shops, Store Shops, Rug and Thrumb Shops abd Shops for Second-Hand Apparel, including some fraudulent Hostlers, small Butchers and Pawn-Brokers: 4,000

8. A class of suspicious Characters, who live partly by pilfering and passing Base Money – ostensibly Costard Mongers, Ass Drivers, Dustmen, Chimney Sweepers, Rabbit Sellers, Fish and Fruit Sellers, Fish and Fruit Sellers, Flash Coachmen, Bear Baiters, Dog Keepers (but in fact dog stealers etc, etc):   1,000

9. Persons in the character of menial Servants, Journey-men, Warehouse porters, and under-Clerks, who are entrusted with property, and who defraud their employers in a little way, under circumstances where they generally elude detection: 3,000

10. A class of Swindlers, Cheats and low Gamblers, composed of idle and dissolute Characters, who have abandoned every honest pursuit, and who live chiefly by fraudulent transactions in the Lottery; as Morocco Men, Ruffians, Bludgeon Men, Clerks, and Assistants during the season; who at other times assume the trade of Duffers, Hawkers and Pedlars, Horse Dealers, Gamblers with E.O. Tables at Fairs, Utterers of Base Money, Horse Stealers etc.   7,440

11. Various other classes of Cheats, not included in the above: 1,000

12. Fraudulent and dissolute Publications who are connected with Criminal People, and who, to accommodate, their companions in iniquity, allow their houses to be rendez-vous for Thieves, Swindlers, and Dealers in Base Money: 1,000

13. A class of inferior Officers belonging to the Customs and Excise, including what are called Supernumaries and Glutmen; many of whom connive at pillage as well as Frauds committed on the Revenue, and share in the plunder to a very considerable extent, principally for their inability to support themselves on the pittance allowed to them in salary: 1,000

14. A numerous class of Persons who keep Chandler's Shops for the sale of provisions, tea and other necessaries to the poor. The total number is estimated at ten thousand in the Metropolis, a certain proportion of whom, as well as small Butchers and others, are known to cheat their customers (especially those to whom they give a little credit) by false weights, for which, excepting in the parish of Mary-le-bone, there is no proper check: 3,500

15. Servants, male and female, Porters, Hostlers, Stable Boys, and Post Boys, etc. out of place principally for ill behaviour and loss of character, whose means of living excite suspicions at all times, about: 10,000

16. Persons called Black Legs, and others proselytised to the passion of Gaming, or pursuing it as trade, who are in the constant habit of frequenting houses opened for the express purposes of play: 2,000

17. Spendthrifts-Rakes-Giddy Young Men inexperienced and in the pursuit of criminal pleasures – Profligate, loose and dissolute Characters, vitiated themselves, and in the daily practice of seducing others to intemperance, lewdness, debauchery, gambling and excess: estimated at: 3,000

18. Foreigners who live chiefly by gambling: 500

19. Bawds who keep houses of ill Fame, Brothels, Lodging-Houses for Prostitutes: 2,000

Prostitutes who had a good sideline pickpocketing clients and dupes divide their spoils.

20. Unfortunate Females of all descriptions, who support themselves chiefly or wholly by prostitution: 50,000

21. Strangers out of work who have who have wandered up to London in search of employment, and without recommendation, generally in consequence of some misdemeanour committed in the Country; at all times above: 1,000

22. Strolling Minstrels, Ballad Singers, Show-Men, Trumpeters, and Gipsies: 1,500

23. Grubbers, Gin-drinking and dissolute Women and destitute Boys and Girls, wandering and prowling about in the streets and by-places after Chips, Nails, Old Metals, Broken Glass, Paper, Twine, etc. etc., who are constantly on the watch to pilfer when an opportunity offers: 2,000

24. Common Beggars and Vagrants asking alms, supposing one to every two streets:
                                                                                                              3,000

THREE

MATTERS OF HONOUR

A MEMORY OF CHAUCER

One of the earliest records of a matter of honour occurred when Chaucer was a student at the Middle Temple during the reign of Edward III. The man who was to go on to write *Canterbury Tales* was insulted by a Franciscan friar in Fleet Street and responded by giving the monk 'a sound thrashing.'

THE DEATH OF MARLOWE

Christopher 'Kit' Marlowe (1564–1593) was a translator, poet of notable blank verse and, above all a dramatist of such a calibre he is arguably the foremost tragedian of his day before Shakespeare. Few realise he was also an active member of the Elizabethan intelligence service and a spy. In early May 1593 a number of scurrilous bills signed with the name 'Tamburlaine' threatening Protestant refugees from France and the Netherlands were posted around London. The text thereon included a number of allusions to the plays of Kit Marlowe. On 11 May the Privy Council ordered the arrest of those responsible for the pamphlets. A certain Thomas Kyd, a colleague of Marlowe was arrested. During a search of Kyd's lodgings a fragment of an old heretical tract, quite unconnected with the recent bills, was discovered. Taken for further questioning, and quite probably tortured, Kyd claimed the piece actually belonged to Marlowe. Arrested on charges of heresy Marlowe was brought before the Privy Council on 20 May. In spite of *prima facie* evidence Marlowe was ordered to 'give his daily attendance on their Lordships, until he shall be licensed to the contrary.' Just ten days later on 30 May Marlowe had spent a long day in deep discussion with three others, namely Ingram Frizer, Nicholas Skeres and Robert Poley at a house in Deptford kept by a widow named Eleanor Bull. All of the men around the table had been employed by Thomas Walsingham, an active operator in the intelligence service; indeed Skeres and Poley had helped to snare the conspirators of the Babington Plot. The coroner's report revealed what happened next. Witnesses testified that Frizer and Marlowe had argued over the bill and exchanged 'divers malicious words.' After a while Marlowe went to lie down on a couch and Frizer sat between Skeres and Poley. Suddenly Marlowe grabbed Frizer's dagger and set about him with it. A struggle ensued, and it was claimed that in the course of this fight Marlowe was accidentally stabbed above the right eye; a blow that killed him instantly. As Marlowe was laid in the churchyard of St Nicholas in Deptford on 1 June 1593 there were no doubt many questions and thoughts of conspiracy over his death. Whether or not Marlowe's death was as a result of his intelligence work, an out lash by a jealous rival or simply an argument over a bill remains a tantalising mystery to this day.

Ben Jonson: dramatist and duellist.

BEN JONSON'S DUEL

In 1598 dramatist and poet Ben Jonson had a quarrel with actor, Gabriel Spencer which ended in a duel on Hogsden Fields at Shoreditch. Spencer was known as a hot head and had only recently returned victorious from another duel. He was also said to have the advantage of a longer blade but fall he did. Jonson and was tried at Old Bailey for murder and only escaped the gallows by pleading benefit of clergy. During his subsequent imprisonment Jonson converted to Roman Catholicism only to convert back to Anglicism over a decade later, in 1610. He was released forfeit of all his possessions, and with a felon's brand on his thumb.

DUEL TO THE DEATH . . . AND BEYOND

A dispute at the gaming table led to a short exchange of acidic letters in which Sir George Wharton, son of Lord Wharton, accused James Stewart, son of Lord Ballantyre and godson to James I of being 'extreme vainglorious' and in reply Stewart described Wharton's behaviour at the table as 'barbarous and uncivil insolvency in such a place and before such a company.' A duel was proposed in a letter from Sir George and accepted by Sir James, who replied: 'To that end I have sent you the length of my rapier, which I will use with a dagger, and so meet you at the farther end of Islington, at three of the clocke in the afternoon.' The date set was 8 November 1609. Distrustful to the last they searched each others' shirts for hidden armour and then the duel commenced. Rapidly both men were mortally wounded and fell together on the field. Two days later in the churchyard of St Mary's, upon the specific instruction of James I, both the duellists were buried together in one grave to sort their differences out in eternity.

A LIFE FOR AN EYE

In sixteenth and seventeenth centuries one of the marks of a true gentleman was proficiency in swordsmanship and tutors would be sought to instruct the young gentry in the art. One of the finest fencing masters of his day was John Turner. Among his elite clientele was the young Robert Crichton, 8th Earl Crichton of Sanquhar. During a practice bout Turner put out Sanquhar's eye. Although a gentleman's agreement of apology was made when Sanquhar was on a visit to France, it is said Henry IV kindly enquired about the accident and asked 'And does the man still live?' This comment is said to have ignited a fuse of revenge which resulted in Sanquhar hiring a man named Carlyle to shoot Turner, an execution he carried out with a single pistol shot in Whitefriars on 11 May 1612 – seven years after the fencing bout! Sanquhar and a number of conspirators were brought to justice. Although a Scottish peer, Sanquhar was not accorded the dignity of trial at High Steward's Court but was brought before the King's Bench as plain Robert Crichton. He and his confederates were all found guilty and sentenced to death, the only concession given to the Lord being a silken noose rather than the common hemp.

THE MYSTERY DUEL

In 1677 the old Maypole on the Strand was the scene of a fatal duel. The body of Robert Percival, a notorious duellist despite just being nineteen years of age, was discovered dead under the Maypole at day break. Closer examination of his blood stained corpse showed a deep wound in his left breast, his drawn and bloody sword lay close beside him. A hat with a bunch of distinctive ribbons in it was also found nearby, which led some to think Beau Fielding was the culprit. Nothing could directly connect Fielding to the scene and the killing – duel or murder was never solved. As a strange postscript Robert's elder brother, Sir Philip was in Dublin a number of years after his brother's death when he leapt upon a man he saw in the street. Spectators parted the fighting men, and Sir Philip, asked to account for his actions swore he was 'urged on by an irresistible conviction that the man he struck was his brother's murderer.'

HAVE YOU SEEN THIS MAN?

Robert Taylor, a dancing master was in the company of several neighbours in Covent Garden late one evening in 1679 when a heated exchange led to him killing Mr Price at the 'Three Tuns' Tavern on Shandois Street. His description was published thus: 'The said R. Taylor is a person of middle stature, hath a cut across his chin, a scar in his left cheek, having two fingers and a thumb of one hand burnt at the ends shorter than the other, round visaged, thick lipt, his own hair being light brown under a periwig; he lived in James Street, Covent Garden.' Whosoever captured Taylor could inform Mr Reynolds, bookseller in Henrietta Street and collect the £10 reward. The 'wanted' notice went on 'it was printed in last week's Intelligence that he was taken you are to take notice that it is most notoriously false.'

THE FALL OF SAVAGE THE POET

In November 1727 Richard Savage the poet, (and a man said to be the bastard son of a lady of high birth) had come up from Richmond to settle a claim for lodgings when he met with two friends, James Gregory and William Merchant, drank until it was too late to get a bed and the revellers were sent to the street. As they passed Robinson's Coffee House at Charing Cross, an establishment with a long established bad name, they saw a light, knocked at the door and were admitted. It was a cold, raw night and seeing the company in the parlour were leaving they pushed through to occupy the seats by the fire, kicking down a table in their rush. A quarrel ensued, swords were drawn and a Mr James Sinclair was delivered a mortal wound by Savage to his lower belly from which he died the following day. Savage and his two companions then fled the scene but were discovered lurking in a back court by the soldiers who had been summoned to stop the affray. The three were taken to Westminster Gate house and thence, in the morning, to Newgate prison. Savage and Gregory were brought up on the capital charge. Justice Page (a man with no reputation for justice) was not kind in his summing up and the jury were hounded to find them both guilty and the sentence of death was passed upon them. The Countess of Hertford, a lady at court, interceded on behalf of Savage and his friend and the sentence was commuted to six month imprisonment in Newgate. Savage never recovered his popularity after the case and died in August, 1743, in his forty-sixth year at Bristol, where he had been imprisoned for debt. Savage was buried in the churchyard of St Peter, at the expense of the gaoler.

'DUEL' OVER THE DIANA

Anne Bracegirdle was hailed as 'the Diana of the stage' in London and poets mused lyrical after her. She was sought after by many suitors much enamoured by her looks and the romantic roles she portrayed; one who felt he had some right to the amours of Mrs Bracegirdle was one Captain Hill 'a half-cracked man-about-town' and a 'drunken, profligate bully, of low character' to boot. Hill was also a friend of that 'sanguinary blackguard' Lord Mohun. In one of Mrs Bracegirdle's performances the romantic interest was played by popular actor William Mountford, the 'frantic extravagance of stage passion' between actor and actress on stage incensed Hill to the degree he believed it real and in a fit of jealousy he swore to be revenged on Mountford and that he would carry Mrs Bracegirdle off by force. On the night of 9 December 1692 after an abortive attempt to kidnap Mrs Bracegirdle, Hill and Mohun remained in front of her home on Howard Street drinking a bottle of wine and plotting their next deranged actions. The Watch were summoned by concerned onlookers but were sent on their way when they arrived by Mohun pulling rank as a peer of the realm. Tragically William Mountford happened to be walking home along Howard Street and had received no warning of the threats made by Hill and Mohun. Upon seeing Mountford, Mohun embraced him and said 'I suppose you were sent for Mr Mountford? To which Mountford replied that he 'came by chance.' Mohun asked Mountford if he had 'heard of the business of Mrs Bracegirdle?' At this point Hill tried to interject telling Mohun to 'hold his tongue.' Mountford continued talking to Lord Mohun and said he was sorry to see the peer assisting Hill 'in such an evil action.' Hill took great exception to this and boxed Mountford's ear. Hardly had Mountford demanded to know what Hill had hit him for when Hill ran him through with his sword. Mounford had no chance to even draw his sword and died the following day of his wound. Hill immediately fled from justice. Lord Mohun saw he could excuse his involvement in this deed by describing it as a duel. Tried in the House of Peers Mohun used his influence to obtain acquittal of murder charges, but this was not to be the last we hear of the duelling Lord Mohun.

THE LAST DUEL OF LORD MOHUN

Lord Mohun's most notorious duel was fought against the Duke of Hamilton on Hyde Park (near 'Price's Lodge' at the north-western angle of the Park where it merges with Kensington Gardens), on 15 November 1712. Caused by a 'grating retort' made by Mohun which questioned the Duke's honesty, the ensuing duel was a savage exchange. Edward Walford recounts the combat in *Old and New London*. 'In a very short time the duke was wounded in both legs, which he returned with interest, piercing his antagonist in the groin, through the arm, and in sundry other parts of his body. The blood flowed freely on both sides, their swords, their faces, and even the grass about them, being reddened with it; but rage lent them that almost supernatural strength which is so often seen in madmen. If they had thought little enough before of attending to their self defence, they now seemed to have adandoned the idea altogether. Each at the same time made a desperate lunge at the other; the duke's weapon passed right through his adversary, up to the very hilt; and the latter, shortening his sword, plunged it into the upper part of the duke's left breast, the wound running downwards into his body, when his grace fell upon him'. Lord Mohun was killed outright and the Duke died in a few minutes. When the body of Mohun was returned to his home, the only remark made by his widow was to express her great displeasure that the men had laid his corpse on her state bed and thus stained her rich and costly furniture with the blood!

SODS' LAW

John Law was once the comptroller-general of the finances of France; he fell from grace after the crash of a speculation and left France for London where he lived a riotous existence as a 'man about town' libertine and notorious gambler. Discovered in a compromising situation involving the sister of Beau Wilson he was challenged to a duel at Bloomsbury Square on 9 April 1694. Both drew their swords, the action happened all to fast, after just one pass Wilson fell to the floor fatally wounded in the stomach. Law was arrested and tried at the Old Bailey, the duel was said to have been unfairly conducted and Law was sentenced to death. The sentence was commuted to a fine on the grounds of the offence, upon reconsideration, amounting only to manslaughter. Wilson's brother lodged an appeal against this and while this hearing was pending Law contrived an escape from the King's Bench and fled to the continent. He was ultimately received a pardon in 1719.

THE SELF HELP DUEL

In 1762 Samuel Martin, a member of parliament known for his truculence had alluded in the House to John Wilkes the witty agitator as a 'stabber in the dark, a cowardly and malignant scoundrel'. Wilkes prided himself on his gallantry and conduct, so took little time to 'demand satisfaction' as soon as the House adjourned. The two men immediately repaired to a copse in Hyde Park with a brace of pistols. They had fired four times when Wilkes fell, wounded in the abdomen. Martin then relented and went to see if he could assist the prostrate Wilkes but, as ever the gentleman, Wilkes told Martin to hurry away to escape arrest.

GAME, HONOUR AND DEATH

William, fifth Lord Byron (grand-uncle of the poet) quarrelled with his neighbour William Chaworth at The Star and Garter Club on 24 January 1765, over who had the most game on their estates. The verbal jousting turned into a matter of honour and Byron challenged Chaworth to a duel over the matter. Fought in a room at the club by the light of a single tallow candle, as Chaworth was shutting the door Byron bid Chaworth to draw, and in turning Chaworth saw Byron's sword was half drawn, upon which he whipped out his own, and made the first pass; lunging his sword through Byron's waistcoat. Chaworth believed he had wounded Byron and asked him if he was mortally wounded. While Chaworth was speaking Byron 'shortened his sword' and stabbed Chaworth in the belly. Chaworth thought he had parried the sword with his left hand 'at which he looked twice, imagining he had cut it in the attempt; that he felt the sword enter his body, and go deep through his back.' A surgeon was sent for but it was clear the wound was going to prove to be fatal and Chaworth died the next day. In his senses to the very end Chaworth lucidly dictated his will on his death bed, recounted the circumstances and events of the duel; he was explicit in his forgiveness of Byron and hoped the world would forgive him too. Byron was committed to the Tower and was tried before the House of Peers at Westminster Hall on 16 and 17 April 1765. For his part in the killing Byron was acquitted of murder but found guilty of manslaughter for which his penance was set at a hefty fine.

THE SEDAN CHAIR DUEL

In 1766 Lord Eldon and his brother (later Lord Stowell) were both at the White Horse coaching inn at the Holborn end of Fleet Street. Both failed to hail a hackney carriage and so they hired sedan chairs, as Eldon wrote: 'Turning out of Fleet Street

into Fetter Lane there was a sort of contest between our chairmen and some persons who were coming up Fleet Street whether they should first pass Fleet Street, or we in our chair first get out of Fleet Street into Fetter Lane. In the struggle the sedan chair was overset with us in it.'

FIGG THE FENCIBLE

In the late eighteenth century the art of duelling and self defence had to be learned by any gentleman – in those days he would carry a sword as a matter of course, not just as a fashion accessory, he would have to know how to use it. One of the foremost instructors in London was one James Figg a legendary prizefighter who acquired

Hogarth's advert for Figg the Fencible.

his reputation from demonstrating his prowess in the ring at Tottenham Fair. Figg even managed to enlist Hogarth to illustrate one of his adverts 'James Figg, Master of ye Noble Science of Defence on ye right hand side in Oxford Road near Adam and Eve Court, teaches Gentlemen in ye use of small backsword and quarterstaff at home and abroad.'

THE FIELD OF FORTY FOOTSTEPS

When Gordon Square was built its paving stones covered one of the legendary 'marvels' of London for here on the waste ground described as 'as ready arena for the idle and lawless dangerous classes' at the rear of Montague House, Bloomsbury was Long Fields, later known as the 'Field of Forty Footsteps.' The tale which accompanied the phenomena was that during the 1680s two brothers were in love with one lady who would not declare which of the brothers received her preference and wickedly sat on the bank of this field to watch the brothers fight a duel over her to settle the matter once and for all. Both brothers died as a result of the combat and, it was said that the grass upon which their footsteps touched as they fought withered and died never to grow on those spots again – even the spot where the woman who was the cause of the duel sat to watch the combat was also said to be made barren of grass.

Southey recorded his visit to the site situated: '. . . about three quarters of a mile north of Montague House, and 500yds east of Tottenham Court Road. The steps are of the size of a large human foot, about 3in deep, and lie nearly from north-east to south-west. We counted only seventy-six; but we were not exact in counting. The place where

The Field of Forty Footsteps, 1830.

one or both the brothers are supposed to have fallen is still bare of grass. The labourer also showed us the bank where the wretched woman sat to see the combat.' Many people came to view these remarkable marks but by the time the Gordon Square came to be erected so many had come to see and retrace the duel marks with their own feet the entire area was blurred beyond recognition.

THE RIVALS

In 1772 a serious disagreement erupted between Richard Brinsley Sheridan and Captain Matthews over Miss Linley, a singer (to whom Sheridan was secretly married). The two men retired to Hyde Park but found the crowds gathered there were too great so they went to the Castle Tavern, Covent Garden where they fought using swords. Both men were cut severely but both were able to leave the field of combat satisfied.

Richard Sheridan.

THE 'MOST PERFECT DUEL'

In 1779 Charles James Fox fought a duel against William Adam on Hyde Park. Fox was slightly wounded after he ignored the advice of his second to place his bulky frame side on to his opponent. Fox said he would have been hit no matter which way he stood as he was 'as thick one way as another.' Horace Walpole commented that this was the 'most perfect of all duels. So much good temper, good sense, propriety, easy good humour and natural good nature.' It was fortunate they didn't kill each other and spoil it!

THE ONE-SIDED DUEL

In 1789 The Duke of York and Charles Lenox, nephew and heir to the Duke of Richmond where respectively Colonel and Lieut-Colonel in the Coldstream Guards. At the time when King George III's mental state appeared to be such his son, the Prince of Wales, supported by his brother (the Duke of York) and the Whigs led by Mr Fox, should be made Regent. The King, however, rallied and there was much public rejoicing. Lieut-Colonel Lenox, a Tory and one who had supported Pitt in his objection to a hasty Regency, proposed a toast to Mr Pitt at a dinner party. His toast was blown out of all proportion and the Duke of York took great exception to what it was claimed he had said. The Duke refused to give up the name of his informant to Lenox and the whole sorry situation resulted in a duel. The Duke, attended by Lord Rawdon and Lieut-Col Lenox seconded by the Earl of Winchelsea met on Wimbledon Common on 26 May 1789. The ground was measured at twelve paces and both parties agreed to fire upon a signal. Signal given Lenox fired and the ball grazed the Duke's side curl. The Duke did not fire. Lord Rawdon then interfered and said he thought enough had been done, the Duke had come out to give Lenox satisfaction, he would not fire as he had no animosity against him. Despite repeated requests for the Duke to return fire he refused and even suggested that if Lenox had not received satisfaction that he should fire again. On this both parties left the ground and Lenox transferred to the thirty-fifth regiment then quartered in Edinburgh where he was warmly welcomed by Jacobite sympathisers.

THROWING DOWN THE GAUNTLET

In 1818 the body of Mary Ashford was discovered badly beaten and drowned. The suspected perpetrator of this horrible deed, one Abraham Thornton was brought to trial for murder. The press covered what became quite lengthy proceedings. The grand jury found a true bill but the petty jury returned a verdict of 'Not Guilty.' Mr Justice Holroyd, who tried the case was satisfied with the verdict but the victim's family were not satisfied and after machinations between counsels the prisoner Thornton claimed his 'right' to trial by wager of battle. The challenge was formally given by the throwing down of a glove upon the floor of the court. The combat did not take place and Thornton was released but was shunned by society, he even had to disguise himself to procure passage to start a new life in America and 'thus relieved this country of his presence.'

THE LITERARY DUEL

John Gibson Lockhart, the outspoken editor of *Blackwood Magazine* was accused, in print, by John Scott the editor of *London Magazine* of forging testimonials and for attacking Coleridge. Lockhart denied all the accusations and sought an explanation for the derision he had received from Scott by using an old college friend, Jonathan Christie and an intermediary. Scott failed to produce and supporting evidence for his accusations and Lockhart went to London intent on calling Scott out for a duel over the matter. Scott did not seem to want to rise to the challenge so Lockhart went home satisfied the matter was over. Once Lockhart had left London Scott carried on the quarrel with Christie – this exchange reached a dramatic climax at Chalk Farm, Primrose Hill on 16 February 1821 when the two men fought a duel by moonlight. Christie deliberately fired in the air but, surprisingly, Scott's second refused to accept this as satisfaction and called for another round. This time he fired in self-defence and Scott was shot through the hip and intestines and was removed from the field to die later that month on the 27th. Even though Lockhart was not present at the duel the sacrifice of his friend affected his already poor health and it was said he was never quite the same again.

FOUR

SOCIETY OUTRAGES & FRAUDSTERS

ASSASSINATION ON PALL MALL

Thomas Thynne had become affianced to Lady Elizabeth Percy, the youthful widow of Lord Ogle, and they were looking forward to a happy life together. She had turned down Count Köningsmark; he did not take that rejection lightly and despatched three assassins to kill Thynne. As Thynne's carriage sped up Pall Mall, opposite the Opera Arcade on the night of Sunday 12 February 1612 the three assassins closed in rather like highwaymen, discharged shots at the unsuspecting Thynne and galloped off to make their escape. Thynne survived just a few hours before he succumbed to his wound. The three killers; Vratz, a German, Stern, a Swede and Borotski, a Pole, were soon traced, and Borotski identified as the man who had fired the fatal shots (no less than five bullets were said to have pierced the victim). They gave up the name of their paymaster and were tried at Hick's Hall, Clerkenwell but Köningsmark used his influence at court to turn a jury and evade prosecution, he then made a swift exit to the continent. The three assassins were executed on gallows at Pall Mall, Stern complaining he had died for a man's fortune whom he never spoke to, for a woman he never saw, and for a dead man he never had sight of. After the execution the corpse of Borotski was suspended in chains a little beyond Mile-End Town. The whole incident is graphically reproduced, carriage, mounted assassins and all on Thynnes' memorial in Westminster Abbey.

The shooting of Thomas Thynne.

RIDDANCE OF A TROUBLESOME HOUSEHOLD

By August 1626 Charles I could not stand the insolence and extravagance of the French household attached to his impetuous wife, Henrietta Maria. Charles gathered them all together and dismissed them *en masse* but they were not going quietly. Behaving 'like sutlers at the sack of a town' they claimed fictitious debts, concocted exorbitant bills and greedily divided among themselves the Queen's wardrobe and jewels 'scarcely leaving her a change of linen.' Charles ended up paying some £50,000 to rid himself of the household and still they delayed departure, so Charles wrote to 'Steenie' the Duke of Buckingham '. . . I command you to send all the French away to-morrow out of the town, if you can by fair means (but stick not long in disputing), otherways force them away – driving them away like so many wild beasts until you have shipped them; and let the devil go with them.' They did not move easily and in the end they had to be removed by force by members of the Yeoman of the Guards in nearly forty coaches.

THE MAIMING OF SIR JOHN COVENTRY

King Charles II, the 'Merry Monarch' did occasionally have his humour pushed too far. During a parliamentary committee debate on playhouse prices when mention of the King's pleasure was made Sir John Coventry rather indiscreetly enquired 'Whether the king's pleasure lay among the men or the women that acted?' When this reached the King's ear he charged the Duke of Monmouth with a reprisal. On the night of 21 December 1669 about twenty of His Majesty's guards under the command of Sir Thomas Sands arrived near Suffolk Street and awaited Sir John to pass that way after an evening at his usual tavern haunt. Spotting the soldiers Sir John divined their

hostile purpose, snatched a flambeau from his servant, drew his sword and placed his back to the wall. Sir John ably defended himself but succumbed to the superior numbers of assailants. Once they had disarmed him they threw him to the ground and cut his nose to the bone. This deed provoked such outrage to prevent such a recurrence parliament passed the Coventry Act whereby 'cutting, maiming and disfiguring of any man was made a felony without benefit of clergy, and punishable with death.'

The attack on Sir John Coventry.

THE GERMAN PRINCESS

Mary Moders was born the daughter of a Canterbury fiddler, after serving as a waiting woman to a lady travelling on the continent and having acquired a smattering of foreign languages she went to London and took up residence at the Exhange Tavern. Speaking confidentially with Mrs King, wife of the landlord, Moders 'confessed' she was in fact Henrietta Maria de Wolway the only daughter and heiress of the Earl of Roscia in Colonia, Germany and that she had fled to London to escape an arranged marriage with an old count. The 'secret' spread to the ears of John Carlton of the Middle Temple, the brother of the hostess. He was introduced to her as a young nobleman, he won her affections with gifts and fine days out and they were soon married, not only in church but also by license. She soon began to show the tastes of a princess in her spending habits but no money from the union came from her side. Soon suspicions were aroused and soon Carlton's father received a letter from Dover in which his daughter in law was described as 'the greatest cheat in the world'. It denied she was a princess and was in fact from a humble background with two husbands already living in that town, where she had been tried for bigamy, and only escaped conviction by preventing her real husband from putting in an appearance at the trial! Mr Carlton challenged the woman at the home she shared with his son in Durham Yard, and no sooner had he seen her he knocked her to the ground, despoiled her of all her counterfeit rings, false pearls and gilded brass wire bracelets and left her 'almost as bare as Mother Eve ere the invention of the apron.' Taken before the magistrates she was committed to the Gatehouse at Westminster. Brought up on trial for bigamy on 4 June 1663, in those days justice was hard, and found guilty she was hanged at Tyburn clutching the portrait of her husband to her breast to the last. She shared the gallows with five young men 'who could not among them all complete the number of 120 years.' Mary Moders was thirty-eight. Her body was given up to her friends who saw her interred in the churchyard of St Martins.

THE CUNNING BRAZIER

The statue of Charles I mounted on horseback by Hubert le Sueur at Charing Cross was removed by order of the Puritan Parliament in 1647 and sold by a local brazier named John Rivit (also spelt Rivet in other accounts) who lived at the Dial near Holborn Conduit. Ordered to break it to pieces Rivit was an enterprising man. He soon had a roaring trade in the sale of various castings and cutlery with handles fashioned from bronze which he claimed came from the melted down statue. His clientele included both Royalists and Roundheads – the former seeking some keepsake of their martyred King, the latter having their own momento of their victory over the monarchical system. After the restoration Rivit revealed he had actually hidden the statue in his garden (another account states he hid it in the crypt of a church!) So with due ceremony, but not after legal wrangle and a suitable remuneration to Rivit, the statue was erected again in 1647 at Charing Cross.

THE KING'S MISTRESSES

Pall Mall, situated so close to the palaces was the residence of a number of mistresses to the Stuarts including Nell Gwynne, Barbara Palmer Duchess of Cleveland and Hortensia Mancini Duchess of Mazarin. In March 1647 John Evelyn recorded a walk he had in St James's Park with Charles II; 'I both heard and saw a very familiar discourse between the King and Mrs Nellie, as they cal'd an impudent comedian, she looked out of her garden (at 79 Pall Mall) on a terrace at the top of a wall, and the king standing on ye greene walke under it. I was heartily sorry at this scene. Thence the king walk'd to the Duchess of Cleveland, another lady of pleasure and the curse of our nation.'

THE ABHORRENT LORD BALTIMORE

Frederick Calvert, Sixth Lord Baltimore was a villain, a disgrace to his family name and the peerage. A widower at thirty-six he desperately desired Sarah Woodcock a pretty twenty-nine-year-old milliner girl who he had encountered at her shop near Tower Hill, but she was engaged and would not entertain the advances of the Lord. Deciding he was to have her whatever the cost in December 1767 Calvert decoyed her to his house on Southampton Row. Held, in effect, as a prisoner over Christmas in that house of luxury, Calvert even tried to buy the girl's maiden head by sending her father £200. He informed Sir John Fielding to raise a hue and cry – much to the outrage of the Lord. Unable to hold off his hideous passion any longer Calvert has Sarah removed to his house at Epsom and there deflowers the poor girl. Tried for rape at Kingston Assizes the case came down to a question of consent, Calvert bought his witnesses and he was acquitted by the court – but not the public. Calvert was shamed again and he died in Naples four years later and his title became extinct.

IMPRUDENCE, ARROGANCE AND A PLETHORA OF SARAHS

In 1782 Lord Westmorland was dining with Robert Child the famous Fleet Street Banker. Westmorland asked Child his advice; 'What would you do if you were in love with a girl and her father would not allow a marriage?' to which Child replied imprudently 'Run away with her of course.' So Westmorland eloped with Child's daughter Mary Anne. They were almost caught in their flight, their carriage almost stopped until Westmorland shot down the leading horse of their pursuers. Mr Child would not forgive them and when he died a few months later he left all his fortune to his eldest child – Sarah. In an attempt to establish some claim on the fortune the Westmorlands christened all their children Sarah, even their son but the fortune remained with the eldest daughter who soon married Lord Jersey.

OLD PATCH

Charles Price, known among the criminal fraternity as 'Old Patch' was a swindler from an early age. A successful forger he trusted no-one but his mistress and even went so far as to make his own ink and paper for his forgeries. He gradually progressed to a series of frauds on the Bank of England in 1780. Adopting the name of Brank he affected a

Charles Price – 'Old Patch'.

disguise including a wide brimmed hat and the eye patch which gave him his nickname and passed his forged notes through honest and unsuspecting people he employed or 'befriended'. In 1782 Price began passing his false notes to tradesmen or by using more innocent folk to go and exchange his forged notes in banks. Finally arrested in January 1786 it was estimated that 'Old Patch' had committed fraudulent acts and forgeries to the value of £100,000. Committed to Tothill Fields Bridewell to await trial, Price knew the case against him would damn him to the gallows so he took matters into his own hands and hanged himself. His body was taken to a crossroads on Tothill Fields and was buried with a stake driven through his heart.

THE MONSTER

Between 1788 and 1790 young ladies of breeding feared an attack by the man dubbed 'The Monster.' This shadowy character would slash the back of pretty young ladies' dresses around their buttocks and hips, or lash out with knives fastened to his knees as they passed by. In another trick, this well dressed young man would offer a

Rhynwick Williams in the dock: was he 'The Monster'?

nosegay for a girl to smell only to lunge at their face with a spike hidden in the flowers. Over two years it was claimed at least fifty women were attacked by The Monster. Despite the vigilance of the Bow Street Runners he always escaping just as help arrived on the scene, and a reward of £100 was offered by philanthropist John Julius Angerstein for the capture of the perpetrator. Such was the fear on the elegant walks of London young men were afraid to approach ladies so a group of them established the 'No Monster Club' of men 'verified' not to be the assailant, and they wore a badge in their lapel to prove it. In June 1790, Anne Porter, one of the victims of The Monster recognised a man she thought to be the attacker in St James's Park. Her admirer, John Coleman trailed the man to his residence. Initially, Coleman confronted the man and challenged him to a duel. The man, one Rhynwick Williams, who was employed by an artificial flower seller, swore there must have been some mistake, a hue and cry arose and Williams was soon brought before magistrates. It soon emerged The Monster had become a 'folk devil' and the ensuing panic had led some women, caught up by the panic to claim they had been attacked when so such attack had ever taken place. The first trial was abandoned but Williams' case was not helped by his defence lawyer, the Irish poet, Theophilus Swift, who had simply set about discrediting Porter by claiming she had made the accusation only to obtain the reward. It only made the case against Williams worse and he was convicted on three counts of defacing clothing (a crime which carried a sterner penalty than assault or attempted murder in the 1790s) and sentenced to a total of six years' imprisonment. Admittedly the attacks stopped after his capture but the debate still goes on over if Williams was, indeed, The Monster or whether he was the unfortunate victim of a mass panic over a serial attacker, who never really existed.

A HAPPY ENDING FOR THE 'WOMAN IN WHITE'

In the early 1790s a most unusual stall holder frequented the Strand Bazaar. Dressed all in white and wearing a white mask this fine seamstress excited great curiosity and suspecting her origins to be noble the curious and the fashionable of London thronged her stall. With such attention surrounding her the identity of the mysterious milliner did not remain a secret for long and she was revealed as the Duchess of Tyrconnell, widow of Talbot, the Lord Deputy of Ireland under James II who 'unable to obtain a secret access to her family' had been compelled to set herself up as a shop woman to pay for food. As soon as her story became known her relatives immediately set about providing for her again.

THE PIG-FACED LADY

One story perpetuated in the broadsheets of London from the seventeenth century was that of the 'Hog-faced Gentlewoman' or 'Pig-Faced Lady.' Although blessed with the physique, manners and deportment of a true lady she had been cursed from birth with the features of the animal and a voice little more than an 'Ough-Ough' (old English for oink-oink) of a pig. Her family were wealthy stock, and having failed to find a suitor by any other means her father broadcast that the fantastical sum of £40,000 was offered to the man who would consent to marry her. Although as fictional as Sweeney Todd the Demon Barber of Fleet Street, when the story enjoyed a revival in the early nineteenth century greedy suitors believed the tale and even sought her out with such advertisements as this one published in the *Morning Herald* of 16 February 1815:

Illustration from an early broadside of the 'Pig-Faced Lady'.

'SECRECY.– A single gentleman, aged thirty one, of a respectable family, and in whom the utmost confidence may be reposed, is desirous of explaining his mind to the friends of a person who has a misfortune in her face, but is prevented for want of an introduction. Being perfectly aware of the principal particulars, and understanding that a final settlement would be preferred to a temporary one, presumes he would be found to answer the full extent of their wishes. His intentions are sincere, honourable and firmly resolved. References of great respectability can be given. Address to M.D. at Mr Spencer's, 22 Great Ormond Street, Queen's Square.' Sideshows soon caught on to the potential attraction and made their own 'Pig-Faced Lady' by obtaining a bear, shaving its head and carefully dressing the tragic beast in a dress, cap, bonnet and wig with ringlets and flowers. Securely tied in an upright position in a large arm chair the restraints holding the poor animal were covered by her clothes and shawl.

IS HE A HE OR IS HE A SHE?

One of the notable characters in the court circulars of the 1760s was the flamboyant chevalier who accompanied the Duke de Nivernois who had been sent to London by Louis XV to negotiate terms of peace. The Chevalier D'Eon was 'of prepossessing appearance, managed the duties of his position with much ability, and displayed a wide range of accomplishments.' When the Chevalier returned to France he was praised by Madame de Pompadour and he was even recommended to become the

French Ambassador or Envoy in England. He was, however, overlooked and given a more junior place on the embassy staff in London. He bit back by leaking diplomatic secrets relating to the court of France including a very damaging accusation against the Count de Guercy (the man who was given the Ambassador position over D'Eon.) and a libel case found against him. D'Eon went to ground but appeared again in 1764 when he issued a charge against de Guercy of attempting to murder or injure him. All of this fizzled away until July 1777 when an action was brought in the Court of King's Bench, the decision of which would depend on the sex of D'Eon. A man had wagered the chevalier was a woman but had lost and brought an action to recover the amount of the debt. Suffice to say from that time the Chevalier appeared in society in female attire and was known as Madame D'Eon. D'Eon received acclaim and rich gifts for the impersonation, a booklet alluding to knowledge of the true sex of the Chevalier explained how D'Eon had been raised as a boy from early life and how 'she' had become a well educated person and how after introduction to Louis XV, D'Eon was selected for a 'delicate position' as a secret agent for France. The true sex of D'Eon was never proved conclusively, some said it was never revealed as D'Eon had a had a massive bet on the matter. Proof was only revealed after D'Eon's death on 22 May 1810 in Millman Street Foundling Hospital. D'Eon had been a man all along.

MURDER AT ST JAMES'S

Ernest Augustus, Duke of Cumberland, brother of George IV was awoken at about 2.30 a.m. on the night of 31 May 1810 by what he claimed sounded like a bat fluttering around his bed chamber. He next claimed he was subjected to a ferocious attack by a man wielding some sharp bladed weapon, the Duke defended himself with his arms and suffered cuts in a number of places. He screamed for help, the running feet of Cornelius Neale his valet caused the attacker to run off. When the valet arrived with a light the Duke's regimental sabre was discovered on the floor by the door, spattered in blood. A doctor was sent for as was the Duke's other valet, Joseph Sellis. On opening Sellis's door a strange gurgling was heard from within. He was discovered on his bed, his throat cut so deeply the head was almost severed from the body. An inquest decided Sellis, possibly possessed by some mania had attacked his master and then committed suicide in his room. Some questions remained unanswered; the Duke's injuries were only found to be superficial, could Sellis really have cut his own throat so ferociously and if Sellis had cut his own throat, why were his hands clean? Court gossip saw rumours erupt of how Sellis had caught the Duke in bed with either his wife or daughter, another later tale suggested that Sellis had discovered the Duke in an 'unnatural act' with Neale and Sellis was murdered to ensure he kept silent.

INFATUATED RECTOR SHOOTS ACTRESS

James Hackman, suffered a fatal infatuation. While guesting at the home of Lord Sandwich he met Martha Reay, a pretty actress and instantly fell in love with her. She did entertain his advances but the flaw was she was also the mistress of the fourth Earl of Sandwich and mother of several of his children. She had to think realistically and Hackman, a young army officer of the 68th Foot could certainly not offer her support and lifestyle of the Earl. In a desperate attempt to offer her a solid home Hackman joined the church and was fortunate enough to be offered a living with a fine parsonage at Wiveton in Norfolk. He wrote to Martha with the good news 'Now my happiness can be deferred no longer. Oh, consent to marry me directly!' In the

The besotted ex-Army officer and clergyman James Hackman, who killed his heart's desire – actress Martha Reay.

meantime Singnora Galli, Martha's singing coach and confidente thought she was helping Martha rid herself of the troublesome Hackman and communicated to him that Martha had tired of him and had taken another lover. This was too much for the impassioned Hackman and in the agony of jealousy he went to London, followed her with Sandwich to the theatre in Covent Garden on 7 April 1779. He then returned home and fuelled with brandy grabbed his brace of pistols and waited in the nearby coffee house on Cockspur Street to watch for her carriage and finally took a brandy in the Bedford Tavern. At the door of the theatre by the side of the Bedford, Martha was getting into her carriage; Hackman pushed through the crowd, pulled at her gown and shot her in the head. He turned his second pistol on himself but this failed and he furiously attempted to kill himself by beating himself about the head with the butt of the pistol. Hackman was arrested, and despite attracting considerable sympathy and the offer of intervention by Lord Sandwich, he was determined his life should end and was satisfied to go to the Tyburn gallows twelve days later.

KNIFE ATTACK ON GEORGE III

On 2 August 1786 George III was stepping out of his carriage in the garden at the rear of St James's Palace when a woman ran out from the crowd, evaded the guards and attempted to stab the King with a dessert knife. The crowd rushed to the King's aid and the woman only narrowly escaped the summary justice of the crowd. The King himself intervened on her behalf, stepping forward to show he was uninjured he exclaimed 'The poor creature is mad: do not hurt her; she has not hurt me.' The woman, later identified as Margaret Nicholson was found to be insane and was sent to Bedlam, where she died in 1828.

THE HOSTESS WITH THE MOSTESS?

Teresa Cornelys loved to entertain. The masked balls and 'fascinating and elegant' entertainments held at her mansion, Carlisle House in Soho Square were the events where high society went to see and be seen. With success comes publicity and competition, and Teresa Cornelys spared no money or pains 'to have everything in keeping with the tastes of her society friends.' In 1765 alone the decorations and furnishings of her mansion amounted to £2,000, a veritable fortune in its day. The opening of an even grander venue, The Pantheon, hit her hard, as did a number of Bills of Indictment proferred before the Grand Jury that insinuated 'that she does keep and maintain a common disorderly house (brothel) and did permit and suffer divers loose, idle and disorderly persons, as well men as women, to be and remain the whole night, rioting and otherwise misbehaving themselves.' Her business declined, Mrs Cornelys retired from society but the creditors could not be paid and she died at an advanced aged in the Fleet Prison on 19 August 1797.

SHAKESPEARE MANUSCRIPTS 'DISCOVERED'

In 1794 young William Henry Ireland, an articled clerk to a London solicitor in New Inn took great pride in showing his father Samuel, a noted London rare book and print dealer, a mortgage deed which appeared to be between an actor named John Heminge and William Shakespeare. The document was authenticated by the college of heralds and soon a host of papers including letters, a love poem to Anne Hathaway, new works and revisions to some of Shakespeare's plays, written in his own hand, emerged from the papers of an anonymous source William Ireland would only name as 'Mr H.' Samuel Ireland staged an exhibition of the discoveries and London society came in their droves to see these previously unknown papers of 'the bard' indeed, even Dr Johnson visited, fell on his knees and kissed 'the relics' thanking God that he had lived to witness the discovery and exclaimed that he could now die in peace. But some were not so hasty to proclaim the papers as authentic, doubts were expressed and soon an authentic signature of John Heminge was compared with that on the Shakespeare deed and it did not match. Clouds of dissent and disbelief fell on the papers, one of the newly discovered plays *Vortigern* opened at Drury Lane on 2 April 1796 but the complex plot and weak prose exposed the work as a clear forgery. The audience jeered, the only mocking cheer raised was in the last act when the lead played by John Kemble delivered the line 'When this solemn mockery is ended.' Shakespearian scholar Edward Malone published a full critique of the forgeries, the press declared 'gross and indecent imposition' and William Ireland was forced to admit to his forgeries in *An Authentic Account of the Shakespearian Manuscripts* in which he was keen to exonerate his father of any involvement or knowledge of the forgeries. Ireland explained he had written the documents on blank pages cut from 200-year-old books and old plain parchments found in the archives of the solicitors office where he worked. Copying the handwriting on other documents of Shakespearian vintage he even copied Shakespeare's signature from one of his father's books. William Ireland concluded 'I should never have gone so far but the world praised the papers too much, and thereby flattered my vanity.' William Ireland faded away from the limelight, eventually became editor of the *York Herald* and died in London on 17 April 1735.

THE MAN WHO FOOLED DARWIN

George Steevens, (1736–1800), one of the leading Shakepearian commentators of his day, did not take criticism well and had no scruples about inventing quotations to back up his texts from rare antiquarian books and tracts that only existed in his own imagination. Some of his hoaxes were malicious, after a grievance with Mr Gough, the director of the Society of Antiquaries of London he contrived a hoax tombstone for Hardicanute, complete with and Anglo-Saxon inscription of his own invention, supposedly dug up in Kennington. One of Steevens' most notorious inventions was his description of the poisonous upas tree of Java and the effluvia killing all things near it. This account, credited by Erasmus Darwin, and introduced in his *Botanic Garden*, spread through general literature as fact; until artists at last were induced to present pictures of the tree and the deadly scene around it. Chambers' *Book of Days* chided the work of Steevens, 'It is impossible to calculate the full amount of mischief that may be produced by such means – literature may be disfigured and falsehood take the place of fact.'

ANOTHER NEAR MISS FOR KING GEORGE

King George III was enjoying an evening at Drury Lane Theatre on 15 May 1800 when a man stood up from the audience and discharged a pistol at the box where the King was sitting. The shot missed the King's head by inches and his attempted assassin was overpowered. The man turned out to be James Hadfield, a soldier of the 15th Regiment of Dragoons. He had been wounded in the head in 1794 and had not been the same since and had become progressively delusional. He believed he was Jesus Christ and therefore should die. Rather than commit the sin of self-murder he resolved to kill the King and thus face the executioner for his crime. Found insane Hadfield was sent to Bedlam, and died there thirty-nine years later.

THE OLD LADY OF THREADNEEDLE STREET

In 1811 Philip Whitehead was an incautious young clerk in the cashier's office at the Bank of England. His high-living lifestyle caused such concern for the directors they brought the lad in and gave him a talking to. The warning was because they feared the young man's debts would reflect badly on the bank but as a good member of staff they were also keen to help the lad get back on track with a more mature sense of responsibility with money. Whitehead was impetuous, took offence and gave up his job at the bank. Whitehead then gambled heavily on the Stock Exchange and ran up huge debts. He tried to clear himself by presenting a forged bill at the Bank. Arrested, and convicted he was subsequently executed at Newgate. His sister Sarah was only a young girl at the time so ex-work colleagues, friends and family sheltered her from what had happened to her beloved older brother. One day an indiscreet clerk let slip what had actually happened and when she discovered the whole truth the poor girl went out of her mind. Every day the next twenty-five years Sarah dressed from head to foot in black, even wearing a crape hood, cape and shawl, she called at the Bank to ask; 'Is my brother here today?' She would chat for a while then as she was leaving say 'Give my love to him

Sarah Whitehead, 'The Old Lady of Threadneedle Street'.

when he returns. I will call tomorrow.' Known variously as 'The Black Nun' and 'The Bank Nun' she was most popularly known as 'The Old Lady of Threadneedle Street' a nickname which passed to the Bank itself after her death.

FAUNTLEROY THE FORGER

Henry Fauntleroy was, to the public, a respectable gentleman, no less than a managing partner of the banking house of Marsh & Co. in Berners Street. In 1824 it was also discovered that he was an adept forger who had manufactured powers of attorney and sold stock to the value of £400,000. It appeared he began his deceit as an act of revenge against the Bank of England, among a list of his forgeries a note was found in his hand stating 'The Bank first began to refuse our acceptances, thereby destroying the credit of our house. The Bank shall smart for it.' By the time Fauntleroy was brought to book he had spent his fortune on a debauched lifestyle maintaining a number of mistresses, dinner parties, houses and high living. Tried at the Old Bailey he was found guilty of forgery and sentenced to death it was rumoured he thought he could beat the noose by swallowing a silver tube into his wind pipe. At his execution in front of Newgate on 30 November 1824 there were no hitches – silver tube or not he went to his doom.

SPRING HEEL'D JACK THE TERROR OF LONDON

In 1837 the first newspaper reports were published of a terrifying creature later dubbed Spring Heel'd Jack. He was described as being an agile and muscular male figure who wore a long, flowing cloak, with tall black high-heeled boots, dressed in a skin tight suit with devil-like features; bulging glowing eyes, pointed ears and nose. Initially he caused no harm, he was simply spotted leaping over high walls and railings in feats far beyond the capacity of any normal human. In September 1837 it became common knowledge that three young women were attacked on Barnes Common. The first was seized by an assailant but managed to struggle free but not without her coat being torn. The second girl was knocked to the ground and touched by 'the vision' who hideously grinned at her 'with eyes of flame'. Luckily her senses returned and she managed to struggle free and flee. The third was knocked over and clothes torn from her body, she lost consciousness and was later discovered by a policeman, she had been left nearly naked. All three women agreed the horror of the attacks was made worse by the maniacal laughter that rose from their assailant. The first named victim was a servant girl named Mary Stevens who was walking to Lavender Hill after visiting her parents in Battersea in the October. As she passed through curiously named Cut-Throat Lane, a figure suddenly leapt upon her, clasped her in his arms and began to kiss her face as he ripped at her clothes and touched her flesh with his clawed hands. She described his hands 'cold and clammy as those of a corpse.' The terror-struck girl screamed and set her attacker to flight. People came to her aid but no trace of the leaping attacker could be found. Later, a coach was running along Streatham High Road when something 'whether man or bird or beast they could not say' leapt out from the shadows and sprung in an inhuman leap across the road causing the horses to fright, the coachman lost control and crashed his coach.

Jack kept on making his shocking appearances over the next couple of months until such a climate of fear had been caused on 9 January 1837 Sir John Cowan, the Lord Mayor of London revealed at a public session held in the Mansion House that he had received an anonymous complaint, which he had withheld for a few days in the hope of obtaining further information. The correspondent, who signed the letter 'a resident of Peckham', wrote:

> It appears that some individuals (of, as the writer believes, the highest ranks of life) have laid a wager with a mischievous and foolhardy companion, that he durst not take upon himself the task of visiting many of the villages near London in three different disguises — a ghost, a bear, and a devil; and moreover, that he will not enter a gentleman's gardens for the purpose of alarming the inmates of the house. The wager has, however, been accepted, and the unmanly villain has succeeded in depriving seven ladies of their senses, two of whom are not likely to recover, but to become burdens to their families.

Recovering the body of Spring Heel'd Jack victim Maria Davis from the Folly Ditch, Jacob's Island, in 1845.

At one house the man rang the bell, and on the servant coming to open door, this worse than brute stood in no less dreadful figure than a spectre clad most perfectly. The consequence was that the poor girl immediately swooned, and has never from that moment been in her senses.

The affair has now been going on for some time, and, strange to say, the papers are still silent on the subject. The writer has reason to believe that they have the whole history at their finger-ends but, through interested motives, are induced to remain silent.

The matter, although cautiously approached for fear of it being the result of panic and 'gossip among the servant girls' was reported in *The Times* and police were instructed to make enquiries and search for those involved in the attacks. Public concern saw many letters sent to the Mayor and other officials. Some took matters into their own hands, notably Admiral Codrington who offered to personally organise a reward fund, and even the old 'Iron Duke' himself, the Duke of Wellington, despite being nearly 70 set out on several nights astride his charger armed with his trusty pistols to hunt down the fiend. More appearances occurred across London, notably in Limehouse and the East End. By the 1840s reports of local instances of a Spring Heel'd Jack could be found in many provincial newspapers. In 1845 Jack was blamed directly for the death of thirteen-year-old prostitute Maria Davis who was described by witnesses as being caught up in the arms of Jack who then threw her into the murky waters of the Folly Ditch at Jacob's Island and sprang off laughing hysterically at his mischief. But there was no joke in the death of poor Maria who died struggling against the oozing mud. Over the years more sightings of Spring Heel'd Jack occurred but they became less frequent. One of his last dramatic appearances occurred in September 1904 in Everton, north Liverpool where he was spotted jumping from Saint Francis Xavier's Chuch in Salisbury Street. He fell to the ground, laughed hysterically at the crowd rushing towards him and then leapt up, clearing them all with a gigantic leap and sprang off over neighbouring houses. Who or what was Spring Heel'd Jack has never been discovered.

DEATH STRUGGLE ON NORTHUMBERLAND STREET

On 12 July 1861, no. 16 Northumberland Street was the scene of a fatal exchange between Major Murray and William Roberts a solicitor and bill discounter, for the sake of gaining the affections of the Major's mistress to whom Roberts had loaned money. Roberts duped Major Murray to his chambers under the pretext of him loaning money to one of the Major's business interests. Once Roberts got Murray in the back room he shot him in the back of the neck and, immediately afterwards, he shot him again in the right temple. Incredibly these shots did not kill the Major and he fell to the floor feigning death. Waiting till Robert's back was turned the Major sprang back onto his feet, grabbed a pair of fire tongs and hit Roberts with such force over the head that the tongs broke into pieces, he then hit him with a bottle and made good his escape out of a window and down the drain pipe. Roberts died a short while later. Murray was brought to trial but a verdict of 'justifiable homicide' was returned and Murray walked free.

THE TICHBOURNE CLAIMANT

Arthur Orton, known to history simply as 'The Tichbourne Claimant' was one of the nineteenth century's most notorious fraudsters. Orton had come to public notice after the wealthy Dowager Lady Tichbourne placed advertisements in newspapers world wide for news of her long lost son, Sir Roger Charles Doughty Tichbourne. He was believed lost at sea after boarding a ship from Rio de Janiero in April 1854. The grief stricken Lady Tichbourne had begun advertising in 1863 when Orton, a Wapping butcher's son, bankrupted and having emigrated to Australia, contacted Lady T. from Wagga-Wagga, claiming to be the lost son and asked to be sent some money! Despite the letter being curiously misspelled she complied and begged her 'son' to return. Although Orton weighed in at a hefty 27st and when Sir Roger was last seen he was weighing about 9st, and all evidence of his Stonyhurst accent had gone, Lady T. accepted him regardless and was delighted to have her son back.

Orton boldly laid claim to the family estates which had passed to a baby boy, Henry Tichbourne, but relatives and friends of Sir Roger had less clouded views and took Orton to court. Proceedings began in 1867 but it was four years before the trial opened. In the meantime Orton had amassed and memorised a huge amount of information about the man he was impersonating, but his opponents had built quite a case against him too and his trump card, Lady Tichbourne had died shortly before the trial opened. What ensued was the longest case in British judicial history – a total of 1,025 days. Orton was caught out again and again on points of fact about the real Sir Roger but his case finally collapsed with the testimony of Lord Bellow, an old schoolfriend of Sir Roger. Bellow knew Sir Roger had a tattoo on his left forearm – Orton had nothing there. After serving a sentence of fourteen years' hard labour Orton was released on 20 October 1884, joined Sanger's circus touring the country and drew large crowds of those who came to hear him tell his story. He died, somewhat ironically, on 1 April 1885, in poverty, having faded from public notoriety and having left the circus he lived by earning a few meagre coppers displaying himself in Kilburn pubs. Despite thousands coming to see his funeral procession Orton was buried in a pauper's grave.

Arthur Orton, the 'Tichbourne Claimant'.

HOW DID SHE DO IT?

Edwin Bartlett was found dead by his wife Adelaide on 1 January 1886. The doctor was called and Edwin's father demanded a post mortem be carried out on the sudden death of his healthy son. The post mortem revealed Edwin had been killed by a large dose of chloroform found in his stomach. The case of 'The Pimlico Poisoning' was to become infamous in the annals of criminal history and the relationship revealed between Mrs Bartlett and Revd George Dyson scandalised Victorian society. Further gasps were made as the sexual proclivities of the Bartletts were discussed in court with such explosive revelations as no less than six contraceptive devices being found in Edwin Bartlett's trousers and a sexual relations and family planning book being found at the Bartletts' Claverton Street apartment. Beyond the scandal the bare facts of the case hinged on the administration of chloroform. If such a chemical had been given to Edwin Bartlett by force or deception it would have would left his throat and digestive passages burnt and inflamed by the chemical on the way to his stomach – there was no evidence of this, the chemical was only found in his stomach. With 'no evidence to show how or by whom the chloroform was administered' Adelaide Bartlett was found not guilty. Sir James Paget commented after the verdict 'Mrs Bartlett was no doubt properly acquitted. But now it is to be hoped that, in the interests of science, she will tell us how she did it!'

FIVE

A WALK ON THE WILD SIDE

DEDICATED FOLLOWER OF FASHION

Phillip Stubbes riled against the excesses of fashion in *The Anatomie of Abuses* (1583), he was particularly disgusted by the procuring of hair for wigs: 'And if there be any poore women . . . that hath faire haire, these nice dames will not rest till they have bought it. Or if any children have faire hair they will entice them into a secrete place, and for a penie or two they will cut of their haire: as I heard on did in the citie of late, who metying a little child with verie faire haire, inveigled her into a house, promised her a penie, and so cutte off her haire.'

DINING WITH THE DEVIL

In the seventeenth and eighteenth century the Devil Tavern on Fleet Street was the haunt of the intellegentsia of the city; the Royal Society held dinners here and others

A country girl is greeted by a city madam. From 'The Harlot's Progress' by William Hogarth.

such as Jonathan Swift and Dr Johnson are recorded as supping here. The club to join here was the Apollo which had a set of rules drawn up by no lesser man than Ben Jonson;

> Let none but guests or clubbers hither come;
> Let dunces, fools and sordid men keep home;
> Let learned, civil, merry men b' invited,
> And modest too; nor be choice liquor slighted;
> Let nothing in the treat offend the guest:
> More for delight than cost prepare the feast.

DELAY FOR DEPILATION

King Charles II was once kept waiting at Covent Garden Theatre by Edward Kynaston, the renowned actor of female parts. Upon enquiry of the reason for delay the reply was given that 'the queen was not shaved yet.'

OFF WITH THEIR HEADS!

The *Gentleman's Magazine* for 1735 under that date of 30 January stated: 'Some young noblemen and gentlemen met at a tavern on Suffolk Street (Charing Cross), called themselves the Calves'-Head Club, dressed up a calves head in a napkin and after some huzzas threw it into a bonfire, and dipt napkins in their red wine and waved them out of windows. The mob had strong beer in them and for a time hallooed with the best but taking some disgust at some (anti-monarchist) healths proposed grew so outrageous they broke all the windows and forced themselves into the house; but the Guards being sent for, preserved further mischief.'

A riotous assembly of the Calves'-Head Club.

Gentlemen admire the beauties of Covent Garden.

THE ILL-VIRTUED CATHERINE STREET

In the eighteenth century 'mazy Drury Lane' and particularly Catherine Street was considered one of 'bad character' where harlots and ladies of ill-virtue could be found. Gay described the courtesans 'with their new-scoured manteaus and riding hoods or muffled pinners standing near the tavern doors, or carrying empty bandboxes, and feigning errands to the Change.'

THE AROMA OF COFFEE

In December 1657 James Farr, barber and keeper of the coffee house at the Rainbow by Inner Temple Gate, Fleet Street was prevented by the parish from 'makinge and sellinge of a drinke called coffee, whereby in making the same he annoyeth his neighbours by evil smells.'

THE UGLIEST IN THE LAND

During the reign of George II some of the gentry bucks during a particularly 'roaring' and drunken party concocted a wager upon their considered opinion that Heidegger, The Master of the Revels had unsurpassable ugliness and that if any of their number could produce someone more unsightly they would win the wager pot. The bucks searched the slums and rookeries on London from top to bottom until one poor old woman was found and brought for comparison with Heidegger, who was happy to oblige comparison. The old woman appeared to win the contest until Heidegger put on the old woman's bonnet. Heidegger was not dislodged from his championship title.

DEAD RECKONING

In the eighteenth century London clubs were homes to gambles and wagers on just about anything, fortunes were won and lost. In September 1750 Horace Walpole recorded 'A man dropped down dead at the door (of White's Club), and was carried in; the club immediately made bets whether he was dead or not; and when they were going to bleed him, the wagerers for his death interposed, and said it would affect the fairness of the bet.'

PETER THE GREAT IN LONDON

In January 1698 Peter the Great arrived in London from Holland. During his stay he moved from residence to residence, each a little more commodious for the number of visitors he entertained, among the residences was a comparatively small lodging on Buckingham Street, another on Norfolk Street, York Buildings and Admiral Benbow's house – Sayes Place, in Deptford. Peter, described, as a 'brave half-savage' would spend his days rowing about the Thames watching the boat building or pulling to Deptford and back. Known for his hard drinking the Czar was known to drink a pint of brandy, a bottle of sherry and eight flasks of sack after which he would calmly visit the play with no outward sign of inebriation. His idea of a relaxing was to settle down for gusty or voracious 'rough evening' with Lord Caermarthen drinking copious flasks of wine crowned off with a nightcap of a pint flagon containing hot brandy and pepper.

THE MOLLIES CLUB

First published in 1709, journalist Ned Ward wrote this account of the infamous Mollies Club for homosexuals.

> There are a particular gang of sodomitical wretches, in this town, who call themselves the Mollies, and are so far degenerated from all masculine deportment, or manly exercises, that they rather fancy themselves women, imitating all the little vanities that custom has reconcil'd to the female sex, affecting to speak, walk, tattle, cursy (curtsy), cry, scold, and to mimick all manner of effeminacy, that ever has fallen within their several observations; not omitting the indecencies of lewd women, that they may tempt one another by such immodest Freedoms to commit those odious bestialities, that ought for ever to be without a name.
>
> At a certain tavern in the City, whose sign I shall not mention, because I am unwilling to fix an odium upon the house; where they have settl'd a constant meeting every evening in the week, that they may have the better opportunity of drawing unwary youth into the like corruption. When they are met together, it is their usual practice to mimick a female gossiping, and fall into all the impertinent tittle tattle, that a merry society of good wives can be subject to, when they have laid aside their modesty for the delights of the bottle.
>
> Not long since, upon one of their Festival Nights, they had cusheon'd up the belly of one of their sodomitical brethren, or rather sisters, as they commonly call'd themselves, disguising him in a woman's nightgown, sarsnet-hod, and nightrale, who, when the company were met, was to mimick the wry Faces of a groaning woman, to be deliver'd of a joynted babie they had provided for that purpose, and to undergo all the formalities of a lying in. The wooden offspring to be afterwards christen'd, and the holy Sacrament of Baptism to be impudently prophan'd, for the diversion of the profligates, who, when their infamous Society were assembl'd in a body, put their wicked Contrivance accordingly into practice (. . .)
>
> No sooner had they ended their feast, and run thro' all the Ceremonies of their Theatrical way of gossiping, but, having wash'd away, with wine, all fear of shame, as well as the checks of modesty, then they began to enter upon their beastly oscenities, and to take those infamous Liberties with one another, that no Man, who is not sunk into a state of devilism, can think on without blushing, or

mention without a Christian abhorrence of all such heathenish brutalities. Thus, without detection, they continu'd their odious Society for some years, till their sodomitical practices were happily discover'd by the cunning management of some of the under-agents to the Reforming-Society; so that several were brought to open shame and punishment; others flying from Justice to escape the Ignominy, that by this means the Diabolical Society were forc'd to put a period to their filthy scandalous revels.'

MOTHER CLAP'S MOLLY HOUSE

The most famous of all London's homosexual brothels was Mother Clap's Molly House. Run by one Margaret Clap, the goings on at her house could not escape the notice of the authorities and eventually it was raided. Mother Clap along with some forty 'mollies' (homosexual prostitutes) were arrested and imprisoned. Clap was brought up on trial in July 1726 on an indictment for keeping a disorderly house in which she procured and encouraged persons to commit sodomy. Samuel Stevens gave the most damning testimony:

On Sunday Night, the 14th of November last, I went to the Prisoner's House in Field-lane in Holbourn, where I found between 40 and 50 men making Love to one another, as they call'd it. Sometimes they would sit in one anothers Laps, kissing in a leud Manner, and using their hand indecently. Then they would get up, dance and make curtsies, and mimick the Voices of Women (exclaiming) 'O, Fire, Sir! — Pray Sir. — Dear Sir. — Lord, how can you serve me so? — I swear I'll cry out. — You're a wicked Devil, — and you're a bold Face. — Eh ye little dear Toad! Come, buss!' Then they'd hug, and play, and toy, and go out by Couples into another Room on the same Floor, to be marry'd, as they call'd it. The Door of that Room was kept by Eccleston, who used to stand pimp for 'em to prevent any Body from disturbing them in their Diversions. When they came out, they used to brag, in plain Terms, of what they had been doing. As for the Prisoner, she was present all the Time, except when she went out to fetch Liquors. There was among them Will Griffin, who has been since hang'd for Sodomy; and Derwin, who had been carried before Sir George Mertins for Sodomitical Practices with a Link-Boy . . . I went to the same House on two or three Sunday Nights following, and found much the same Practices as before. The Company talk'd all manner of gross and vile Obscenity in the Prisoner's hearing, and she appear'd to be wonderfully pleas'd with it.

Mother Clap was found guilty as charged but unlike some of those who actually indulged in homosexual activities (a number were hanged for sodomy as a result of the raid), she got off comparatively lightly and was sentenced to stand in the pillory in Smithfield market, to pay a fine of 20 marks, and two years' imprisonment.

MAN GIVES BIRTH

In April 1727 the *Daily Post* recorded: 'A young woman that had been apprentice to a mantua-maker near Fetter-Lane, who afterwards put on man's cloaths, going by the name of Tom Shammy, and became Servant at a Tavern of good note, within Temple Bar near the Gate, was last Friday brought to bed of a daughter: We hear that one of the midwives that were present at her labour, declared her to be an hermaphrodite, grounding her wise judgment, as is supposed, upon the impudent Creature's being aparelled as a man.'

SALE OF A WIFE IN SMITHFIELD MARKET.

Now is your time Gemmen ; here's my Fat Heifer and ten pounds worth of bad Halfpence , all for half a Guinea , why her Hide's worth more to a Tanner, I'll warrant She's Beef to the Heels, and tho' her Horns ben't Visible ,yet he that buys her will soon feel their Sharpness.___there hant been such a Beast in the Market for Years.___ Zounds says the Fool in the Blue Apron, I think I'll take her of thee , She, and the Halfpence ,must be worth the Money, I have had two Wives, and wou'd have Sold 'em both for half' that Sum.

Published 25th July 1797 by LAURIE & WHITTLE, 53 Fleet Street London .

An eighteenth-century cartoon comment on wife-selling.

WIFE-SELLING

In the days when divorces (and church marriages for that matter) were hard to afford or procure for 'common' folk 'hand fasting' marriages were often taken instead of the full church marriage ceremony. Equally, the simplified divorces of the eighteenth century could be such as that recorded in *Country Journal* in September 1729 '. . . one Everet of Fleet Lane, sold his wife to one Griffin of Long Lane for a 3/- bowl of punch; who, we hear, hath since complained of having a bad bargain.'

THE LION CHILD

In April 1746 it was reported in *Gentleman's Magazine* 'The wife of one Richard Haynes of Chelsea, aged thirty-five, and mother of sixteen fine children, was delivered of a monster with a nose and eyes like a lyon, no palate to the mouth, hair on the shoulders, claws like a lion instead of fingers, no breast bone, something surprising out of the navel as big as an egg, and one foot longer than the other – she had been to see the lyons in the Tower where she was much terrified with the old lyon's noise.'

A HAZARDOUS GAME

An account in *Gentleman's Magazine* 1753 carried the story of a game of hazard played on Saturday 6 January by HM King George II and other members of the Royal family and court at St James's Palace. One of the Royal players took away the veritable fortune of £3,000, the article goes on to record The Duke of Grafton was one of those who lost heavily.

THE PLACE FOR SECRET MARRIAGES

In the times when a disapproving father or family had legally or physically taken steps to prevent marriages they disapproved of, or couples needed to wed in secret to avoid scandal, one chapel did advertise itself thus in *Public Advertiser* of 2 January 1754 'By Authority – Marriages performed with utmost privacy, secrecy and regularity, at the ancient royal chapel of St John the Baptist in the Savoy, where regular and authentic registers from the time of the Reformation . . . The expense not more than one guinea, the five shilling stamp included. There are five private ways by land to this chapel, and two by water.'

THE FIRST SPEEDBOAT . . . ALMOST

In 1765 a wager for a thousand guineas was made in 1765 between two noblemen, one of whom had constructed a machine which he maintained could propel a boat at a rate of twenty-five miles an hour. A canal was prepared for the test near the banks of the Thames but the working tackle of the machine broke and the wager lost before the apparatus was tested.

KITTY PIE

A girl remembered to history as simply 'Kitty' was probably London's most successful high-class prostitute of the eighteenth century. Described as 'one of the most beautiful and talented demi-mondaines of the eighteenth century' she could command an average of 100 guineas a night. On one occasion the Duke of York dared to insult her with a mere £50, with the excuse that it was all he had on him. Kitty dismissed the financially challenged peer and refused to see him again. Her contempt for the payment did not end there – she sent the banknote to a pastry chef with the instruction that it be baked into a tart and served up for breakfast.

THE GASTRONOMIC BOY OF WHITECHAPEL

Recorded in *Annual Register*, a young apprentice of fifteen who worked for a Whitechapel carman had built quite a reputation for his gastronomic capacity. In April 1765 he faced his biggest challenge, for a wager of two guineas he was to consume 7lbs of all solid meat beef steaks, a large quartern loaf and all washed down with two quarts of porter. The lad was allowed two hours – he devoured the lot with thirty minutes to spare.

WITH THE LOSS OF AN EYE AND FOUR GUINEAS . . .

In the *Annual Register* of May 1766 a fight between a lamp lighter and a baker is recorded as being fought upon Bunhill Fields for a handsome wager of four guineas for the victor. The hand to hand combat lasted for one hour and five minutes by which time the baker had lost an eye and yielded to the lamp lighter.

FOR YOUR OWN PROTECTION

An advert in an eighteenth-century newspaper read:

This advertisement is to inform our customers and others, that the woman who pretended the name of Philips, in Orange Court, is now dead, and that the business is carried on at Mrs Philip's Warehouse, that has been at the Green Canister in Bedford (late Half-Moon) Street, seven door from the Strand, on the left side, still continues in its original state of reputation; where all gentlemen of intrigue may be supplied with those Bladder Policies, or implements of safety, which infallibly secure the health of our customers . . . we defy any one to equal our goods in England, and have lately had several orders from France, Spain, Portugal, Italy and other foreign places.
N.B. Ambassadors, foreigners, gentlemen and captains of ships etc. going abroad, may be supplied with any quantity of the best goods in England . . .

> To gard yourself from shame or fear,
> Votaries to Venus, hasten here;
> None IN our wares e'er found a flaw,
> Self-preservation's nature's law

Letters (post paid) duly answered.'

THE THAMES CROSSING WAGER

A wager was made in 1766 by a man who claimed he could cross the Thames in a butcher's tray. It was estimated that the sum of £1,400 was placed upon the success of the feat. Using nothing more than his hands and wearing only a cork jacket in case of accident the man set out from Somerset Stairs across the water. Upwards of seventy boats full of spectators watched aghast as the man achieved the crossing and landed with ease upon the Surrey shore to claim his prize.

THE ENGLISH APHRODITES

The most exclusive sex club of the eighteenth century was known as 'The English Aphrodites' which arranged wife-swapping and sexual encounters for its exclusive clientele. Membership was then, and is even by today's standards a fortune – £10,000 for a gentleman and £5,000 for a lady, plus a gift comparable and reflecting their economic status. Little is known of the exchanges and parties held in this most elitist and debauched society but one of the members recorded her liaisons over a twenty-year period, among her lovers, the tally reads:

72 princes and prelates	342 financiers
93 rabbis	420 society men
439 monks	117 valets
288 commoners	12 cousins
2 uncles	47 negroes
119 musicians	and 1,614 foreigners.
929 Officers	

Casanova and fellow sexplorers find novel uses for condoms.

WAKING THE DEAD?

In the 1780s a party of revellers in a fit of bravado dared one of their number to enter one of the vaults beneath Westminster Abbey, and to prove he had done it was agreed he would stick a fork into one of the coffins deposited there. In the dark, sepulchral gloom the man accomplished the challenge and was ready to return to his compatriots and collect his glory and prize but as he turned to leave he felt something tug his cloak, he pulled to get away but whatever was holding onto him would not release its grip. This was too much for the man and he fainted. Alarmed by his long absence his friends descended with a lantern to ascertain what was wrong. There was their friend in a dead faint on the floor and there was the fork plunged into the coffin lid – what their friend had not realised in the blackness and his frightened haste that he had also pinned part of his long cloak to the coffin with one of the fork tines!

COME SEE THE EIDOPHUSIKON

In the 1790s an upper room in Exeter Change exhibited De Loutherbourg's Eidophusikon, a clever optical entertainment similar to magic lantern with glass slides and lamps, only on a larger scale with more depth. Occupying a stage about 6ft wide and 8ft deep such scenes as 'the view from One-tree Hill in Greenwich Park,' the loss of the East Indiaman Halsewell and the 'Rising of Pandemonium.' One account survives of how a real thunderstorm broke out when the shipwreck scene was being played causing some audience members to leave declaring 'the exhibition was presumptuous.'

COURT BROTHEL

During the reign of George III some of the innermost members of the court set about starting their own brothel in a group of houses near St James's Palace in a lane which became known as 'King's Place.' The girls in the employ of this brothel were only allowed to walk in the royal parks and access to these women was only granted to those who set it up or strictly by invitation only.

DON'T LAUGH AT THE PRINCE REGENT!

In 1812 Leigh and John Hunt, the founders of the *Examiner* whose offices were based near Waterloo Bridge were found guilty of satirising the Prince Regent as 'the Prince of Whales' and called him 'a fat Adonis at fifty.' They were sentenced to two years' imprisonment in Horsemonger Lane Prison and fined £500.

MISS BERKLEY AND HER HORSE

Among the high-class brothels of nineteenth-century London one of the most famous was run by Theresa Berkley at 28 Charlotte Street. Her services were only for specific tastes and very wealthy clients, for she worked as a 'Governess' specialising in chastisement and flagellation. She was credited with being the inventor and exponent of the Berkley Horse – a device very similar in design and purpose to the flogging horse used in Newgate Prison. A nameless source quoted by Henry Spencer Ashbee said of Miss Berkley: 'Her instruments of torture were more numerous than those of any other governess. Her supply of birch was extensive, and kept in water, so that it was always green and pliant: she had shafts with a dozen whip thongs on each of them; a dozen different sizes of cat-o'-nine-tails, some with needle points worked into them; various kinds of thin bending canes; leather straps like coach traces; battledoors, made of thick sole-leather, with inch nails run through to docket, and currycomb tough hides rendered callous by many years flagellation. Holly brushes, furze brushes; a prickly evergreen, called butcher's bush; and during the summer, a glass and China vases, filled with a constant supply of green nettles, with which she often restored the dead to life. Thus, at her shop, whoever went with plenty of money, could be birched, whipped, fustigated, scourged, needle-pricked, half-hanged, holly-brushed, furze-brushed, butcher-brushed, stinging-nettled, curry-combed, phletbotomised, and tortured till he had a belly full. Mrs Berkley has also in her second floor, a hook and pulley attached to the ceiling, by which she could draw a man up by his hands. This operation is also represented in her memoirs.' There were also those who wished to flog a woman, to which Miss Berkley would submit herself, to some extent 'but if they were gluttons at it, she had women in attendance who would take any number of lashes the flogger pleased, provided he forked out an *ad valorem* duty. Among these were Miss Ring, Hannah Jones, Sally Taylor, One-eyed Peg, Bauld-cunted Poll, and a black girl, called Ebony Bet.' After the death of Theresa in 1836, Dr Vance, her medical attendant and executor came into possession of her correspondence, which ran into several boxes brimming with letters 'from the highest aristocracy, both male and female, in the land.' It was claimed the letters were so outrageous in the wrong hands they could have threatened the very fabric of society and were destroyed.

THE QUEEN OF LONDON WHOREDOM

The most successful London prostitute of the nineteenth century was Laura Bell. Born in Ireland she spent her early working life after a move to London working as a shop girl in Jay's General Mourning House. Her favours were always in demand by only the most wealthy clients. She was well recalled by Sir William Hardman 'I remember several notorious Hetaerae being pointed out to me as they rode in spanking style in the Row and were driven in open Landaus or charioteered themselves about Hyde Park in the season. The most memorable of these was Laura Bell. Clearly I do call to mind Laura's pretty, doll-like face, her big eyes, not ignorant of an artistic touch that added a lustre to their natural brilliance and her quick, vivacious glances as she sat in an open phaeton, vivaciously talking with a variety of men, all swells of the period, of course, at the corner of the drive near the Achilles statue, while her smart little 'tiger' stood at the horses' head. What strange stories I used to hear of her recklessness, her prodigality, her luxury and her cleverness'. She made her fortune as the mistress of the Nepalese dignitary Jung Bahadoor. Over the course of their three-month relationship she was said to have earned some £250,000 – and was not yet twenty-one years old. In 1856 Laura married Captain Augustus Thistlewaytes and they settled in Grosvenor Square. Despite their relationship, Laura 'got religion' and 'she was, by all accounts as successful a preacher as she had been a whore' – no mean achievement.

KING OF THE GAMBLERS

In the early nineteenth century London was full of gentlemen's clubs, most of them with a regular set of gamblers. The founder of one such club that bore his name was James Crockford, of whom it was said 'he won all the disposable money of the men of fashion of London, which was supposed to be near two millions.'

*Lee and Harper's booth
in the heyday of
Bartholemew Fair.*

THE BARTHOLOMEW FAIR

By the eighteenth century the district around Smithfield had become one of the most degraded of London and the ancient Bartholomew Fair held there the attraction of 'every thief and purveyor of vice in the city.' It is hardly surprising the Fair's popularity declined after such instances in 1801 when 'a lewd band of toughs attacked every decent woman on the fair ground and tore their clothes to sheds.' The following year a gang known as 'Lady Holland's Mob' took the fair as an opportunity to beat, pelt or rob every passer by who ventured into their range. In 1815 the death knell was sounding when forty-five cases of assault, misdemeanour and felony committed on the fairground were brought before the Guildhall. The fair gradually dissipated and shows removed themselves to Islington. By 1855 the fair had disappeared entirely.

Of Bucks and Beasts . . . bear-baiting in the early nineteenth century.

THE BEAR BITES BACK

One of the most hideous spectator sports of Regency London, and indeed a 'sport' which could be traced back hundreds of years was Bear Baiting where a poor old bear would be chained to a post and dogs set upon it – the sport being the wagers laid on who would die first, how long it would take or how many dogs would be killed before the bear succumbs to the pack. Hideous behaviour but on at least one occasion during bear baiting in Tothill Fields in May 1806 one of the bears broke loose and fastened upon a jeering spectator named Shawe 'whom he tore very much with his paws and would have he destroyed him but for the assistance of the people.'

THE MORNING AFTER THE NIGHT BEFORE

In June 1811 the society gossip papers were drawn to report an incident at Carlton House, the home of the Prince of Wales (later George IV) when a number of stray shoes were found in the court yard. They filled a bran tub from which those who had lost their footwear were able to claim their 'lost property.' No suggestion was implied as to how the shoes had ended up in the court yard but further comment was made that many ladies and also gentlemen were seen walking about in their stocking feet (shock, horror!) and 'About a dozen females were so completely disrobed they were obliged to send home for clothes, before they could venture out in the streets, and one lady was so completely disencumbered of all dress, a female domestic, in kind compassion, wrapped her up in an apron.'

THE RISE AND FALL OF CORA PEARL

Cora Pearl was another very successful high class nineteenth-century prostitute. Certainly a young beauty, born the daughter of a minor composer, she was blessed with being socially acceptable, intelligent, witty and above all, discreet. She became mistress to a number of gentlemen while still in her teens. Among her benefactors were Prince Willem of Orange, son of King William III of the Netherlands, Prince Napoleon – cousin to Emporer Napoleon III and Prince Achille Murat. By the 1860s Cora owner several houses with all the trappings of the wealthy. Just one of her accounts from a supplier in Paris reveals just one of her bills for underwear came to £18,000. Cora did not live out her life without major scandal. While travelling as an actress in France she did enjoy some acclaim but maintained a few liaisons. One wealthy man, Alexandre Duval, became obsessed with her, lavished great sums of money on her and became jealous of her seeing other men. When she called off their 'relationship' he shot himself on her doorstep. She left France immediately but the news travelled to London and she had to give up her acting career and it seemed men were put off for fear of being driven to a similar fate by her fatal kiss. Cora had acquired a taste for gambling but had always had a wealthy benefactor to bail her out, but they were not around any more and her debts mounted up. Drifting in and out of prostitution Cora ended her days in a shabby rooming house where she died alone and almost unnoticed in 1886.

INNOCENCE, TRUST AND NAIVETY

On 8 March 1888 Mrs Eliza Ann Smith (aged twenty-six) appeared at Thames Police Court for attempting to procure a girl, Kate Spencer (under twenty-one years), to become a prostitute. Also charged in the case was Eliza Millings (alias Pea) the keeper of a brothel at 3 Ernest Street, Stepney. Smith has induced the Spencer girl to come to London 'to seek a husband' and paid her fare from Gloucester. Smith met Spencer in London and took her to the house on Ernest Street. Over tea when Spencer explained she had no money for rent to stay there and had nowhere else to stay Millings had said, 'You had better go out and get men and money.' In the evening the girl was taken by Millings to the Paragon Music Hall to meet and attract clients, Spencer started crying. Luckily PC Barnes 280H was on duty and enquired of the young girl what was wrong and the whole sordid story spilled out. Mullings and Smith were soon apprehended, found guilty of their crimes and sentenced to two years and one-and-a-half years with hard labour respectively.

MURDER IN MAYFAIR

Mme Reil, Mistress of Crimean War hero Lord Lucan, was found dead in the cellar pantry at her house at 13 Park Lane on 8 April 1871. She had been battered to death at the foot of the cellar stair and a rope had been put about her neck so she could be dragged like a side of meat into the more secluded cellar pantry. News of the dreadful deed soon spread – murder in Mayfair was so uncommon the last incident of this kind had been thirty years before. It soon became apparent the Belgian cook, Marguerite Diblanc (aged twenty-nine) and some money were missing. Diblanc was traced and extradited from Paris. At her trial it became apparent Mme. Reil was a hard employer and had made accusations against Diblanc of listening at doors and drinking, and summarily dismissed her. The jury agreed there had been extreme provocation and her death sentence was soon commuted to life imprisonment.

THE MANNERED MURDERER

James Simms (aged forty-three), a former American seaman, executed at Newgate on 24 March 1879 for the murder of Lucy Graham 'a woman of loose character' in a public house at Shadwell. Simms had been 'paid off' from his ship in the port of London. With his money burning a hole in his pocket and plenty of people to help him spend it, his money was soon gone (or possibly stolen). Simms had lost his fair weather 'friends' when he saw Lucy Graham (a woman he claimed had stolen his money at a previous assignation) and struck out and cut her throat with a razor in a fit of desperate and bitter revenge. Resigned to his fate, Simms was a model prisoner who went to the scaffold with a firm step. As executioner Marwood was pulling the cap over Simms's head he said he wished to speak to the prison governor. The cap was lifted and he said 'I wish to thank you, Sir, in particular, and also all the rest of the officers, for your great kindness. I am satisfied; that is all.' The bolt was drawn, the trap fell and Simms died instantly.

PSSSST! WANNA BUY SOME DIRTY PHOTOS?

Joseph Berger (aged twenty-nine) and Mike Paster (aged eighteen) appeared at Thames Police Court on 12 May 1888 charged 'with exposing indecent photos for sale' on barrows on the Whitechapel Road. Arrested by Inspector Reid of H Division, Berger was found to be offering 173 indecent photos and Paster 83. Berger was fined 40s and Paster 20s or one month imprisonment for default. The photos were destroyed upon application of Inspector Reid.

JUST KEEPING THE NOISE DOWN

On 26 October 1888 Arthur Wilkinson (aged twenty-one), a fish frier and Charles Smith (aged twenty), a bootmaker appeared at Worship Street Court for having been the principals at an illegal prize fight at the Morning Star Club, East Road, City Road on the nineteenth. Inspector Capp admitted in cross examination that he was aware boxing matches took place all over London at the like of St James's Hall and Agricultural Hall. He also admitted he was aware that Smith disputed Wilkinson's claim to be the 8st champion. Capp came to the conclusion '. . . gloves were not being used because the sound of the blows was so loud.' Each witness was similarly dealt with by the skilful defence team. The only damning evidence that stuck was a letter found on Smith in which the writer said betting was 30–40 on him. Wilkinson and Smith were bailed for £100 each.

MAN AND MONSTER

In October 1888 American actor Richard Mansfield trod the boards of Henry Irving's Lyceum Theatre in his acclaimed stage adaptation of Robert Louis Stevenson's *Dr Jekyll and Mr Hyde*. Since the book was first published in 1886 Victorian sensibilities were outraged by the premise that every human being (even the respectable ones) has a demon imprisoned within them that the right concoctions of chemicals could release on society to gorge themselves on an orgy of debauchery and malevolence. Mansfield's transformation from the upright Doctor Jekyll to hideous Mr Hyde 'in all his blood curdling repulsiveness' was remarked upon for the convincing and complete transformation of man to half human beast, a transformation made more shocking and horrible because it was done in full view of the audience without 'screens, gauzes or traps.' Due to accusations that the play was responsible in some way for the Jack the Ripper murders (on the grounds of his performance, some even suspected Mansfield himself of being the Ripper) the run of the play was cut short and terminated in its tenth week.

William T. Stead.

THE MAIDEN TRIBUTE OF MODERN BABYLON

William Stead was one of London's most prolific journalists, his stories in the *Pall Mall Gazette* were anticipated with bated breath as his next revelation to shock and concern society would be splashed over the pages while rival editors regarded the maverick Stead with dislike, suspicion and undoubted jealousy. Stead smashed onto the journalist scene in 1885 with a series of articles about young girl prostitutes. Despite being against the law, the white slave trade was alive and well in London and

Stead wanted to expose the whole sordid business. Co-opting William Booth, founder of The Salvation Army and his Salvationist son Bramwell, both men doyens of propriety, onto the scheme to oversee no harm or abuse was involved Stead set out to buy a virgin girl. After making contact with underworld 'fixers' the deal was done and the story published where he revealed he 'purchased' Eliza Armstrong, a girl of thirteen for £5. Despite exposing this hideous trade in his articles entitled 'The Maiden Tribute of Modern Babylon' what Stead had done was still against the law and accordingly he was arrested. The trial was short, Booth was lucky to escape prosecution, the fixers – the procuress and the midwife who confirmed the girl's virginity both got six months each, Stead was sent down for three on 10 November. Every year (until his death on the RMS *Titanic* in 1912) after his imprisonment Stead wore his prison uniform on the day of his sentence in memory of his time in 'happy Holloway.'

SCANDAL ON CLEVELAND STREET

On July 6 1889 Inspector Frederick Abberline the officer who led the investigation 'on the ground' of the Jack the Ripper crimes of 1888 arrived at 19 Cleveland Street in the West End to arrest Charles Hammond. The house had been identified after Thomas Swinscow, a telegraph boy at the London Central Telegraph Office had been caught in possession of 18s during an investigation into a cash theft from the office. The terrified boy explained he had such a sum of money having earned it as a rent boy in a male brothel run by Hammond. The warrant Abberline carried pulled no punches, spelling out the charges that he did '. . . unlawfully, wickedly, and corruptly conspire, combine, confederate and agree to . . . procure teenage prostitutes to commit the abominable crime of buggery.' Hammond had fled but his accomplice and procurer of the boys, Henry Newlove (aged eighteen) was soon traced and apprehended. Closure of a homosexual brothel and the prosecution of its' keepers was hardly headline news but this case was different. Soon the names of eminent and titled gentlemen were being given and corroborated by the brothels' operatives. The whiffs of scandal began to leak out when the Earl of Euston and Lord Arthur Somerset head of the Prince of Wales' stables were immediately named by the boys found in the brothel but press coverage was stamped on with a heavy boot from the highest levels when Eddy, HRH the Duke of Clarence, son of Edward Prince of Wales (later Edward VII) and imminent heir to the throne of England was implicated and named for his involvement in 'The Cleveland Street Scandal' in the foreign press.

HOUSE OF INTERNATIONAL SCANDAL

On 15 August 1899 Amy Hopkins appeared before West London Police Court for permitting her house at 86, Finborough Road, Kensington to be used as a brothel. Her husband John, a supervisor at the Earl's Court Exhibition also appeared on charges of living off immoral earnings. Inspector Seabright of F Division in describing the character of the house stated 'On a recent occasion I saw one of the South African natives enter the house with a woman . . .' After a stream of convincing incidents were related the couple were found guilty and sentenced to six week imprisonment or £15 fine for Amy and three months hard labour for John. Three young children, all girls, were rescued from the house; they were ordered by the magistrate to be taken to the workhouse with a view of sending them to industrial schools.

THE LAST COURTESAN

The woman regarded by many as the last of the great courtesans was Catherine Walters (1839–1920), known to those who walked on the rich wild side as 'Skittles' a name said to have stuck from her early years as a prostitute (she began aged thirteen) working behind the skittle alley of a London pub. It may have stuck because her waist was also said to have been as small as a skittle. A strikingly beautiful woman who was also a brilliant horsewoman, Skittles caught many an eye of the gentlemen as she rode out on the fashionable 'Rotten Row' in Hyde Park. Such was the favour in high places, and the attention she received as her arrival at the Row was eagerly anticipated, hundreds were said to envy her and many copied the cut of her clothes or affected the same hats Catherine wore. She was, above all, the soul and epitome of discretion. Loyal to her benefactors, the rumours would circulate of her involvement with certain members of high society but she never gave up a name, thus her career was a long and lucrative one and enabled her to retire from society, a very wealthy woman, in 1890.

SIX

CABINET OF CURIOSITIES

A LOST GIANT?

In an account written in 1631, Weever mentions that in the cloister of the church of St Mary Aldermanbury hung 'the shank-bone of a man, wondrous great and large, measuiring twenty-eight inches and a half, with the portrait of a giant-like person and some metrical lines.'

THE ITALIAN ON THE BRIDGE

On 19 March 1638 John Rous entered in his diary; 'I saw in Holborn, London, near the bridge, an Italian who with his mouth did lay certain sheets of paper together, one upon another lengthwise . . . he then took a needle and pricked it through one end, and so then the other, so that the paper lay sure. Then he took a short-text pen, and dipped it in a Standish or ink-horn of lead, and therewith wrote Laus Doe semper, in a very fair text hand (not written with his hand but his mouth).' The Italian then went on to embellish the lettering with flourishes, thread a needle and sew with his feet. The end of his display was the loading and discharge of a flintlock, even deftly rolled dice – all with his feet on account of his arms being 'both shrimped and lame.'

TRADESKIN'S ARK

The South Lambeth 'physic garden' and collection of curiosities, stuffed animals, idols, chemicals, weapons and relics from around the world created by John Tradescant during the 1640s and '50s was one of the most popular visitor attractions of the London. After John's death his son published a catalogue of the curiosities from 'Tradeskin's Ark' in 1656 under the title of *Museum Tradescantium*. A few selected items give an idea of what was on display: a dodo (described as a Dodad) from the island of Mauritius; a bustard as big as a turkey of the type 'usually taken by greyhounds on Newmarket Heath;' A cow's tale from Arabia; 'landskips, stories, trees and figures cut in paper by some of the emperors;' half a hazel nut with seventy pieces of household stuff in it; a set of chess men in a peppercorn; a trunnion from Drake's ship, the knife that killed Hudson in Hudson's Bay, Anne Boleyn's night veil, and Edward the Confessor's gloves.

'Mermaids' displayed in nineteenth-century London were cunning taxidermists' amalgamations of fish and monkeys.

THE LONG AND THE SHORT OF IT

A curious stone sculpture once adorned the entrance to Bull Head Court on Newgate Street. It depicted the starkly contrasted figures of William Evans, the giant porter of Charles I with Sir Jeffrey Hudson the dwarf of Henrietta Maria who could travel in the giant's pocket. Evans stood 7ft 6ins tall, truly a giant in his day. Hudson stood 3ft 9ins but he was a fiery man if his height was derided too much, to the degree he challenged and killed a Mr Crofts in a duel over the matter.

WORTH A LOOK?

In 1664 a collection of curiosities was advertised at the Mitre pub near the west end of St Paul's. In it was 'a rare collection of curiosityes, much resorted to, and admired by persons of great learning and quality'; among which were to be seen 'a choice Egyptian Mummy with hieroglyphics; the Ant-Beare of Brazil; a Remora; a Torpedo; the huge Thigh bone of a Gyant; a Moon-Fish; a Tropick-bird etc.'

THE RUNAWAY

In 1664 Mrs Manby was very concerned to lose 'her' little boy and placed this appeal in a number of public journals: 'Lost upon the 13th inst. A little blackamoor boy in a blew livery, about 10 years old, his hair not much curled, with a silver collar about his neck, inscribed 'Mrs Manby's blackamoor, in Warwick Lane.' Whoever shall give notice of him to Mrs Manby, living in the said lane or to the 'Three Cranes' in Pater-Noster Row shall be well rewarded for his peynes.'

THE CHANGELING CHILD

Appearing next door to the Black Raven in West Smithfield in 1698 'A Changeling Child' (a child left or changed by fairies for the parents' own child) '. . . being a living skeleton, taken by a Venetian galley from a Turkish vessel in the Archipelago. This is a fairy child supposed to be born of Hungarian parents, but chang'd in the nursing, aged nine years and more, not exceeding a foot and a half high. The legs, thighs and arms are so very small, that they scarce exceed the bigness of a man's thumb, and the face no bigger than the palm of one's hand; and seems so grave and solid, as if it were threescore years old. You may see the whole anatomy of its body by setting it against the sun. It never speaks. And when passion moves it, it cries like a cat. It has no teeth, but is the most voracious and hungry creature in the world, devouring more victuals than the stoutest man in England.'

'The Spotted Boy'.

THE 'PAINTED PRINCE'

In 1699 Prince Giolo, Son of the King of Moangis from Gilolo, 'a fruitful island' lying under the equator 'abounding with rich spices and other commodities', was displayed at the Blew Boar's Head in Fleet Street, near Water Lane. It was claimed the prince's boat was caught in a storm as he sailed with his mother and sister to a neighbouring island to celebrate the imminent marriage of his sibling with the king of that island. Driven ashore on the island of Mindaneo, they were all taken prisoner, except the sister who was taken by that chief as his wife. The mother and son were sold into slavery, the mother died but the young prince was brought to England. Described as 'The Painted Prince' his whole body except the face, hands and feet was 'curiously and most exquisitely painted or stained, full of variety of invention, with prodigious art and skill performed.' Some of the tattoos were described thus 'The more admirable back parts afford us a lively representation of one quarter part of the world upon and betwixt his shoulders, where the arctick and tropic circles centre in the north pole on his neck.' If this was not enough the advert continued to point out the ink for the tattooing was from a certain plant peculiar to the prince's island. The royal privilage being such head to foot tattooing that once completed it would render the young man impervious to 'the deadly poison and hurt of any venomous creatures whatsoever.'

THE CURIOSITIES OF DON SALTERO

James Salter, one time valet to Sir Hans Sloane and later barber surgeon proficient in bleeding and tooth-drawing set up a coffee house in 1693. He had been given a few curiosities to help attract trade. Quite a character in his own right, Salter was soon nicknamed Don Saltero after the resemblance he was said to have to the celebrated knight of woeful countenance. The coffee shop became a popular meeting house for both naval and military pensioners who sold and donated some of their 'trophies' collected while on their campaigns around the world. Among the curiosities on display recorded in the catalogues of the collection (which went through forty-five editions up to when Salters daughter kept the house in the 1760s) were: a piece of Solomon's temple; Job's tears that grow on a tree; a curious piece of metal from Troy; a set of beads made from the bones of St Anthony of Padua, a curious flea trap, a piece of Queen Catherine's skin, Pontius Pilate's wife's great-grandmother's hat, a lignified pig, Manna from Canaan, a cockatrice serpent; the lance of Captain How Tow Sham, King of the Darien Indians, with which he killed six Spaniards and took a tooth out of each head and put in his lance as a trophy. Saltero kept as many provenances for his items as possible including a page from the Tatler confirming the elaborately carved and gilded coffin and its contents was sent as a present from the Emperor of Japan to the King of Portugal, and had been captured by an English privateer whose captain gave it to Saltero. Despite all of these amazing items the house came to an end in 1799 when what remained of the collection was auctioned and raised £50.

THE COCK LANE GHOST

Well into the nineteenth century visitors to St John's Church would descend into the crypt to visit the coffin of 'Scratching Fanny the Cock Lane Ghost'. The interest had begun in 1762 when it was widely circulated that the poltergeist of a young lady, poisoned by the lover to whom she had bequeathed her property made her presence known with mysterious noises. Her fame grew and even luminaries such as Horace Walpole and Dr Johnson came to investigate. If the ghost did not manifest on Cock Lane suggestion was made to visit St John's and knock upon her coffin. Walpole and Johnson suspected the girl named Parsons who was said to be the object of the spirit visits was a fraud. It was eventually found that the girl's father, the parish clerk of

Cock Lane in the nineteenth century.

St Sepulchre's had set up the deceit to frighten 'a gentleman of Norfolk' by creating the ghost to accuse him of the murder of 'Scratching Fanny' and thus by this contrivance cause the gentleman to repay a loan he owed to him (a type of blackmail to ensure Parsons kept quiet about what he knew). Mr Parsons was placed in the pillory on three occasions but drew no malice – instead of maltreating him the crowd raised a subscription in his favour! Parsons did however spend a year in the King's Bench prison.

ONE OF THE FIRST TO BE FREED?

In 1810 a woman described as 'The Hottentot Venus' was displayed at Mr Bullock's Museum of Curiosities in London. She was exhibited on a stage two foot high, along which she was led by her 'keeper.' Treated like a wild beast she was obliged to walk, stand or sit as he ordered her. It was clear to all that the princess was not a willing participator in this humiliating display. The exhibition was so offensive and disgraceful it was brought to the notice of the attorney general who called for the Lord Chancellor to intervene. The publicity given to the matter in the Court of Chancery soon saw the Hottentot Venus removed from public gaze but what her ultimate fate was does not appear to have been recorded.

DON'T LOSE YOUR HEAD

At the Theatre on Patrick Street on the evening of 24 February 1812 an event was publicised as 'positively and definitely the last night' Signor Belzoni introduced 'a feat of Legerdemain, which he flatters will astonish the spectators, as such a feat never was attempted in Great Britain or Ireland. After a number of entertainments, he will cut a man's head off – and put it on again!'

SEVEN

PLAGUE & PESTILENCE

THE BLACK PLAGUE

When the Black Plague hit London (1348–9) no accurate number of all those who succumbed is recorded but numbers in the high thousands can be safely assumed. An idea of how many can be obtained after the Lord Mayor, Sir Walter Manny was caused to buy 'thirteen acres and a rod of ground' outside the walls because the city graves were full. The area, now occupied by Charterhouse Square, was said to have been filled in the year 1349 with more than fifty thousand buried. Ralph Stratford, Bishop of London did similar by purchasing 'three desolate acres' between the Abbey of Westminster and the Knights of St John in Clerkenwell and called it 'Pardon Churchyard.'

NOT SO CLOSE TO ME!

Bartholomew James, Lord Mayor of London in 1479 fined his Sheriff £50 for kneeling too close to him and for cursing him when spoken to. James had brought his charges against the Sheriff because he was afraid of catching the plague.

PLAGUE IN ELIZABETHAN LONDON

Plague stalked London on a number of occasions in the sixteenth century. In 1563 bubonic plague saw bills of mortality return deaths of 1,000 people a week in mid-August, 1,600 per week in September and 1,800 per week in October. Many people who could afford to do so, moved out of London. Good Queen Bess moved her court to Windsor Castle where once ensconced she ordered the erection of a gallows to swing any who came there from London, and ordered a block on the import of goods to prevent the spread of plague to her court. In total about 80,000 people were killed in this plague outbreak – this was about a third of the population of London at the time.

THE GREAT PLAGUE

The first announcements of plague appeared in the parish of St Giles in the Fields in April 1664. The plague was carried by the fleas on rats and on the clothes of anyone contacted by them; even bolts of cloth could carry the fleas. The warm summer saw the insects breed and the disease spread rapidly. Initially pest houses were set up on the outskirts to remove plague victims out of the city. Each pest house was intended for about 100 patients but these soon became hideously filthy and overcrowded. Despite precautions of scattering and burning herbs and the nailing up of houses, painting red crosses on the door and observing the quarantine of forty days by 1665 the plague had spread in unprecedented ways right across London. Soon streets of houses appeared abandoned and grass literally began to grow on the roads. Even markets were cancelled. Country folk refused to enter the city, preferring to meet with traders far out on the outskirts at Spitalfields, St Georges Field in Southwark, Bunhill fields and especially at Islington where any money exchanged would be sluiced in vinegar before it was

Solomon Eccles, Prophet of Doom, declaiming the fate of London during the Great Plague of 1664.

exchanged. As the plague took hold of its victims they started to lose their senses, some choosing to throw themselves out of windows, shoot themselves or murder their own children rather than go through the hideous and agonising death from plague. Defoe observed the physicians treatment of those in the advanced stages of plague, 'The swellings in some grew hard, and they applied violent drawing plasters or poultices to break them; and, if these did not do they cut and scarified them in a terrible manner. In some those swellings were made hard, partly by the force of the distemper and partly by their being too violently drawn, and were so hard that no instrument could cut them, and then they burned them with caustics, so that many died raving mad with torment . . . some broke out on the streets, perhaps naked and would run directly down to the river, if they were not stopped by the watchmen, or other officers and plunge themselves into the water . . . It often pierced my very soul to hear the groans and cries of those who were thus tormented.' The dead were eventually removed on carts by bearers who rang a bell and cried, 'Bring out your dead.' Most of these bearers developed the most crude and macabre sense of humour to pass the time in their job; some with full loads on their way to the plague pits cried out, 'Faggots, faggots! Five for sixpence!' Others were known to undress once attractive young women and practice necrophilia. An estimated 100,000 Londoners died in the Great Plague, only with a cooling down of temperatures and the hard winter of 1665/6 did the plague abate. In 1666 those who had fled the city began to return. It has been suggested the city was only truly cleansed of the plague with the Great Fire of London in September 1666.

GAOL FEVER

London had the greatest concentration of gaols, prisons and bridewells in the country so it is hardly surprising the most severe and frequent instances of gaol fever occurred in the capitol. The fever not only carried away the prisoners but often claimed those who worked closely with them to the degree that in 1750, in a single session of the London courts the gaol fever struck down the Lord Mayor, three judges, an under sheriff, several counsel and a number of jurymen.

PANIC PLAGUE

On 29 July 1760 a rumour spread across London that plague had broken out in St Thomas's Hospital. Panic buying of rue and wormwood at Covent Garden, the old mainstays of plague repellence saw prices rise the following day by forty per cent. Public fear and businesses cashing in on the groundless panic, saw the following notice signed by a number of surgeons, physicians and an apothecary appointed to St Thomas's Hospital printed in public journals 'Whereas the town has been alarmed with a false and wicked report that the plague is broke out in St Thomas's Hospital; we the underwritten . . . do hereby certify that the said report is absolutely without foundation; and that there are no other diseases amongst the patients than what are usual in this and all other hospitals.' No reason or person was ever identified as the source of the rumour.

SCREWED DOWN — LIKE IT OR NOT!

During the cholera epidemics of the 1840s the sufferers were removed to temporary cholera hospitals away from the population centres of the city. As soon as a patient died it was imperative to get them out of the bed to free it for another and into the wooden shell (a wooden box one could hardly dignify by calling it a coffin) and screw the lid down ready for burial. As there was a backlog in burials the shells were stacked up in a shed and more than one account tells of how the hospital workers and coffin handlers heard 'kicking in the coffins.' The lids were seldom unscrewed – 'we knew they were going to die anyway.'

THE "SILENT HIGHWAY"-MAN.

Punch's satire on the 'fatal stench' of the River Thames in 1858.

DIRTY FATHER THAMES, KING CHOLERA AND THE GREAT STINK

By the mid-nineteenth century the increased volume of water used by new flush toilets and water closets fitted in the more affluent households of London caused the 200,000 old cesspits to overflow into the old rainwater drains of the streets and ultimately carried the raw sewage into the Thames along with a host of unsavoury and unsanitary detritus from the factories and slaughterhouses of the metropolis. Papers and Magazines depicted Old Father Thames as a filthy old man who bred sick children and carried disease. In 1848, *Punch* published a satirical cartoon and the poem, 'Dirty Father Thames':

> Filthy river, filthy river,
> Foul from London to the Nore,
> What art thou but one vast gutter,
> One tremendous common shore?
> All beside thy sludgy waters,
> All beside thy reeking ooze,
> Christian folks inhale mephitis,
> Which thy bubbly bosom brews.

'King Cholera,' the nemesis of many Victorians, was thought to be carried on the air
what was termed a 'miasma' but it was not formally realised the disease was water
borne until Dr John Snow provided proof by removing the handle of a public water
pump he identified as the source of the outbreak of cholera in Soho in 1854. When
no more water could be drawn from it the instances of cholera ceased in that area.
After this discovery wheels were sent in motion for sanitary improvement but progress
was slow. The eminent Professor Michael Faraday wrote to the editor of *The Times*
and his 'Observations on the Filth of the Thames' were published in July 1855:

SIR,
I traversed this day by steam-boat the space between London and Hangerford
Bridges between half-past one and two o'clock; it was low water, and I think the
tide must have been near the turn. The appearance and the smell of the water
forced themselves at once on my attention. The whole of the river was an opaque
pale brown fluid. In order to test the degree of opacity, I tore up some white
cards into pieces, moistened them so as to make them sink easily below the
surface, and then dropped some of these pieces into the water at every pier the
boat came to; before they had sunk an inch below the surface they were
indistinguishable, though the sun shone brightly at the time; and when the
pieces fell edgeways the lower part was hidden from sight before the upper part
was under water. This happened at St Paul's Wharf, Blackfriars Bridge, Temple
Wharf, Southwark Bridge, and Hungerford; and I have no doubt would have
occurred further up and down the river. Near the bridges the feculence rolled up
in clouds so dense that they were visible at the surface, even in water of this kind.
    The smell was very bad, and common to the whole of the water; it was the
same as that which now comes up from the gully-holes in the streets; the whole
river was for the time a real sewer. Having just returned from out of the country
air, I was, perhaps, more affected by it than others; but I do not think I could
have gone on to Lambeth or Chelsea, and I was glad to enter the streets for an
atmosphere which, except near the sink-holes, I found much sweeter than that
on the river . . . If there be sufficient authority to remove a putrescent pond
from the neighbourhood of a few simple dwellings, surely the river which flows
for so many miles through London ought not to be allowed to become a
fermenting sewer. The condition in which I saw the Thames may perhaps be
considered as exceptional, but it ought to be an impossible stat, instead of which
I fear it is rapidly becoming the general condition. If we neglect this subject, we
cannot expect to do so with impunity; nor ought we to be surprised if, ere many
years are over, a hot season give us sad proof of the folly of our carelessness.

Faraday's words were uncannily prophetic because just three years later in 1858 there
occurred an unusually hot and humid summer which caused the bacteria in the
sewage-ridden Thames to thrive and London was engulfed by the resultant stench. So
bad was it that even in the House of Commons the curtains were soaked in chloride
of lime in an attempt to deaden the smell but to no avail and the sitting of Parliament
was disrupted because of the unbearable stench from the nearby Thames. Members
considered moving to Hampton Court to conduct the business of the House and the
Law Court made plans to evacuate to Oxford and St Albans. Luckily, heavy rains soon
came and lessened the stench but effective measures to avoid a repetition were set in

PUNCH, OR THE LONDON CHARIVARI.—July 21, 1855.

FARADAY GIVING HIS CARD TO FATHER THAMES;
And we hope the Dirty Fellow will consult the learned Professor.

Punch's poignant satire on Faraday's card experiment in July 1855.

motion and a select committee appointed to report on the Stink and recommend how to put an end to the problem. In 1859 the Metropolitan Board of Works accepted a sewerage scheme proposed by their own Chief Engineer, Joseph Bazalgette and over the next six years the most advanced sewage system in the world was established under London.

KILLER YELLOW SMOG FOG

On 22 November 1891 London was enveloped in a dense yellow fog from Christmas time until New Year. 'Russian' influenza (so named after its first appearance in Bokara, Russia in May 1889) spread to England via St Petersburg and spread to epidemic proportions, and clogged the wards of the capitols' hospitals especially The London Hospital who admitted hundreds from Whitechapel. Because of the terrible conditions in which many from the East Enders existed they had the least chance of survival and hundreds succumbed to this virulent strain of broncho-pneumonia. It has been suggested that it was from this epidemic Prince Edward, (Eddy) the Duke of Clarence caught his illness and died after being moved away to Sandringham, the country retreat of the Royal family in Norfolk.

EIGHT

MEDICINE:
QUACK & CHYRURGICAL

KING'S EVIL — CURED BY THE KING

From the time of Edward the Confessor is was believed the touch of a monarch's hand upon the part of the body afflicted by scrofula would alleviate if not entirely cure the condition that became known as 'King's Evil.' By the sixteenth and seventeenth century this laying on of the Monarch's hands had become a grand

Charles II delivering his 'touch' to cure 'King's Evil'.

religious ceremony. Sufferers were brought individually before the King, a service was read and the King stroked the affected part with an 'angel', a coin minted for giving to the sick. The sufferer would then wear the coin around the neck until the cure was complete. Between 1660 and 1664 King Charles II was reputed to have touched and cured over 92,000 sick people. On one occasion in 1664 the sufferers rushed forward at the sight of the king and seven were trampled to death in the ensuing mob.

THE GOLDEN ELIXIR

Dr Francis Anthony believed and even published a learned defence of the extraordinary medicine 'after inexpressible labour, watching, and expense' he had discovered 'through the blessing of God.' Based on 'extract or honey of gold' and known as *aurum portabile* the medicine, which could be dissolved in any liquid, was said to be a 'universal cure.' Popular during the reign of James I, Dr Anthony lived a comfortable life in Bartholomew Close, Smithfield on the profits of his elixir until his death in 1623.

FANCY A COFFEE?

When the first coffee shops emerged in London in the 1650s the brew was extolled as having many virtues. In *The Publick Advertiser* of May 1657 it stated 'In Bartholomew Lane, on the back side of the old Exchange, the drink called coffee, which is a very wholesome and physical drink having many virtues, closes the orifice of the stomach, fortifies the heat within, helpeth digestion, quickneth the spirits, maketh the heart lightsom, is godd against eye-sores, coughs, colds, rhumes, consumptions, headache, dropsie, gout, scurvy, King's Evil and many others, is to be sold both in the morning and three of the clock in the afternoon.'

TO END PLAGUE

The cure for plague commonly used in London during 1665 was to, 'Take the inward bark of the Ash Tree . . . Walnut with the Green outward Shells, to the number of Fifty, cut these small: of Scabious, of Vervin, of each a Handful, of Saffron two Drams, pour upon these the strongest Vinegar you can get, four pints, let them a little boil together upon a very soft fire, and then stand in a very close Pot, well stopt all night upon the embers. After distil them with a soft fire, and receive the Water close Kept. Give unto the patient laid in Bed and well covered with cloaths, two ounces of this water to drink, and let him be proved to Sweat: every eight hours (during the space of four and twenty hours) give him the same quantity to drink.' As the plague wore on another less involved recipe was 'An Ale Posset-drink with Pimpernel seethed in it, till it taste strong of it, drunk often, removes the infection, tho' it had reached the very heart.'

TEETHING TROUBLE

In 1679 the 'much approved necklaces of Joynts, of the great traveller J.C.' that were sold with the promise that they 'absolutely ease children in breeding teeth by cutting them' and thereby 'prevented feavers, convulsions etc' were sold by T. Burrel at the 'Golden Ball' under St Dunstan's Church in Fleet Street.

CONTINUED SUPPORT

In 1680 this advert was placed in a London periodical: 'Whereas John Pippin, whose grandfather, father and himself have been for above 190 years past famous throughout all England for curing the rupture, making the most easie trusses of all sorts, both for men, women and children, being lately deceased; This is to certifie to all person that Eleanor Pippin, the widow, who in his lifetime made all the trusses which he sold, lives still at 'The Three Naked Boys' near the Strand Bridge, where she makes all manner of trusses. She also hath a gentleman to assist in the fitting of them upon men, he being intrusted by the said John Pippin in his lifetime.'

STOP PRESS! ALE THAT MAY CAUSE WIND

Dr Butler's Ale, sold on Newgate Market and at Tobias' Coffee-House was a typical late seventeenth-century cure-all described thus in the accompanying literature; 'It is an excellent stomack drink, it helps digestion, expels wind and dissolves congealed phlegm upon the lungs, and is therefore good against colds, coughs, ptisical and consumptive distempers; and being drunk in the evening, it moderately fortifies nature, causeth good rest and hugely corroborates the brain and memory.'

QUACK OR NOT?

Dr Joshua Ward was 'celebrated for his drop and pill' in the eighteenth century. Best known as the inventor of 'Friar's Balsam' he was praised by General Churchill and Lord Chief Baron Reynolds. He also prescribed for the King for which he was awarded a vote of thanks from the Commons and granted the privilege of driving his carriage through St James's Park. Despite the acclaim he was still considered a quack, the King's recovery being made 'in spite of the quack, "Spot" Ward.' Sadly he will be best remembered for his conspicuous inclusion in the one of Hogarth's caricatures, Ward can always be identified by the 'spot' or 'claret mark' covering 'half his brazen face.' (see p. 200.)

An eighteenth-century advertisement offering a cure for the pox.

BLISTER OR DIE?

After her husband's death in 1722 the formidable Sarah, Duchess of Marlborough kept up the high standards on pomp and ceremony in the family residence Marlborough House to the last days of her life. In her 84th year she was warned by her physician that she must either be blistered or die, her retort was swift 'I won't be blistered, and I won't die.'

THE TAPPING OF MARY PAGE

Dame Mary Page was one of the most notorious cases of dropsy in London. Her tomb erected in 1728 on Bunhill Fields stated 'In 67 months she was tapped 66 times and had taken away 240 gallons of water, without ever repining at her case or ever fearing the operation.'

SHE COULD NOT MEND HER BROKEN HEART

Mrs Sarah Mapp the bone-setter was a strong-framed woman with a fine reputation built on her 'cures' effected more by personal strength than skill – she was a sort of eighteenth-century physiotherapist. Based in Epsom she held performances at the Grecian Coffee House where she would arrive in coach and four and leave 'bearing away the crutches of her patients as trophies of honour.' On just one of her weekly visits she successfully operated on the niece of Sir Hans Sloane and upon the same day 'straightened the body of a man whose back had stuck out two inches for nine years.' She became the 'toast of the town,' a comedy was written about her entitled *The husband's relief, or The Female Bone-setter and the Worm-doctor* and her success saw her set up a permanent establishment on Pall Mall. In 1736 her joy was completed with a marriage to an Epsom footman – who ran off abruptly with all her savings just a week later. Her heart broken, she was inconsolable and went into rapid decline. Mrs Mapp died at her lodgings near the Seven Dials in December 1737, 'so miserably poor, that the parish was obliged to bury her.' (see p. 200.)

WORMING OUT OF AN ILLNESS

In January 1737 the *Daily Journal* published the following advert:

> These are to certify that, whereas, I, Hannah Goph, dwelling with M.——, Distiller at Richmond Green, was troubled with a great Pain in my stomach and side, a swimming in my head, a Shortness of Breath, my stomach being also swelled; for relief of which disorders I applied to
>
> MR JOHN MOORE, Apothecary
> At the Pestle & Mortar in Laurence-Pountney's Lane, the first great gates on the Left Hand from Cannon Street. Of whom I had some of his worm medicines, which brought from me a worm thirteen yards and a half long; since the coming away of which I am much better in my head, stomach, side and breath
> December 6, 1736   HANNAH GOPH

> NB— This Worm is to be seen at the said Mr Moore's and any person, for further satisfaction may enquire at Mrs Ellen's near the Playhouse, at Mrs Pattingall's at the Fountain in Cruicifix Lane, near St John's Church, Southwark or at Mrs Lark's over against St Olave's workhouse in Southwark.

RAISED FROM THE 'DEAD'

On 24 November 1740 the body of a seventeen year old William Duell who had just been executed at Tyburn for the robbery and murder of Sarah Griffin was brought to Surgeons' Hall for dissection. He had been strung up for over 20 minutes before

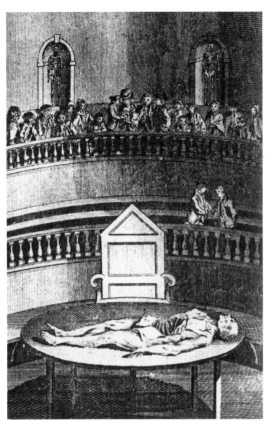

he was cut down and removed and had laid on the dissecting table for over an hour. As one of the servants was washing Duell's naked body in preparation for the first cuts to be delivered by the surgeon, he perceived signs of life in the executed felon. A surgeon was summoned, he bled Duell and recovered him so much he threw his hand in the surgeon's face and accidentally cut his lips with the lancet. Within two hours Duell was sitting up in a chair, groaning and apparently in some agitation. He could not speak. Kept in Surgeon's Hall until midnight the Sheriff's Officers were summoned and Duell was returned to Newgate, shocked but almost totally recovered. Although, officially, the dread sentence had been carried out upon him, Duell did not evade punishment, although he did avoid a return visit to the gallows, as he was transported instead. That was the true story, a more embroidered tale once repeated in London guides told of how the Surgeons hid Duell and raised the young felon among themselves in secret and how they paid for his passage abroad. The story was capped off with Duell becoming a successful merchant

The body of a murderer, initial incisions and openings made, exposed in the Theatre of the Surgeons' Hall before full anatomisation.

in Levant and how he had sent the company a magnificent screen as a small token of his gratitude. Sadly, the story was not all it seemed, later research revealed the screen implicated in the tale was in the Surgeons' company inventory some thirty years before Duell went to Tyburn and, in fact, no longer exists as it was destroyed in the London blitz during the Second World War.

TO CURE A WEN

In 1758 brothers James and Walter White were executed at Kennington Common for breaking and entering the home of farmer Vincent of Crawley. As the two were freshly dangled on the nooses, a child of about nine months old was placed in the hands of the executioner who then stroked the child's face nine times with one hand of each of the executed men. The reason for this strange procedure was the child was suffering with a wen upon one of its cheeks. The stroke of the executed felon's hand was a long established folk medicine 'cure' for the condition.

MRS BROWNRIGG

Elizabeth Brownrigg opened a private lying-in hospital in Flower de Luce (Fleur de Lys) Court on Fetter Lane in 1765. Having a large number of children of her own her priority was always towards them, not her paying patients. Any staff employed would have to be cheap so she employed orphaned girls for household duties. For some reason, possibly a mental condition, or more likely perverted pleasure Browrigg sadistically tortured her orphan girl staff. One poor girl named Mary Jones, was stripped naked and stretched out between two chairs, and flogged until Mrs Brownrigg's arms gave out. Mary Clifford was stripped and suspended by her bound hands naked from the ceiling and flogged mercilessly over a prolonged period of hours rather than minutes. Treated worse than a dog this poor child was then forced to sleep on a filthy mat in the coal cellar. A concerned neighbour was moved to investigate and discovered yet another girl named Mary Mitchell covered in ulcerated sores. The matter reported to authorities saw warrants issued for the Brownriggs. By the time the case was brought to court poor Mary Clifford had died of the wounds inflicted on her by Mrs Brownrigg – she was found guilty of murder, her husband and her son who had also been complicit in the beatings were given six months. Hanged at Tyburn on 14 September 1767, Mrs Brownrigg was scorned as the worst of her sort, she drew no sympathy, unlike her dissected body that drew visitors by the hundred when it was exhibited at Surgeons' Hall.

Elizabeth Brownrigg.

DR GRAHAM'S TEMPLE OF HEALTH AND HYMEN

In the late eighteenth century, Dr James Graham, one of London's most successful quack doctors opened his original 'Temple of Health and Hymen' in Adelphi Terrace and enjoyed success, and attracted such society clientele it he moved it to larger premises on Pall Mall in 1781. The rooms were sumptuous in their hangings and decorations of marble statues, ornamental dragons and stained glass. Areas of the house showed the discarded crutches, eartrumpets, trusses and trophies from those he had 'cured.' Graham was joined in his Temple by about twenty other assistants, among them a provocative 'priestess' – Amy Lyon (who changed her name to Emma Hart and one and the same woman who later became Lady Emma Hamilton, the mistress of Admiral Nelson), a woman described 'as beautiful as she were vulgar and abandoned.' The rooms were also filled with glass globes, 'medico-electric apparatus' and other such impedimenta to inspire mystical 'cures' all of which was complimented by tinted lamp lighting and the air 'drugged with incense and strains of music.' Here,

*The celestial bed at
Dr Graham's Temple
of Health and Hymen.*

such treatments could be procured as 'earth baths' (mudbaths) or 'divine balm' for a
guinea or for £50 a night one could sleep on the magneto-electric bed where
'electricity and perfumes were laid on in glass tubes from adjoining reservoirs. The
beds rested on six massy transparent columns. The perfumed curtains were of purple
and celestial blue . . .' But these were nothing compared to the bed Graham alleged
cost £60,000; this was his 'celestial bed' supported by forty pillars of glass, and
situated under a mirror-lined dome which after just one night any couple rich enough
to spend a night within its folds could, or at least Graham claimed, 'obtain the desire
of their lives' and be blessed with children. Graham also sold an 'elixir of life' for
£1,000, payable in advance of course. By 1787 most had seen Graham for the fraud
he was, patronage left him so he became a religious fanatic. Committed to a lunatic
asylum he died in 1794.

HELL'S KITCHEN

In April 1801 a group of young lads were larking around Wych Street when they looked through the keyhole of the former Queen of Bohemia Tavern which they believed to have been desserted. Inside they beheld hell's kitchen when persons were seen 'cutting up human bodies.' The boys ran to raise the alarm and soon an angry mob had assembled in front of the building and forced an entry. There they discovered several human bodies in various states of dissection, one of a man 'who appeared to have been not long dead' along with several tubs of human flesh, fat and eviscera; 'The stench was so great that many were glad to return (to the street) without viewing the disgusting scene, many who went in were seized with sickness.' The mob was angry, fears were that they would set fire to the building. It was only in the nick of time that a party of Bow Street officers arrived on the scene. Some order was restored and enquiries soon revealed the old pub had been used as a legitimate anatomical theatre and boiling house. They surgeons were still advised to leave the house at speed by the back entrance.

UNFORESEEN EVENTS

In July 1871 Charles (aged forty-one) and Sarah de Baddeley (aged thirty-seven) of 4 Exeter Villas, Kensington were brought up before the Central Criminal Court. They had placed an advertisement in a spiritualist journal inviting people to consult at the house. Police sent a woman named Hansard with a fictitious enquiry on behalf of a pregnant friend to visit 'Madame de Baddeley' to elicit her mode of procedure. After being put into 'a so-called state of clairvoyance' Madame advised Hansard what to do in the case of a young woman she mentioned and gave her a quantity of ergot of rye to procure abortion. The sum of 6*l*. was paid in total to Madame de Baddeley. Mr and Mrs de Baddeley insisted they had committed no crime and criticised the police for laying a trap. Jury found both guilty and the Baddeleys were sentenced to 12 months' hard labour.

A PATENT CURE FOR ALL WOES

On 19 August 1888 an inquest was held at the City Mortuary into the death of Mr G.H. Hall, a brewer of Beckenham. It transpired Hall had had 'business worries' purchased three separate bottles of a patent medicine named 'chloral' and went to the City Central Hotel and was discovered dead in his bed the following day. After examination of the medicine it was revealed each bottle contained about 180 grains – a full sleeping dose being 30 grains. Jury returned a verdict of suicide while temporarily insane and recommended steps should be taken to prevent the ready sale of chloral.

MACKILL'S ASTHMA-CURE

Does for the CHEST and LUNGS what the SWEEP'S BRUSH does for a smoky chimney.

The Rational Cure for
ASTHMA, BRONCHITIS, SHORTNESS OF BREATH, INFLUENZA, &c.

Being inhaled it enters directly into the respiratory passages, allays all inflammatory developments, clears the air tubes and valves, thus relieving the chest oppression, and rendering the breathing easy and regular.

It gives instant relief followed by a Permanent Cure.

Sold by Chemists every where, in Tins at
1/9, 2/9, and 4/6.
FREE SAMPLE TINS
ON APPLICATION TO
Wholesale Agents

THE NEW APOTHECARIES' CO.,
GLASSFORD ST., GLASGOW.

A popular asthma cure advertised in London magazines in the 1880s.

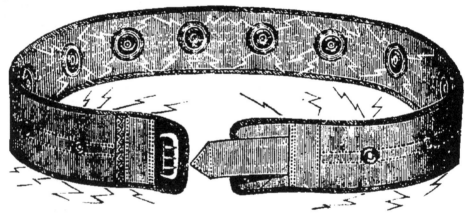
The 'miracle' cures offered by the Electric Belt in the 1880s.

THE WONDERS OF THE ELECTROPATHIC BELT

In the 1880s the Medical Battery Co. of Oxford Street took out large panel adverts in many of the leading magazines of the day to advertise their 'Electropathic (Battery) Belt.' Claimed and often illustrated being worn by Mr Gladstone the Prime Minister, the advert would go on to ask 'Can you afford to die?' and claimed that if you wore the belt 'all disorders of the nervous system, impaired vitality and defective organic action can be speedily, effectually and permanently cured.' Alleged testimonials surrounded the adverts extolling the efficacy of the device's cures for complaints as diverse as gout, hysteria, kidney disorders, bronchitis and writer's cramp, female complaints, constipation and piles – and this miracle cure was yours (post free) for only 21*s*.

HARDLY HERBAL REMEDIES

On 10 May 1889 George Hare, a man who described himself as a Herballist of Portobello Road and his housekeeper Lillian Ayliffe appeared before the Central Criminal Court. Not to put too fine a point on it Hare and Ayliffe were back street abortionists. They stood accused of two cases of conducting operations 'with an instrument' (probably a crochet hook) 'with intent to procure a miscarriage' by which means Elizabeth Louisa Davies had been seriously injured and Rhoda Fayers met her death. Found guilty Ayliff the assistant received five years and Hare ten.

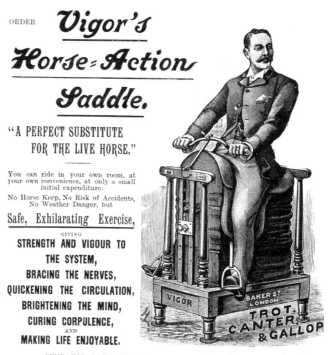

The horse riding experience in your own home!

CURES EVERYTHING BUT DEATH

The last word should come from the epitaph of eighteenth-century London quack doctor Lionel Lockyer who was buried in Southwark Cathedral. He claimed to be the inventor of a pill 'capable of curing every disease known and unknown' (clearly with the exception of death). I assume, he could not see the irony of shamelessly advertising his wonder pills on his memorial stone;

> His virtues and his PILLS are so well known,
> That envy can't confine them under stone,
> But they'll survive his dust and not expire,
> Till all things else th'universal fire.
> This verse is lost his pill embalms him safe
> To future times, without an epitaph.

NINE

GUNPOWDER, TREASON, PLOT & PROTEST

GOD SAVE THE KING! BUT DON'T SHOUT IT TOO LOUD

One of the earliest riots on record was in 1066 at the Coronation of William the Conqueror in the original Westminster Abbey. The Norman guards outside heard the acclamations in the Abbey and mistook them for the battle cries of insurgent Englishmen and fearing an attack they set fire to the houses that surrounded the Abbey. The English then feared they had been tricked and lured to the occasion and feared massacre. They left the Abbey to try to damp the fires outside and find arms with which to defend themselves. William was left inside with a fragment of his guests and a lot of frightened and confused clerics. William insisted the coronation proceed; it did, but was concluded quickly and with very little ceremony.

MASSACRE AT THE CORONATION

The coronation of Richard I in 1189 was severely marred after the uncrowned King had passed an edict that no Jews would be admitted to the Abbey or Westminster Hall on the day of his coronation. Many Jews still wanted to witness the occasion on the streets with the rest of the cheering public but many of the guards and public took offence that the Jews even dared to come into the crowds near the occasion and after a minor fracas the crowd erupted into an attack on all non-gentiles. Many Jews who fled from the fight were even pursued to their homes that were summarily torched – with the occupants still inside.

THE PEASANTS' REVOLT

In 1381 the peasants revolt marched on London under Wat Tyler. Thousands of peasants had successfully entered the city and took the Tower and had even beheaded the Archbishop of Canterbury. On 15 June 1381 King Richard II agreed to meet the peasants and hear their terms at Smithfield, the exchange between them has entered into legend. It was said that Wat Tyler was insolent and drew his dagger upon the knights the king had sent to meet him, when he finally approached the king Tyler grabbed the bridle of the monarch's horse. This was one insult too many and Sir William Walworth the Lord Mayor plunged a dagger into Tyler's throat. The peasants, outraged by the killing of their leader were ready to attack again when the legend tells of the King riding up to their lines and addressed them 'Why this clamour, my liegemen? What are ye doing? Will you kill your King? Be not displeased for the death of a traitor and a scoundrel. I will be your captain and your leader: follow me into the fields, and I will grant you all you ask.' The peasants trusted the words of the King and he led them into Islington Fields where they dispersed. Jack Straw, Tyler's second in command was afterwards hanged in Smithfield.

THE END OF BRAVEHEART

William 'Braveheart' Wallace was brought to London after raising revolt in Scotland. Condemned for his treason he was dragged by horses from the Tower to Smithfield on St Bartholomew's Eve 1305. He was hanged, drawn and then quartered while he was still living. Quarters of his body were divided between Newcastle-upon-Tyne, Berwick, Stirling and Perth – as a warning to the people in those rebel areas who might think of challenged English rule again. Wallace's head remained in the city, impaled on a spike on London Bridge.

THE SMITHFIELD MARTYRS

Hundreds of martyrs (a figure of 269 executed in the reign of 'Bloody' Mary I alone is recorded), who were persecuted for their religious beliefs, met horrific deaths at the stake on Smithfield between the fifteenth and sixteenth centuries. In many ways the death of John Badley in 1409 was typical of them all but in one respect it was unique; for the use of a tun (a barrel) in his execution. According to Nicholas' *Chronicle of London*, when Badley was bound to the stake no lesser man than Henry, Prince of Wales implored Badley to forsake his heresy and 'hold the righte way of holy chirche.' Offered sacrament Badley was asked what it was, and he stated 'it was hallowed bred and nought Godes body.' The tun was then put over him and a fire kindled within. As the flames burnt into Badley's flesh he cried for mercy. The prince commanded the tun be removed and then asked Badley again if he would forsake heresy, take the faith of the Holy Church and his life would be spared. Nicholas concludes 'the cursed shrewe wolde nought, but continued forth in his heresye,' the fire was rekindled and Badley was burnt to cinders.

THE ROBUST OLD GATE

In 1471 Aldgate, one of the great defensive gates of the city was attacked by the rebellious Thomas Nevill 'the Bastard of Falconbeigh.' Affecting an entrance the portcullis was suddenly let down, and Nevill and his men were surrounded and slain where they stood.

RACK AND FLAME

Anne Askew the beautiful young daughter of Sir William Askew was a condemned as a heretic in 1546 and tortured on the rack at the hands of Lord Chancellor Wriothesley to give up the names of those court ladies of Queen Catherine Parr who shared her opinions. She did not divulge a name but she lost the use of her feet after her stretch on the rack, and was carried to the Smithfield stake on a chair. After she was tied to the stake round the middle by a chain that was to also hold up her body, and the sermon had been delivered, the dignitaries, which included Wriothley, the Duke of Norfolk, Duke of Bedford and Lord Mayor, on the bench by St Bartholomew's Church were concerned that before the fire was set to the faggots heaped around Anne, a check should be made for the strength of gunpowder in them to hasten the poor girl to her death, lest they exploded and sent a hail of twigs at them. Bedford was recorded as assuring his fellow dignitaries the powder was only about her body. Anne was given a chance to recant, but declined. The Lord Mayor then cried in a loud voice 'Fiat Justicia,' fire was put to the faggots and Anne was soon 'compassed in the flames of fire;' one of many martyred for the Protestant cause.

THE GUNPOWDER PLOT

Undoubtedly the most infamous plot in the history of London, and indeed, Britain is the Gunpowder Plot. Still remembered every year, children still recite the old poem:

> Remember, remember,
> The Fifth of November:
> Gunpowder, Treason and Plot.
> I see no reason
> Why gunpowder treason
> Should ever be forgot.

The plot was created by a group of Catholic fanatics who wanted to blow up James I as he opened the new session of Parliament on 5 November 1605, thus destroying the Protestant King and his Government. They would then ensure James's daughter Elizabeth (who was a Catholic) and put her on the throne in his stead to restore the old Catholic Church to England. The man said to have organised the plot was one John Grant; those identified as the key members of the conspiracy were Robert and Thomas Wintour, Thomas Percy, Christopher and John Wright, Francis Tresham, Everard Digby, Ambrose Rookwood, Thomas Bates, Robert Keyes, Hugh Owen, Robert Catesby and their explosives expert Guy Fawkes. By the night of 4 November Fawkes and the conspirators had managed to get thirty-six barrels of gunpowder under the House of Lords and all was set, but the cataclysmic blast was not to be. Over a week before on 26 October an anonymous letter had been received by Lord Monteagle warning him to stay away from parliament, which was to receive 'a terrible blow.' Historical research over subsequent years has suggested to some historians that government intelligence may well have known of the plot for some time before the letter, which may have actually been a contrivance of the intelligence service to

The Gunpowder Plotters.

officially set in motion the investigation of the plot without revealing its sources. What we know for sure is that the king ordered a search of the undercrofts and cellars of the House on 4 November and Westminister magistrate Sir Thomas Knyvet and his men caught Guy Fawkes and his lethal explosives red handed. Dragged before the King, Fawkes was defiant and declared that 'a desperate deed requires a desperate remedy.' The king sought a remedy of his own for the treasonous Fawkes and sent him to The Tower. Sir William Wade, Lieutenant of the Tower, was given orders directly from the King to use any means to get information, especially the names of the fellow conspirators, from Fawkes. Guy Fawkes withstood three days of torture before he finally betrayed the names of others involved in the plot. The comparison between Fawkes signature before and after the torture tell a story of a man broken in mind, soul and body. Catesby, Percy and Winter were hunted down to Staffordshire and all bar Winter died after a fierce fight when the men came to arrest them. The rest of the named conspirators were tried at Westminster Hall. All were found guilty of high treason; their plot may have been bloodless but James's retribution saw justice was served swift, public and bloody; all were to be hanged, drawn and quartered. On 30 January 1606 five of the plotters were executed in St Paul's Churchyard, Fawkes and two others were executed in Old Palace Yard, Westminster. Still crippled by the torture he had suffered Fawkes had to be assisted up the ladder of the gallows. Others said to have been named by conspirators were to suffer the same fate over the following months. All of their heads were displayed on spikes and poles around London as a lasting reminder for anyone who dared to forget or conspired to plan another fifth of November.

THE WALLER PLOT

In 1643 while the Civil War was raging a plot was hatched by poet and former MP Edmund Waller with two conspirators named Nathaniel Tomkins and Richard Challoner. The plan was to instigate an armed uprising from within London to deliver the city and the Tower to the King. Doomed to failure, the conspirators were brought to trial at the Guildhall before the Earl of Manchester. Waller quickly confessed all and gave up his co-conspirators. Tomkins and Challoner went to the gallows. Tomkins was hanged on Fetter Lane within sight of the Magpie and Stump pub where it was said the plot was hatched. Waller was far more fortunate, after an eloquent defence and plea bargain where Waller offered to pay the financially desperate Parliament a £10,000 fine he was allowed to keep his life and went into exile in France until the Restoration.

THE KILLING OF THE KING

The ultimate act of the English Civil War was enacted on a high-raised platform outside the Banqueting House, Whitehall when shortly after 2 p.m. on 30 January 1649, King Charles I was executed. The King chose St James's Park as the route of his final walk, a sombre procession in which the King was escorted by soldiers with companies of halberdiers in front and behind complete with their drums beating and colours flying. As the King stepped out he surveyed the block which only stood about 10ins high and objected for this would cause him to have to lay prostrate rather than the more dignified kneeling afforded by the block in the Tower. His executioner simply said it 'It can be no higher, Sir.' As Charles prepared to lay his neck on the block, he told his executioner to wait until he stretched out his hands as

The execution of Charles I, 30 January 1649.

a sign he had finished his prayers – then to strike with the axe. Conscious of the presence of his executioner and fearing impatience Charles's last words were 'Wait for the sign! Wait for the sign'. A pause later the King spread his arms wide and the headsman did his duty removing the King's head with one deft blow. Rather than a cheer the assembled crowd gave 'a universal groan, the like never before heard.' The assistant executioner then picked up and held the head aloft for all the crowd to see with the words 'Behold the Head of a Traitor.' Once removed from the scene of execution the King's head was sewn back on his body and removed to St James's to be embalmed. Charles I was finally laid to rest a few days later in St George's Chapel, Windsor.

THE MAN WHO KILLED THE KING

The executioner and his assistant who executed Charles I were both masked and heavily disguised with false beards and thick coats. Much speculation was made about who they were in the years afterwards. The most likely candidate for the man who assisted was one William Lowen, a former dunghill cleaner but the man who actually wielded the axe was almost certainly Richard Brandon, a rag shop proprietor from Rosemary Lane, Whitechapel. At his burial on 21 July 1649 the people realised

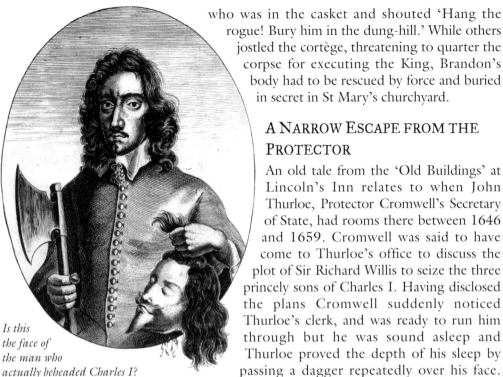

*Is this
the face of
the man who
actually beheaded Charles I?
Or is it a satire on Thomas Fairfax?*

who was in the casket and shouted 'Hang the rogue! Bury him in the dung-hill.' While others jostled the cortège, threatening to quarter the corpse for executing the King, Brandon's body had to be rescued by force and buried in secret in St Mary's churchyard.

A NARROW ESCAPE FROM THE PROTECTOR

An old tale from the 'Old Buildings' at Lincoln's Inn relates to when John Thurloe, Protector Cromwell's Secretary of State, had rooms there between 1646 and 1659. Cromwell was said to have come to Thurloe's office to discuss the plot of Sir Richard Willis to seize the three princely sons of Charles I. Having disclosed the plans Cromwell suddenly noticed Thurloe's clerk, and was ready to run him through but he was sound asleep and Thurloe proved the depth of his sleep by passing a dagger repeatedly over his face. Cromwell was satisfied and the clerk, who was not really asleep, but had just managed to keep his cool and had heard everything and sent a secret warning sent to the princes. It seems Thurloe was an astute man, with a keen sense of preservation. After the restoration he looked out all the incriminating papers naming him and many of his friends and hid them in a false ceiling of his offices. They were not discovered until William III was on the throne and Thurloe had peacefully died.

THE MURDER OF JUSTICE GODFREY

Magistrate Edmund Berry Godfrey became embroiled in the alleged Popish Plot concocted by Titus Oates in 1678. When Oates and one of his cohorts names Israel Tonge appeared before Godfrey, they asked him to give his oath that the papers they presented as evidence were based on truth. Godfrey said he could give no such oath if he did not know the contents of the papers so a copy was delivered to him on 28 September 1678. Upon examination of the papers, Godfrey was undoubtedly concerned he may be a target but took no extra precautions for security. Perhaps he saw through the scaremongering of Oates and appeared to be obstructive to his plans. The truth will probably never be known. On the night of 12 October 1678 Godfrey did not return home and was discovered in a ditch on Primrose Hill on 17 October. Lying face down, he was impaled upon his own sword. There was no sign of struggle near the scene, he still had his jewellery on him but his body was bruised and marks around his neck indicated strangulation, the sword wound had not bled and thus had been committed post mortem. Two committees of investigation and a £500 reward saw Miles Prance, an unreliable witness to say the least, name Robert Green, Lawrence Hill and Henry Berry as the men who lured Godfrey to Somerset House under the pretext of being called to keep the peace between two servants who were fighting in the yard. Once the justice arrived his assassins leapt from the shadows and strangled him with such force it broke his neck. The body was then removed in a Sedan chair to Soho where it was hidden for a few days and eventually moved again to be dumped in the ditch on Primrose Hill. These three men were executed on Greenberry Hill on 5 February 1679. Prance's story was later discredited and he pleaded guilty to perjury. Upon this confession it appears the three men were sent to the gallows in error and who really killed Justice Godfrey remains a mystery.

TAKEN FOR A MUG?

On 23 July 1716 a tavern in Salisbury Court off Fleet Street was attacked by a violent mob and bloodshed took place before order was restored. The riot stemmed from the new accession of the house of Hanover to the British monarchy after the death of Queen Anne. 'Mug Houses' were established across London (simply named so after the mugs the beer was drunk from that were also hung outside the taverns in the forenoon to show the number of regulars and thus the growing numbers of new

A mug-house riot, c. 1716.

supporters for the house of Hanover). In these taverns the friends of the Protestant Hanover succession drank loyal toasts to 'Good King George' and rallied against the Jacobite partisans of the popish pretender. By the Autumn of 1715 taverns proved to become recruiting grounds and meeting places for those who set out to defend the house of Hanover and bands of drink fuelled men began to march in disorderly manner along the streets after dark to fight with the Jacobites. The troubles and rioting mobs grew in size and intensity until the attack on the Salisbury Court mug-house by a large mob that was fought off through the night but eventually the greater numbers of the invading mob finally forced their way in and Read the keeper of the coffee house, in a fit of desperation blasted one of the ringleaders dead with his blunderbuss. The mob got hold of Read, beat him mercilessly and left him for dead. The rest of the beaten, bruised and bleeding loyalists retreated to the upper rooms of the building where they were imprisoned while the Jacobite mob gutted the bar and drank the majority of the cellar contents. The mob was only dispersed by the arrival of the military. At the inquest on the dead ringleader a verdict of wilful murder was returned against Read, but he was acquitted at his trial. A number of the rioters were not as lucky and were hanged for their part in the insurrection and peace, slowly, but surely returned to the mug-houses.

FIRING OF THE KING'S PRINTING HOUSE

When James II took flight from London after his abdication in 1688 riotous crowds took to the streets, recorded by Macaulay thus: 'When the night, the longest night, as it chanced, of the year approached, forth came from every den of vice . . . thousands of housebreakers and highwaymen, cut purses and ring droppers. With these were mingled thousands of idle apprentices, who wished merely for the excitement of a riot. Even men of peaceable and honest habits were impelled by religious animosity to join the lawless part of the population.' The target of the crowds were mostly Catholic churches and prominent Papists, even the King's Printing House from which Catholic tracts were published was torched and the pamphlets inside heaped up in the street and burnt in a huge bonfire.

FIREWORKS AT KING'S BENCH

On 14 July 1737 an inconspicuous parcel wrapped in brown paper was placed unobserved by person or persons near the side-bar of the Court of the King's Bench in Westminster Hall. While the court was sitting, between one and two o' clock in the afternoon the device inside the parcel exploded causing panic and commotion, but it was soon clear that the contents were simply fireworks. As the crackers rattled and burst, they threw out balls of printed bills that stated on the last day of term, five libels (five unpopular Acts of Parliament) would be publicly burned in Westminster Hall. The grand jury considered this whole incident 'wicked and audacious outrage.' A reward of £200 was offered for the author or printer of the bills but they were never discovered.

MESSAGE RECEIVED LOUD AND CLEAR

In October 1763 several thousand journeymen weavers assembled in Spitalfields and marched on the house of one of their masters. Their anger boiled into riot and they gained entry, smashed the looms and cut a great quantity of rich silk to pieces. They then set an effigy of the master into a cart with a halter (noose) about his neck with an executioner on one side and a coffin on the other and drove it in true 'carting to Tyburn' style through the streets then hanged the figure on a gibbet and burnt it to ashes. Their anger demonstrated, they dispersed 'without further mischief.'

HARDLY AN APRIL FOOL

During the middle ages and well into the nineteenth century groups of rioters fearful of retribution after over-reaction by their employers and local authorities would often make their point by staging parades or costumed festivals which would hopefully not be construed as too aggressive. In April 1771 such protest or complaint was well evinced when two carts preceded by a hearse were drawn through the City to Tower Hill. In the first cart was a man dressed as the executioner with three near life size figures, complete with caps and handkerchiefs over their eyes, painted on board strung up in a wooden gallows, in the second cart were similar. All of the dangling figures had names of people of rank such as Aldermen painted on their backs. At Tower Hill all the figures were ceremonially burnt to masses of cheers from the large crowd who had walked with the procession. One man in the mob was seen to be noting down the names painted on the figures – seized as a spy he was ducked in the Tower ditch until the mob were really convinced he had simply copied the names down to satisfy his own curiosity.

THE GORDON RIOTS

One of the most dramatic illustrations of the volatility of the London Mob occurred in 1780. Rumblings of disquiet had been heard since the inception of the Catholic Relief Act of 1778 which relieved 'His Majesty's subjects, of the Catholic Religion, from certain penalties and disabilities imposed upon them during the reign of William

The attack of the rioters upon Newgate during the Gordon Riots, June 1780.

III,' notably removing the obligation of Catholics from taking the religious oath when joining the Army or Navy. The eccentric rabid anti-Catholic Lord George Gordon set up The Protestant Association in 1780 to fight for the repeal of the legislation and inflamed the London mob with his scaremongering of Papism and a return to absolute monarchical rule. At a mass meeting on 29 May 1780 Gordon declared they would march on the House of Commons to deliver their petition of protest. On 2 June a mob numbering between 40,000–60,000 assembled at St George's Fields, Southwark carrying banners and placards demanding 'No Popery' many of them wore blue cockades in their hats, a symbol of allegiance to The Protestant Association. Led with Gordon at their head they marched to parliament, their numbers swelled along the route and more and more joined the throng. Their mood was not improved as Lord Gordon appeared to have difficulty in having his petition received at the House. He did manage to present it to the Lower House but the mob outside were impatient, soon got out of hand and a riot erupted. The mob expressed their anger by damaging, defacing, smashing and firing many Catholic churches, chapels, businesses and homes of known followers, supporters and sympathisers of the faith. The Bank of England, Fleet Prison, Clerkenwell and the Lord Chief Justice were all attacked. The worst damage was inflicted on Newgate Prison where the mob attacked the walls and started a fire that largely destroyed the old prison. On 7 June the army was mobilized to put down the riot, it was a bloody quelling as 285 of the rioters were killed, 173 wounded and 139 arrested, and an estimated £180,000 worth of property had been destroyed in the rioting. A variety of custodial sentences were meted out to the rioters brought before the courts, but 21 of Gordon's followers identified as ring leaders were executed. Lord George Gordon was arrested and charged with high treason but he was found not guilty.

THE IGNOMINY OF COLONEL DESPARD

Colonel Edward Marcus Despard was once a respected soldier who had distinguished himself by his skill as an engineer and as the commander of a successful expedition against the Spanish possessions on the Black River in 1782. Tragically he was attacked on frivolous charges levelled by ambitious enemies during his time as Superintendent of the Bay of Honduras, was recalled to England and between 1790 and 1792 he was suspended on half pay. Further charges were brought and Despard landed up in King's Bench debtors prison from 1792–4. More suspicions were to stain the Colonel in 1794 as he was accused of involvement in the Irish Rebellion and was held in London prisons (notably Coldbath Fields) for over three years without charge. He was released without any charges pressed in 1802. Now in his fiftieth year and fired with hatred for the system that had treated him so badly Despard gathered together a group of similarly disaffected soldiers and Irishmen and began plotting their greatest campaign – the taking of the seat of power of Great Britain. The scheme involved the seizure of the Tower and the Bank of England and even the assassination of George III. This last detail was to be signalled by the stopping of the mail coaches so the people in the country would know 'that revolt had taken place in town.' Despard was informed upon, arrested in the Oakley Arms, Oakley Street with a number of his co-conspirators and brought to trial. Despite a dramatic personal appearance by Lord Nelson who had served with Despard on the Spanish Main and spoke in Despard's favour as 'a loyal man and a good officer' the jury would not be turned and Despard, with six other conspirators (namely private soldiers John Francis (aged twenty-three) and John Wood (aged thirty-six); carpenters Thomas Broughton (aged twenty-six) and John Macnamara (aged fifty), slater Arthur Graham (aged fifty-three) and shoemaker James Sedgwick Wratton (aged thirty-five), were found guilty of treason and sentenced to be hanged, drawn and quartered, a dread sentence carried out at Horsemonger Lane Gaol, Southwark on 21 February 1803. As each were taken down their bodies were placed upon sawdust with the head on a block and beheaded, Despard's head being held aloft by the hair with the exclamation 'This is the head of a traitor, Edward Marcus Despard!' Despard's body was removed by his friends on 1 March who saw to it his body was taken by hearse accompanied by three mourning coaches to near the south door of St Paul's Cathedral where he was finally interred. The City Marshal was present, lest there should be any disturbance on this occasion.

THE O.P. RIOTS

After the fire at Covent Garden that burnt the old Theatre to the ground on 20 September 1808 valiant efforts were made to rebuild it and almost a year to the day after the fire the new Covent Garden Theatre opened its doors again. But all was not well, the expense of rebuilding and the increased ground rent meant that prices had to be raised for tickets to the boxes and the pit. This not did sit well with the audience and rather than simply do something else they started to protest for the restoration of the old prices. They still came to theatre but wore hats and coats marked with the letters 'O.P.' This peaceful protest, not receiving any gesture of recognition, progressed to placards and shouts being made in performances which in turn escalated to a cacophony of groaning, singing, laughing and whistling with occasional accompaniment of coachmen's horns, showmen's trumpets, dustman's bells and watchman's rattles. There was even the 'O.P.' dance which consisted of alternate stamping of the feet, accompanied with the regular cry of 'O.P!' in noisy and monotonous unison. The theatre proprietors sought to quell the 'rioters' by organising a corps of prize fighters to act as bouncers led by the noted pugilist 'Dutch Sam.' This was seen as rather heavy handed and after an incident where it appeared a more formal legal action was imminent between O.P. Rioters and the box manager, the theatre management met with the protestors, dropped all charges and listened to the objections raised, the Treaty of Peace being ratified at a dinner a few weeks later.

THE CATO STREET CONSPIRACY

In the stable loft of a house on Cato Street a group of plotters led by Arthur Thistlewood devised a scheme to assassinate the entire cabinet as they dined with Lord Harrowby in Grosvenor Square. After the slaughter the heads of three ministers, including the Home Secretary were to be carried off in a bag. The conspirators were then going to storm and plunder The Bank of England, fire the King Street Barracks and capture the cannon on the artillery ground to take the Royal Exchange, Mansion House, Bank and even The Tower where they planned to proclaim their new provisional government! As the date set for the deed approached, one of the conspirators, probably George Edwards, informed the authorities and on the night of 23 February 1820, the night planned for the coup, the Bow Street Runners and a detachment of Coldstream Guards stormed into the loft on Cato Street. As the raiders forced their way in Thistlewood ran through Richard Smithers, one of the law officers, with his sword exclaiming 'Oh, my God, I am done' and made good his

Arthur Thistlewood runs through Richard Smithers, one of the Bow Street Runners who raided the Cato Street conspirators.

escape. A number of conspirators were arrested on the spot, the eleven others who got away that night were brought in to Bow Street over the next few days. Thistlewood was arrested the day after the raid when he was traced to a house in Little Moorfields. Found guilty of the conspiracy five were transported and Thistlewood and the other ring leaders, namely James Ings, William Davidson, John Brunt and Richard Tidd were executed before a large crowd at Newgate on 1 May 1820. The conspirators had been sentenced to be hanged, drawn and quartered but in the end public pressure and sympathy saw them hanged and then beheaded. Thistlewood died stoically sucking an orange after his final defiant exclamation of 'Albion is still in the chains of slavery. I quit without regret.'

THE ACCUSATION OF BURKING

During the bodysnatching scares and trials of the 1830s those involved in the business were particularly hated by the public. In December 1831 'an elderly masculine-looking woman' commonly known as Nanny Newman, a launderess, bore a grudge against one of her neighbours, Mrs Ann Kerr who kept a lodging house at 2 Rogers Court near the Hermitage Bridge, Wapping. The grudge was said to have arisen after Mrs Kerr prosecuted Richard Banks, a ship's mate and one of her lodgers whom she accused of stealing a silver watch. Perhaps Newman was sweet on Banks or simply wanted an excuse to vent a petty jealousy on Kerr, whatever the motive since that time she had taken every opportunity to abuse poor Mrs Kerr when she passed her on the street and called her a 'Burker' (bodysnatcher) and shouted 'They have burked poor Banks' if she spotted anyone coming to the Kerr's door. Not content with this, Newman spread rumours that Kerr had actually 'burked' several persons to the surgeons. Kerr was shunned by many who believed the tale. Matters came to a head when Newman gathered a mob in from of Rogers Court 'who made a most discordant noise, and appeared inclined to make an attack on the premises.' Newman was restrained and the mob dispersed. Brought before Thames Police Office, when called to account for her behaviour Newman struck the bar with great violence and exclaimed 'I did say Mrs Kerr and her daughters were Burkers, and I'll stick to them yet: nothing is so sweet as revenge.' The newspaper account of the hearing notes she 'accompanied these words with the most threatening gesticulations towards the complainant.' Newman was ordered to find sureties, herself in 28*l.*, and two sureties of 10*l.* each to keep the peace towards the complainant for the next 12 months.

THE IRON DUKE ON THE DEFENCES OF PARLIAMENT

After the fire which gutted much of the Houses of Parliament in 1835 suggestions were put forward that it may be a good time to relocate this seat of power to somewhere such as Green Park or Trafalgar Square but the old Duke of Wellington was having none of it. The 'Iron Duke,' victor of Waterloo argued the old site was the only place for Parliament because with the river it its back it could never be surrounded by any 'revolutionary or hostile mob.'

THE EIGHT LIVES OF QUEEN VICTORIA

There were no less than seven assassination attempts on the life of Queen Victoria. The first came hardly three years after her accession to the throne. The Queen and her Consort Albert were riding in their carriage along Constitution Hill on 10 June 1840. A labourer named Edward Oxford (aged eighteen) drew a pistol which he had concealed in the breast of his jacket and discharged it at the Queen, the ball passed so close it was heard to 'whiz by' but thinking nothing of the noise nor anyone having reached Oxford to obstruct his act, he drew another pistol. Her Majesty saw this second pistol drawn and stooped down, Oxford fired and the ball whizzed by again. A crowd had reached the scene and Oxford was overpowered by a man named Lowe who took the pistols from him and the attempted assassin was removed to custody. Despite fears of a Chartist or other conspiracies Oxford was found insane and he was detained in Bedlam 'during Her Majesty's pleasure.' The second attempt was on 29 May 1842 when John Francis fired a pistol as the Queen was being driven through St James's Park. Francis was immediately seized by PC William Trounce (hence the term to be 'trounced' meaning to foil), put on trial and found guilty of high treason but his sentence was commuted to transportation for life. Just days after Francis's sentence was commuted a third attack came on 3 July 1842 when a boy named John William Bean shot the Queen. No doubt a stupid publicity stunt as his gun was only loaded with paper and tobacco. This lad was given eighteen months imprisonment. The fourth attack was made by a disgruntled Irishmen named William Hamilton on 19 May 1849 who fired a pistol filled only with powder at the Queen as her carriage passed down Constitution Hill. Hamilton was given seven years' transportation. The only time the Queen sustained any injury from attack occurred with the fifth attempt carried out on 27 June 1850 by mentally unstable Robert Pate an army officer on half pay, late of the 10th Hussars, who struck out at the Queen in her carriage with his

John Francis about to be trounced as he fires his pistol at Queen Victoria.

cane near the gates of Cambridge House, Piccadilly. He crushed her bonnet and caused bruising to her face. Pate never gave a reason for his attack. His plea of insanity was not proved so he was given seven years' transportation. The sixth attempt on Queen Victoria came on 30 April 1872 when Arthur O'Conner (aged seventeen) came running towards the Queen's carriage with a pistol in one hand and a petition for the release of Fenian prisoners in the other. Seized and restrained by John Brown the Queen's loyal retainer, O'Conner was sentenced to one year of imprisonment and twenty stokes of the birch rod. The seventh and final attempt on Victoria's life came on 2 March 1882. Roderick Maclean, a Scot, had developed a grievance with Her Majesty after allegedly receiving a 'curt reply' after he had mailed some of his poetry to the Queen. As the Queen was leaving Windsor Railway station in her carriage Maclean shot her but missed. Overpowered and taken into custody he was found insane and lived out the rest of his life in an asylum. No more attempts on her life, Queen Victoria lived on and died peacefully in 1901.

SCOTLAND YARD BOMBED

Shortly before 9 p.m. on 30 May 1884 a bomb planted by Fenians tore through the gable end of the CID and Special Irish branch headquarters in Great Scotland Yard. Smashed glass and brick rubble was strewn across the road and a 30ft high hole was blasted out but luckily no-one was injured but the damage to the reputation of the police, having had a bomb go off literally under their noses, was inestimable. Matters were compounded with other bombs being exploded at the Junior Carlton Club and outside Sir Watkin-Wynne's house; there was even an unexploded device found at the foot of Nelson's Column – luckily the fuse attached to the 16 sticks of dynamite which would almost certainly have brought the great monument down, was defective.

THE SAVING OF WESTMINISTER HALL

On 24 January 1885 Fenian bombs exploded in some of the most significant and historic buildings of London. A device exploded at the Tower of London scattering stands of arms and armour in its wake, creating havoc in the Old Banqueting Hall. A second bomb was discovered on the steps going down to St Stephen's Crypt in the Palace of Westminister and was reported to PCs Cole and Cox of A (Whitehall) Division. Lifting the parcel with its burning envelope PC William Cole carried the device up the stairs into Westminister Hall where his hands were so badly burnt he was caused to drop the bomb and it exploded. Bravely tended by PC Cox who was on duty in the hall, Cole was later awarded the Albert Medal for his gallantry. A third bomb was detonated in the House of Commons, luckily the house was not in session at the time but extensive damage was caused to the Division Hall Strangers and Peers galleries. Two men were convicted of complicity in the bombings and were sentenced to penal servitude for life.

BLACK MONDAY

On 8 February 1886 saw the occurrence of the 'Black Monday' Riot in Trafalgar Square. Two rival radical movements, The London United Workmen's Committee and H.F. Hyndman's pro-revolution Social Democratic Federation both made it known they wanted to hold rallies in Trafalgar Square on this day, neither would back out and a violent clash was almost imminent. The new Home Secretary was preoccupied with getting a grip on the reins of his new office, both meetings were approved and force constables designated to police the square with 563 reserves standing by. The meetings went without incident in the square but as the mob, fired up by the speeches, streamed along Pall Mall a garbled message was sent that there was trouble in the Mall rather than Pall Mall. The reserves rushed to defend Buckingham Palace and the mob was left to run amock in Pall Mall and St James's. An unofficial rally in Hyde Park saw the mob whipped into a frenzy of window smashing and looting along Oxford Street. Inspector James Cuthbert was routinely parading his sergeant and constables ready for their duties when he heard the mob. His actions were swift, brave and decisive. He marched his men to Oxford Street, seventeen in number and with truncheons drawn they charged the crowd and ended the riot. Two days later a further panic of a large mob assembling to attack Oxford Street saw businesses barricade themselves and fear for the worst – the mob never came and was probably only ever a paranoid over reaction by police officials on unreliable information. An enquiry was called into the incidents and Metropolitan Police Commissioner Henderson took the only option open to him and resigned. A man with a strong military background was needed to head the police and deal decisively with such incidents so he was replaced by General Sir Charles Warren.

BLOODY SUNDAY

Unemployment and poverty driven desperation had grown to such proportions in London that jobless agitators started camping in Trafalgar Square in an attempt to draw attention to their plight. Political meetings began to be held in the square with increasing regularity and with speeches becoming more and more inciteful and impassioned. Sir Charles Warren saw the warning signs and pressured Home Secretary Matthews to declare such meetings in and around the square illegal. A meeting the challenge this prohibition was called for at 2.30 p.m. on 13 November 1887. Warren personally took 2,000 of his men to Trafalgar Square to meet this challenge. He also had two Squadrons of Life Guards on standby at Horse Guards Parade with two Magistrates to read the Riot Act if necessary. At 3.45 p.m. an unruly mob, armed with sticks, iron bars, knives, stones and bricks approached the square intent on storming it. The police held firm but concerned with the escalating violence, Warren ordered the Life Guards in at 4.05 p.m. In all, four thousand constables, 300 mounted police, 300 Grenadier Guards and three hundred Life Guards were deployed to quell the riot. Over 300 were arrested. Most were dismissed with warnings or fines, some got imprisonment with hard labour varying between one and six months. It was incredible that no-one was killed outright on Bloody Sunday, over 150 were treated for injuries and hospitals swelled with serious cases for weeks afterwards. On 5 December 1887 an inquest was conducted at St Martin's Vestry Hall, Charing Cross, into the circumstances of death of Alfred Linnell (aged forty-one), a Law Writer of Took's Court, Cursitor Street who died from injuries received in Northumberland Avenue during the 'Bloody Sunday' riots. Slipping he had fallen down, and was trampled by a mounted policeman and several others while they were clearing the streets. Rushed to Charing Cross Hospital he was operated on for a compound fracture of the thigh. All appearances suggested full recovery but blood poisoning set in and it killed him. Accidental death was recorded.

POLICE ON STRIKE

On 7 June 1890 Policemen disgruntled by lack of proper pension provision, pay scales and desirous of starting a union came out on strike at Bow Street. Joined by socialist activists and an unruly mob of 'supporters' they threatened to knock down any man seen going on duty at Bow Street, marched up and down the street singing 'Rule Britannia' and then hung around the area armed with flour bombs and rotten vegetables – these they hurled at the mounted police officers when they arrived to control the situation. The strike ended when Assistant Commissioner Howard invited the policemen on the Station steps to come in and discuss their grievances, the mob was dowsed with a bowl of water from the upper windows of the police station and were already dispersing as two troops of Life Guards trotted into Bow Street.

TEN

TALES FROM THE TOWER

A DOUBLE FIRST?

The first recorded prisoner in The Tower of London was Ranulf Flambard, Bishop of Durham. He was imprisoned in the White Tower, for extortions carried out under William II under order of Henry I in 1100. In 1101 he managed to escape using a rope smuggled in to him hidden in a pot of wine – using the wine to get his guards drunk he lowered himself out of his cell by the rope and made good his escape to Normandy. Thus Ranulf also has the distinction of being the first recorded escapee from the Tower of London.

THE PRINCES IN THE TOWER

In 1483, Richard Duke of Gloucester brought his two nephews, the twelve year old uncrowned boy King Edward V and his younger brother the Duke of York to the Tower of London under the guise of it being for their own protection. What next happened to the boys remains a debate which rages to this day. Tudor historians would have us believe that under the instructions of the Princes' wicked uncle and guardian, Sir James Tyrell arranged and oversaw John Dighton his horsekeeper and Miles Forrest, one of the boys' four Tower guardians, suffocate the uncrowned Edward V and his ten-year-old brother with pillows so that their twisted uncle could usurp the throne and be crowned Richard III. It is even claimed that under sentence of death for treason in 1502 Tyrell finally confessed to this heinous deed. Two hundred years after the disappearance of the princes the bones of two young boys were discovered under a stair during renovations. Charles II believed these to be the remains of the princes and had them removed and given a Royal burial in Westminster Abbey. In 1933 the bones were removed from their burial urn and examined again; they were said to be those of two boys, apparently related and aged comparably to the princes at the time of their disappearance.

THE END OF BARON HASTINGS

Richard III, the man accused of being behind the murder of the Princes in the Tower has blood on his hands from a less well known incident. William, Baron Hastings refused to pledge allegiance to Richard after his assumption of the throne. A message was sent to Hastings inviting him to a council meeting at the Tower on 13 June 1483. The meeting convened, Richard feigned anger and crashing his hand to the table cried 'Treason, Treason!' accusingly at Hastings. Soldiers burst in to the chamber, Richard accused Hastings of treacherous plotting, one account has Richard exclaiming 'By God, I will not dine until thy head is struck from thy shoulders!' Manhandled outside to beneath the walls of the Keep, a log used for odd repairs was improvised as a block, and Baron Hastings was beheaded.

BY SWORD NOT AXE

On 19 May 1536 Queen Anne Boleyn, second wife of King Henry VIII was executed on Tower Green at the Tower of London after being found guilty of trumped up charges of adultery and treason. Contrary to popular belief she was not decapitated on the block with an axe but was, by her own special request, executed by a swordsman from Calais, France. Blindfolded and kneeling upright the executioner's assistant walked towards her on a pre-arranged signal from the executioner to distract her and instinctively move her head, then made just one sweep of his blade and the executioner severed her head. To avoid manhandling of her head her ladies in waiting wrapped it with her body in 'a white covering' and because there was not even a coffin provided for her it was said Queen Anne was buried with little ceremony in an arrow chest in the Chapel of St Peter ad Vincula within the walls of the Tower. A curious postscript to this even is recorded in *Ghostly Visitors* by 'Spectre Stricken' in 1882, a Captain of the Guard one night saw a light glowing from the chapel and obtained a ladder to look inside and saw 'Slowly down the aisle moved a stately procession of knights and ladies, attired in ancient costumes; and in front walked an elegant lady whose face was averted from him, but whose figure greatly resembled the one he had seen in reputed portraits of Anne Boleyn. After having repeatedly paced the chapel, the entire procession, together with the light, disappeared.'

THE LAST OF MORE

Sir Thomas More was a noble and wise statesman but as a staunch believer in the Pope's supremacy he would play no part in Henry VIII's schism with Rome nor would he acquiesce to take an oath recognising the king's marriage or King Henry as head of the English Church in place of the Pope. After maintaining a dignified silence that spoke volumes of his opinion of the king's behaviour, he was imprisoned in The Tower and was eventually sentenced to execution by beheading on Tower Green in 1535. Upon mounting the scaffold More, in time honoured tradition, forgave his executioner and said 'Pluck up thy spirits, man, and be not afraid to do thine office. My neck is very short – take heed therefore thou strike not awry for saving thine honesty!' More was an old man at the time of his execution and he asked the executioner to be patient while he placed his head on the block and pushed his whiskers aside, he remarked that his beard 'had committed to treason.' The executioner did his job well and beheaded the saintly Sir Thomas with one blow.

EXECUTION OF THE EXECUTIONER

Cratwell, the London hangman and executioner who probably beheaded both Sir Thomas More and The Bishop of Rochester received a taste of his own medicine on 1 September 1538. According to Hall's Chronicles he, '. . . was hanged at the wrestling place on the backside of Clerkenwel beside London, for robbing of a bouthe in Batholomew's Fayre, at which execution was above 20,000 people attending.'

SHE WAS NO TRAITOR, SHE WOULD NOT GO QUIETLY!

Henry VIII took retribution seriously. After Cardinal Pole's brave denunciation of Henry's religious doctrines and for his divorce from Catherine of Aragon, Henry wanted to mete out some sign of his objection to the outspoken priest. Pole was safely in France so Henry took revenge on his family, throwing the Cardinal's nearest and dearest into the Tower without trial, warmth or adequate clothing for some two years. The cruellest punishment was finally visited upon Pole's mother, The Countess of Salisbury on 27 May 1571. Aged over seventy at the time she faced the executioner, the elderly lady was not going to go quietly. When so commanded she refused to lay her head on the block saying 'So should traitors do, and I am none.' The Countess would not be still, as Lord Herbert recorded, 'so turning her grey head every way, shee bid him if hee would have her hedd, to get it off as best be could; so that he was constrained to fetch it off slovenly.' It took numerous wields of the executioner's axe to finally silence and part the head from the body of the Countess of Salisbury.

THE END OF THE NINE-DAY QUEEN

Tuesday 22 August 1553 was a bloody day even by the standards of the Tower. The tragedy was that Edward VI had named his cousin, Lady Jane Grey to be his successor, his half sister Mary and her many supporters had other ideas. After just nine days Lady Jane was removed by Mary and thrown in the Tower along with the other main 'conspirators' who had sought to place Lady Jane on the throne of England. Suffering the bitter reprisals of Mary I, Jane's father-in-law the Duke of Northumberland was first to be beheaded along with supporters Sir Henry Gates and Sir Thomas Palmer – although in these last moments they accused each other of being the 'authors of the treason' but eventually went to their maker as penitent men. They were followed by Northumberland's nephew, Guildford Dudley, the man he had paired as husband to Lady Jane. From the window of her lodging in Master Partridge's house Lady Jane witnessed her husband being led away for execution and saw his trunk with decapitated head delivered to the chapel, the pretty, young Lady Jane Grey became distraught and only just recovered her composure to be led to the scaffold. All others on that day had been executed before a vast crowd on Tower Hill, Lady Jane was granted the comparative seclusion of Tower Green. Fearing some instant fall of the axe she timidly implored the executioner 'Will you take my head off before I lay me down?' The tall, masked executioner reassured her he would do nothing till she was ready. She bound her own eyes with a kerchief but then panicked, reaching her arms out for the block she said 'What shall I do? Where is it? Where is it?' One of her ladies guided the young neck onto the block, weeping as she did so. The axe then fell and with one blow decapitated the queen of nine days. She was followed eleven days later by her father The Duke of Suffolk (see p. 208). What is often forgotten is that at the time of her execution Lady Jane Grey was just sixteen years old.

THE RIP VAN WINKLE OF THE TOWER

Stow recorded the case of William Foxley, a pot maker for the Mint in the Tower of London who, on 27 April 1546 'being Tuesday on Easter week . . . fell asleep, and so continued sleeping, and could not be wakened by pinching, cramping or otherwise burning, till the first day of term, which was fourteen days and fifteen nights.' When he awoke he complained of no ill effects and despite examination by physicians no cause could be found for this phenomena. Foxley was just as bemused, he thought he had simply slept for one night! He lived for over forty years more but never experienced the same long sleep.

THE VIRGIN PRINCESS IN THE TOWER

Princess Elizabeth, the future Elizabeth I, was imprisoned in the Bell Tower for over two months in 1554 while she was interrogated about her knowledge of plots against her half-sister Mary I.

ESCAPE FROM THE TOWER

One of the rare instances of an escape from the Tower was achieved by Father John Gerard and John Arden in 1599. They managed to swing to freedom on a rope stretched from the Cradle Tower across the moat where they were met by accomplices waiting for them in a boat.

THE POISONING OF SIR ROGER OVERBURY

Robert Carr, Earl of Rochester, favourite of King James I made the mistake of falling in love with the Countess of Essex who was indeed beautiful and young but also married. After securing a divorce all seemed set for the union but Rochester's old friend and confidante Sir Roger Overbury warned Rochester against the union with the mischievous and depraved Countess. She was having nothing stand in her way and first offered £1,000 to Sir John Wood to murder Overbury under the guise of a duel. This was turned down so the couple concocted a charge of contempt for royal authority against Sir Roger and had him committed to the tower where bribes were made to introduce poison to Overbury's food. His constitution was strong and despite the administration of 'arsenic, catharides, lunar caustic, mercury and powdered diamonds' Sir Roger lived on. Only with stronger doses and finally 'a clyste' put an end to his sufferings on 15 September 1613. He was hastily buried and it was said he said 'of a loathsome, contagious disease.' A few days later Rochester, by then Earl of Somerset married his Countess. About a year later the story of the poisoning of Sir Roger leaked out. The conspirators were arrested under warrant from Lord Chief Justice Coke. Mrs Turner, the confidante of the Countess and a woman who may well have used poison to despatch her own husband, Elwes the Lieutenant of the Tower, Weston the warder who had been directly responsible for Overbury and Franklin the apothecary stood trial along with the Count and Countess. The nobles received the King's pardon, the four lesser conspirators were hanged at Tyburn.

SHARP MEDICINE FOR SIR WALTER

The famous explorer, statesman and courtier Sir Walter Raleigh was imprisoned in the Bloody Tower on charges of plotting against James I for thirteen years between 1603 and 1616. His time was not spent in some hideous cell but rather well fitted out accommodation where he wrote his *History of the World* and even had an early type of chemical laboratory. But, Sir Walter did face the execution axe in the end. After sentence was passed he was lodged in the gatehouse of Westminster. At 8 o'clock on 29 October 1618 he was conducted to the scaffold in Old Palace Yard. After a short speech where he refuted all the charges against him, Sir Walter knelt and prayed, rising with the words 'Now I am going to God,' he walked courageously towards the executioner and picked up the axe, passed it on his hand and felt the edge of it and said with a smile 'This is sharp medicine, but it will cure all diseases.' He bade his final farewells and manfully laid his head on the block. There seemed to be a pause, a delay perhaps by a less intrepid executioner. Raleigh barked 'What dost thou fear? Strike man!' The nervous executioner took two stokes to behead the noble Sir Walter.

ATTEMPTED THEFT OF THE CROWN JEWELS!

After making the acquaintance and friendship of Mr Talbot Edwards, the custodian of the Crown Jewels a certain 'Parson' and Mrs Blood proposed the marriage of the Edward's pretty daughter to their highly eligible nephew. A date of May 9th 1671 was set for the pair to meet. Arriving early on the day with three male companions Blood explained that his wife had been delayed. While they were waiting it was suggested that they should see the jewels. Edwards was delighted to do so and led them in. As he closed the door the three villains sprang upon the old man, threw a cloak over his head and forced a gag into his mouth and told him he would be killed if he made a sound. Edwards bravely attempted to make as much noise as he could but was resolutely knocked to the ground with blows from a wooden mallet where he lay feigning death. Blood seized the crown, his companion the orb but the third man seizing the sceptre found it too long for easy concealment and attempted to file it through! They were disturbed by the surprise arrival of Edwards' son, a soldier on leave. As the son rushed in Edwards spat out his gag and shouted 'Treason! Murder!,' his daughter heard the cries and raised the alarm. Blood evaded the son and discarding the sceptre the robbers made off with the

Colonel Thomas Blood.

crown and orb. A warder attempted to stop them at the drawbridge but was shot at by Blood. In the rush to escape the three robbers evaded capture by pretending, themselves, to be in pursuit of the thieves but they were finally overpowered while making for St Katherine's Gate. Blood said of his attempt 'It was a gallant attempt, however unsuccessful; it was for a crown.' Charles II seemed to warm to the daring Colonel Blood, in reality a daring Irish solider of fortune, and rather than let him go to the gallows gave him a pardon and returned his forfeited estates to him. Although it has been suggested that this gesture from the Merry Monarch may also have been importuned as he was in fact involved with the plot and would have received his share of the proceeds had the robbery been successful!

IGNOMINIOUS END OF THE 'HANGING JUDGE'

The infamous and unpopular Judge George Jeffreys presided over the 'Bloody Assizes' following the Monmouth's attempt to usurp the crown. Unabashed at equally handing out whippings and death sentences, by the end of his tour of duty through the seat of the rebellion in the West Country he had passed 333 death sentences and ordered more than 800 people for transportation to the West Indies or America. When James II fled England Jeffreys attempted to follow; one account states Jeffreys adopted the disguise of a woman but was spotted by a law clerk from the window of the Red Cow tavern in Wapping, another says he was discovered disguised as a sailor at the same place. Either way his disguise was soon seen through, a raging mob soon surrounded Jeffreys and he narrowly escaped being lynched. Incarcerated in the comparative safety of a cell in the Bloody Tower he died there of natural causes on 18 April 1689.

THE ADMIRABLE LADY NITHDALE

Lord Nithdale, a Scottish peer was confined to the Tower under sentence of death after the Jacobite Rebellion of 1745. Lady Nithdale followed her husband to London and set about endearing herself to the guards entrusted to his captivity. The day before Nithdale's execution her ladyship came to visit the Lord with two friends. Quickly they disguised the Lord as another woman, painted his face and dressed him in petticoats, hood and muffler. When all was ready they opened the door and the grief stricken group of what appeared to be women left the cell. Lady Nithdale then returned to the cell and pretended to talk with her husband for some considerable time and assured her husband had made good his escape. Lady Nithdale was arrested, but pardoned and the devoted couple lived some 32 years together in Italy.

THE LAST JUDICIAL BEHEADING WITH AXE AND BLOCK

The last execution with axe and block on Tower Hill conducted on 9 April 1746 was that of the debauched Simon Fraser, twelfth Baron Lovat after his part in the second Jacobite Rebellion. Lovat had petitioned the king with his wish that he should be executed in a manner befitting Scots nobility by use of 'the Maiden,' an early type of

Simon Fraser, twelfth Baron Lovat.

guillotine. This request denied, Lovat, who was in his eighties, was to face the axe and block. He had rehearsed what he had to do with a Yeoman Warder, on the morning of the execution but when he was brought out he had not anticipated so many spectators. Such was the interest that rickety wooden grandstands had been erected for better views – at a cost of course. One of these seating arrangements by the Ship ale house, near Barking Alley collapsed under the weight of about 1,000 spectators killing about ten instantly and at least ten more of them died in hospital over the next few days (the casualties included the carpenter who had built the stand and his wife who was selling beer beneath it.). At the time of the collapse Lovat was just leaving the Tower for Tower Hill. The old Nobleman still had some humour in him and said upon seeing this 'The more mischief, the more sport!' And went to his doom with a gruff chuckle on his lips.

A LAST WORD ON LOVAT

Lord Selwyn, a man of culture, who had become a collector of morbid spectacles when rebuked for witnessing Lovat's execution argued he made up for it by calling at the undertakers to see the head sewn on again.

The executioner's axe, block and mask displayed at the Tower of London, 1875.

ELEVEN

THE TYBURN TREE & OTHER PUNISHMENTS

THE TERRIBLE PUNISHMENT OF THE TEMPLARS

The earliest recorded judicial punishments are often those meted out by the church. One of the most devout medieval orders were the Knights Templar who visited terrible punishments upon refractory members of the Order after their move to what later became known as the Temple in 1184. Several are recorded as being starved to death locked in the penitential cell 4ft 6ins by 2ft 6ins – so small the prisoner would not be able to lie down. Among those punished here was Walter le Batchelor, Grand Preceptor of Ireland who was starved to death for disobedience of the Master of Templars. Another who deserted the Templars was recaptured and sentenced to fast four days each week, to eat his food with dogs for a whole year and to be scourged naked before the priest at the high altar every Monday.

THE EXECUTION OF THE LORD CHIEF JUSTICE

In 1388 the 'merciless parliament' persecuted those who had remained loyal to Richard II. Among those to be punished was Sir Robert Tresilian, the Lord Chief Justice of England. Rumours abounded that Sir Robert was protected by witches' charms and it was recorded that when he was stripped by soldiers, amulets depicting astrological signs, a demon's head and 'several diabolical names' were found about his person. No charms saved poor Sir Robert from the noose, but the executioner did take the precaution of cutting the late Lord Chief Justice's throat – just to make sure!

BURNING OF THE FIRST ENGLISH MARTYR

William Sawtre, priest of St Benet Sherehog on Pancras Lane, the first English martyr of the English Reformation to be burnt at the stake, had his vestments stripped from him in St Paul's cathedral before he was sent to his death at the stake at Smithfield on 19 February 1401.

SHAMED FOR SORCERY

In 1441 Eleanor Cobham, Duchess of Gloucester and aunt of King Henry VI was ordered to walk bareheaded along Fleet Street to St Paul's with a lighted taper of 2lbs weight in her hand as a penance for 'having made a wax figure of the young king and melted it before a slow fire, praying that his life might melt like the wax.' She was said to have had 'diabolical conferences' with a number of others including priest and supposed necromancer Sir Roger Bolinbroke and Margaret Jourdain, a witch of Eye, near Westminster. These confederates had far worse fates for their treasonable witchcraft for which Jourdain was burned at Smithfield and Bolingbroke, having been imprisoned at the Tower, condemned at Guildhall then drawn to Tyburn where he was hanged, beheaded and quartered – his head set up on London Bridge and his quarters displayed at Hereford, Oxford, York and Cambridge.

THE PENANCE OF THE MERRIE HARLOT

Jane Shore, courtier and mistress of Edward IV, a woman desribed by the king as 'the merriest harlot in the realm' found herself on the wrong side of the Lancastian and Yorkist divide after the death of Edward in 1483. The Protector, Richard of Gloucester suspected her of aiding the escape of the Queen's oldest son, Thomas Grey (another one of Jane's lovers) and had her arrested in June 1483. Being a freewoman of London she had the right to chose her prison and she selected Ludgate Gaol. No evidence could be produced against Jane for aiding the escape so the old fall-back of sorcery was used against her. This also failed so with no other resort Richard had his pound of flesh by denouncing her as a harlot and she was sentenced to open penance at St Paul's Cross. The penance drew a large but sympathetic crowd. Dressed in only her kertle, she carried the lighted taper and was seen to blush. A contemporary account stated she was 'so faire and lovelie hir great shame wan her much praise among those that were more amorous of hir bodie, than curious of hir soule.'

THE FIRST BRIDEWELL

In 1553 Edward VI presented the dilapidated Bridewell Palace (named after the nearby St Bride's Well) to the City of London authorities who converted it into the first house of correction for minor offenders, 'masterless people,' tramps and vagabonds. The name of Bridewell was adopted by all other such buildings as they were established in counties across Britain over the next 300 years.

Bridewell in the eighteenth century. Note the stocks and whipping post in the courtyard.

HOISTED UPON HIS OWN PETARD

One of a number of executioners to fall foul of the law over the years was one recorded for posterity simply as 'Stumpleg.' This man, thought to have been the bungling headsman who took two attempts to decapitate to Duke of Suffolk and sent hundreds to their death on the end of the rope or 'Tyburn Halter' was found guilty of theft in 1558 and was executed upon the gallows he knew and worked so well. They did, however, find another executioner to carry out the job upon him.

SUBJUGATION OF THE LAWYERS

During the reign of Mary I (1553–8) the young lawyers of the Inns of the Temple had become so notorious and foppish an Act was passed to restrain them. Henceforth none were to 'wear beards of more than three weeks growth upon pain of a fine of forty shillings; and they must refrain their passion for Spanish cloaks, swords, bucklers, rapiers, gowns, hats or daggers at their girdles. Only Knights and Benchers might luxuriate in doublet or hose of bright colours, except scarlet or crimson; and forbibben be velvet caps, scarf-wigs to their gowns, white jerkins, buskins, velvet shoes, double shirt-cuffs, or feathers and ribbons in their caps.'

FIRST ON THE TRIPLE TREE

By the mid-sixteenth century the old uprights and single cross-piece of the old Tyburn gallows were found wanting. More criminals than ever faced sentence of death so a new device with no less than a triangle of three sturdy uprights and cross beams capable of accommodating twenty-four felons at the same time were erected and the Tyburn 'Triple Tree' began a legend. The first to be strung up upon the fatal tree was Dr John Story, a Roman Catholic who came to the prominence for his assiduous persecution of Protestants during the reign of Mary I ('Bloody Mary'). After the death of Mary, Story went out of favour and fled the country with the aid of the Spanish Ambassador's Chaplain. Story obtained a very lucrative post with customs at Antwerp. One day he was recognised by the Protestant owner of a ship who still, like many, bore a grudge against him. Tricked into the hold of the ship under pretence of inspecting the cargo, the hatches were battened down and the ship set sail for England where Story faced trial. Taken to the Tower, he was tried and found guilty, facing the death sentence the Spanish ambassador tried to intervene; upon being presented with the request it was said Good Queen Bess retorted; 'The King of Spain may have his head if he wants it, but his body shall be left in England.' On 1 June 1571 Story was drawn on a hurdle to Tyburn to be hanged, drawn and quartered. Cut down while still alive, it was said after the executioner drew his knife across the stomach and was 'rifling through his bowels' Story sat up and dealt him a blow before finally succumbing to dismemberment.

THE FATE OF THOSE WHO CHALLENGED GOOD QUEEN BESS

After an abortive attempt to raise a rebellion against and murder Elizabeth I to gain the throne for Mary Queen of Scots, Sir Anthony Babington and his fellow conspirators were found guilty of treason and condemned to death. The executions were carried out over two days, September 20th and 21st 1586 in Lincoln's Inn Fields, near the site where it was said the conspirators met to 'conferre of their traitorous purposes.' Those executed on the first day were 'hanged, bowelled and quartered', those on the second day were simply hanged.

EXECUTION IN THE CHURCHYARD

On 3 May 1606 Father Garnet was executed in the churchyard of St Paul's cathedral after being accused of playing a part in the conspiracy of the Gunpowder Plot. He died protesting his innocence.

THE TEARS OF A CLOWN

The court jester or fool for James I and his son Charles I was a witty little chap known as Archie Armstrong. Taking Archbishop Laud as one of his regular foils was an unwise one because he could only stand so much teasing and eventually complained to the Council about the jester and he was accordingly sentenced to 'have his coat pulled over his head and to be discharged of the King's service and banished from the Court.'

THE AGONIES OF WILLIAM PRYNNE

William Prynne was a puritan in every way, in dress, word and deed. A barrister of Lincoln's Inn, he published *Histriomastix* a tome of a thousand pages in which he slammed theatres as 'the chapels of Satan', the players, his ministers, and all their frequenters were rushing headlong to hell. His next target was dancing, an activity

Prynne in the pillory.

which he believed caused the ladies of England to become 'frizzled madams' and 'destroyed their modesty.' Prynne then attacked many things the reforming Bishop Laud had been supporting, such as maypoles, public festivals, church ales, music and Christmas carols. Laud attempted to lay hold on his pestilent satirist but he was defeated twice by injunctions from Westminster Hall. The third attempt accused Prynne of reflecting his diatribes upon the king and queen. This could not be ignored; in May 1634 Prynne was excluded from the Bar and from Lincoln's Inn, he was deprived of his university degree, fined £1,000, his books were ceremonially burnt before him by the hangman and worse was yet to come. Prynne was sentenced to two stands in the pillory at both Westminster and in Cheapside – at each place once his head and hands were secured in the holes of the pillory he was to be branded on the forehead, a slit made in his nose and one of his ears was to be cut off. He was sentenced to life in prison. Prynne carried on publishing from prison and got into trouble again in June 1637 and was sent back to the pillory for similar treatment. Whether the hangman relented the first time or whether he left some sort of stump where his ears were when Prynne was shut in the pillory at Old Palace Yard, as if spurred on by the jeers and shouts of the crowd his torturer sawed and gouged out every vestage of Prynne's ears. So harsh was this treatment that even the crowds turned to booing and hissing at the macabre display.

THE BRAVE PURITAN

Despite the horrific punishments inflicted on Prynne, a man recorded for posterity as 'free born John Lilburne' ignored the lessons of the pillory and reprinted one of Prynne's books and similar literature. Arrested in December 1637 and brought before the Court of Star Chamber, Lilburne obstinately refused to take the oath and claimed that his prosecution was unlawful. His sentence was carried out on 18 April 1638 when he was whipped at the cart-tail from the Fleet prison to the Palace Yard, Westminster, where he was ordered to stand in the pillory, then imprisoned until he conformed and admitted his guilt. Throughout his public punishments Lilburne proclaimed he had committed no crime against the law or the state but that he was a victim of the bishops' cruelty. He drew popular support but still remained in prison for three years until he was released after the personal pleas of Oliver Cromwell to the more sympathetic Long Parliament.

'Free-born' John Lilburne.

THE RETRIBUTION OF THE 'MERRY MONARCH'

After the Restoration of Charles II his retribution against those responsible for the execution of his father knew no bounds. Present at the execution of the 'regicide' Thomas Harrison on 13 October 1660, the diarist Samuel Pepys noted: 'I went to Charing Cross to see Major-General Harrison hanged, drawn and quartered; which was done there, he looking as cheerful as any man could do in that condition. He was presently cut down and his head and heart shown to the people, at which there was great shouts of joy. Thus it was my chance to see the King beheaded at White Hall, and to see the first blood shed in revenge for the blood of the King at Charing Cross.' Harrison was followed to the gallows three days later by parliamentarian 'regicides' John Carew and John Cooke (sometimes spelled John Cook) Cromwell's Solicitor General and the leading prosecutor at the trial of Charles I. Hugh Peters, Cromwell's chaplain was forced to sit within the rails of the gallows to behold the death of Cook. As Cook was cut down Colonel Peters, the officer overseeing the executions, ordered the Sheriff's men to bring Peters to see the body as it was being disembowelled. The hangman grinning horribly and rubbing his gory hands together with savage joy, asked Peters 'Come, how do you like this – how do you like this work?' Peters maintained his dignity with the reply 'I am not, I thank God, terrified at it – you may do your worst.' Peters suffered the same fate a short while later, as he died Peters proclaimed 'What, flesh! art thou unwilling to go to God through the fire and jaws of death. Oh! This is a good day. He is come that I have long looked for, and I shall soon be with Him in glory.' He then smiled, he did make one final statement but 'what Peters said further it could not be taken, in regard his voice was low at the time and the people uncivil.' John Evelyn did not witness the execution, but 'met their quarters, mangled and cut and reeking as they were brought from the gallows in baskets.' The quarters of their bodies were then impaled and exhibited as a warning to others on the City Gates.

SAVED BY THE QUIP

George Wither was always one to 'stick his head out' and was lucky not to lose it. A seventeenth-century poet, satirist and idyllist, he had served time in the Marshalsea prison for his satire *Abuses*, been stripped and whipped and could count himself one of Cromwell's Major-Generals, so it was hardly surprising he would be in for a hard time after the Restoration. He was fortunate to have friends who petitioned for his life, the Merry Monarch appreciating the clever quip from Denham 'As long as Wither lives I should not be considered the worst poet in England.' Wither died peacefully in 1667 and was buried in the Chapel of St Mary, Savoy.

THE FIRST QUARTERS

In 1670 the last, 'original' Temple Bar was built with Sir Christopher Wren as architect and Joshua Marshall as mason. This edifice was one of a number in London upon which the quartered remains of traitors were displayed. The first to adorn the Bar were the boiled and pitch-covered quarters of Sir William Armstrong, Master of the Horse to Charles II, who was executed for his connection to the Rye House plot to assassinate Charles II in 1684.

The 'Crown' of Temple Bar, 1746.

THE 'CROWN' OF TEMPLE BAR

On a number of eighteenth-century engravings an unusual 'crown' of three poles with baubles on top appear to adorn the Temple Bar. The baubles are in fact heads, all of them Jacobites – Oxburgh, Townley and Fletcher. The heads of Jacobite sympathisers on Temple Bar goes back to Sir William Perkins and Sir John Friend who were found guilty of involvement in an abortive plot in 1696 to waylay the carriage and kill William III in a secluded lane between Brentford and Turnham Green as he returned from hunting at Richmond. Perkins and Friend were executed at Tyburn; where three nonjuring clergymen absolved them, much to the indignation of the loyalists in the crowd. In 1716 the head of Colonel Henry Oxburgh was added to make the trio. A Colonel in the Pretender's army, he had the unenviable task of proposing terms of surrender to the King's troops at Preston. Executed at Tyburn on 14 May 1716 Oxburgh's body was buried at St Giles' but his head was displayed on Temple Bar. The next two heads due for poles were Colonel Francis Townley and George Fletcher who had been hanged, drawn and quartered upon the scaffold on Kennington Common along with a number of other rebels for their involvement in the 1745 Rebellion. These two heads were put up upon Temple Bar on 2 August 1746. The old heads of Perkins and Friend having fallen off some time before, leaving this new and soon familiar 'crown' atop the central gate of the Bar until the last of these heads tumbled off in 1772.

THE END OF NOBLE LORD RUSSELL

William, Lord Russell was executed for alleged high treason on Lincoln's Inn Field on 21 July 1683. One of those who accompanied him to the end wrote 'Some of the crowd that filled the streets wept, while others insulted; he was touched with the tenderness that the one gave him, but did not seem at all provoked by the other. He was singing psalms a great deal of the way; he said he hoped to sing better soon. As he observed the great crowd of people all the way, he said 'I hope I shall quickly see a much better assembly' . . . He laid his head on the block, without the least change of countenance: and it was cut off at two strokes.

THE LAST WOMAN TO BURN FOR HIGH TREASON

The last woman to be burnt at Tyburn for full blown treason was Elizabeth Gaunt 'an ancient matron of the Baptist persuasion' in 1685. She had assisted James Burton, one of the Rye House Plotters, when a reward was advertised for his apprehension to escape to Gravesend by boat where she then gave him some considerable sum of money and he boarded a ship bound for Holland. But Burton did not stay there, he returned to fight for Monmouth in his rebellion, which also failed and he fled to the house of John Fernley, a Whitechapel barber. Despite being on hard times Fernley did not betray Burton, but when Burton heard the King delivered far harder retribution on those who harboured rebels than the rebels themselves, he lost no time in betraying Fernley and even the kindly Elizabeth Gaunt! Fernley was sent to the gallows but poor Elizabeth was burnt at the stake. Denied the privilage of stangulation or a sack of gunpowder around her neck to speed and minimise the pain of her death, she was literally burnt to death.

THE PEOPLES' PENALTY FOR DISRESPECTING SANCTUARY

In 1696 a creditor dared to ignore the rights of sanctuary possessed by the church of St Mary le Savoy and entered it to demand a debt from one who had entered there. The creditor was hastily manhandled from the church and exposed to a gathering crowd who beat him almost insensible, tarred and feathered him, trundled him in a wheelbarrow up the Strand where they left him tied to the Maypole. Worse may have been inflicted but constables came and dispersed the rabble and rescued the tormented man.

KNOCK, KNOCK

By the seventeenth and eighteenth centuries London's Bridewell had become notorious for its floggings, carried out in the presence of the Court of Governors.

Sir Robert Clayton the president of the court sat with his gavel in hand, poised to hammer down when the offender had been seen to receive his or her sentence of lashes. A familiar cry at this time, especially heard from the lips of females 'Oh, good Sir Robert, knock! Pray, good Sir Robert, knock!' The phrase entered into popular parlance as a reproach against those who had been imprisoned in Bridewell.

TO PUBLISH AND NOT BE DAMNED

In 1727 Edmund Curll, the 'publisher of all the filth and slander of his age,' was sentenced to a stand in the pillory at Charing Cross for printing 'a vile word' entitled *Venus in a Cloyster*. Using the 'lying and cunning of his reptile nature' he circulated broadsheets telling people he was sentenced to his stand for daring to vindicate the memory of Queen Anne. The mob allowed no one to pelt him and once he was released from his stand he was carried off in triumph to a neighbouring tavern.

JAMMY JAPHET CROOK?

Japhet Crook (aka Sir Peter Stranger), a one time brewer on Tower Hill was a serial forger who was finally brought to trial and convicted of forging a conveyance, to himself, of an estate to the value and draining it of several thousand pounds. Convicted as charged in June 1731 he was condemned to imprisonment for life but not before an horrific stand in the pillory at Charing Cross where the stern sentence of law prescribed further punishments inflicted upon him. Seated in an elbow chair the common hangman cut off both of Crook's ears with an incision knife. The ears were then delivered to Mr Watson, a sheriff's officer. Crook's nostrils were then slit with a pair of scissors and then seared with a hot iron. A surgeon attended and 'applied styptics to prevent the effusion of blood.' Crook bore his punishments with remarkable courage, even laughing on the pillory and denying his guilt to the last! It is worthy of note that Crook was the last to face such punishments for this crime. As he stood in dock the law was changing, Crook was sentenced according to the old law but just six days later Richard Cooper, a Stepney victualler was subject to the new legal edict and was hanged for forgery at Tyburn. Crook did, at least, live to tell the tale and after his stand in the pillory was removed to the Ship Tavern at Charing Cross and thence to King's Bench prison where he spent the rest of his life – quietly leaving his ill gotten fortune to his executor.

SAVED FROM EXECUTION DOCK

In December 1738 *Gentleman's Magazine* reported 'James Buchanan, a sailor condemned at the Admiralty Sessions for the murder of Mr Smith in China, was hanged at Execution Dock (at Wapping), but after a few minutes was cut down by a gang of sailors, and was carried off in a boat and was brought to life but retaken. The compassion thus shown this criminal by his brother tars, is said to arise from his good character, and being without cause was more severely beat by Smith who was a petty officer than any Englishman ought to bear without resenting.'

THE END OF JENNY DIVER

Mary Young alias Murphy or Webb went to the gallows at Tyburn in March 1741. A proficient 'directress' (distraction thief) and pickpocket, she was known in the criminal fraternity as 'Jenny Diver.' Her favourite trick was to dress as a lady and put on a false belly to give the appearance of pregnancy. Her accomplice, dressed as a footman would knock at their target's door and claim 'her ladyship' was 'in the pains.' Frequently she was given admission, her 'pains' increasing the household would set about procuring medical assistance which Mary and her accomplice set about packing away the moveable valuables and making their escape.

  As she bid farewell to her children for the last time at Newgate it was recorded that even the hardened gaoler shed a tear. She went to her doom in a mourning coach dressed in the height of fashion. There was also a heavy guard surrounding the carriages as it was anticipated a rescue could well be attempted at the last minute. The execution of Jenny Diver was conducted without a hitch.

THE PUNISHMENT FOR TREASON ON THE HIGH SEAS

In January 1743 Thomas Rounce, having been found guilty of fighting against his country aboard two Spanish privateers, was dragged from Newgate to Execution Dock upon a hurdle. The executioner travelled beside Rounce, the scimitar with which he was to wreak the final destruction upon Rounce on full view to the condemned man and public throughout the journey. Rounce was strung up upon the gallows and cut down after but a short swing, his head was then cut with a slice of the scimeter then 'ripped up his stomach, and took out the heart etc, exposing them to the crowd which was so very great that many were hurt.'

THE CUSS BOX TARIFF

In September 1746 the first case in London following an Act for fining those caught swearing saw its first conviction of a man in the capitol; a ticket porter brought before the Lord Mayor. Found guilty he was fined 3*s*, a considerable sum for such a working man. A Tariff based on class was soon established viz:

Every day labourer, common soldier, common sailor, and common seaman, 1*s*.

Every other person under the degree of a gentleman, 2*s*.

Every person of or above the degree of a gentleman, 2*s*.

The Idle 'Prentice executed at Tyburn. An engraving by William Hogarth, 1747.

SMASHING THE TYBURN STANDS

Many folks wishing to get a really good view of the proceedings at the 'three legged mare' or 'triple tree' scaffold at Tyburn would pay for a seat on the wooden grandstands. The amount charged for the seats would often be increased if a notable or infamous criminal was to be 'swung' but the crowd could also show its displeasure such as when having paid premiums to see Dr Henesey executed in 1758; the doctor was reprieved and the crowd, deprived of its morbid show smashed the stands down in anger and disappointment.

SCHOOL DISCIPLINE

The punishments meted out on the boys educated at Christ's Hospital in the 1780s were recorded by Brandt in his *Life of Samuel Taylor Coleridge*: 'Discipline was upheld by substantial methods. The masters flogged, the monitors flogged, and the beadles flogged. The superintendent of the dormitories would haul half-a-dozen boys at a time out of their beds on the coldest nights for the slightest disturbance, and flog them . . . For a boy who ran away, imprisonment and the leather strap were the award.' As late as 1877 a boy who ran away knew his fate and chose to commit suicide rather than face the consequences.

THE PILLORY OF PILLORIES

The pillory near Temple Bar was always a favourite setting for punishments inflicted on malfactors in London. Here those who had defrauded their customers with diluted milk, doctored measures or adulterated flour would face the wrath of their customers. Salacious speakers, perjurers would also face a stand, some repeat offenders may even have their ears nailed to the wood of the pillory or even have their tongue skewered by a red hot poker – all to the delight of the crowd who would then pelt the unfortunates with the likes of excrement (animal and human), rotten fruit and vegetables, stones, mud and even dead animals. Daniel Defoe was sentenced to a stand in the pillory for his satirical writings against the government in 1703 – the crowd agreed with his stance – the people gave him an ovation, drank his health and decorated the pillory with flowers. A deservedly less understanding crowd faced Titus Oates – a man described by a contemporary as 'a most consummate cheat, blasphemer, vicious perjurer, impudent and saucy foul-mouthed wretch'. Oates was the perjurer who had concocted an anti-popish plot implicating Spanish Catholics, French Benedictines, Irish and English malcontents who were conspiring to massacre Protestants and kill the king with nothing less than silver bullets. Oates saw some thirty-five 'suspects' arrested and

Titus Oates in the pillory.

executed. His lies caught up with him in 1685 and he was denounced and arrested at the Amsterdam Coffee House behind the Royal Exchange. Convicted of perjury he was fined, whipped from Aldgate to Tyburn and sentenced to perpetual imprisonment with only brief release from his prison walls when he was taken for his annual stand in the pillory on 10 August.

TO PRESS FOR AN ANSWER

Between the court house in the old Old Bailey and Newgate Prison was a large open space known as the Press Yard. William Spiggot was taken here in 1720, after refusing to plead his case and was subjected to one of the most horrible tortures inflicted at Newgate; the Peine Fort et Dure or pressing. Pressing had been used for centuries upon those who refused to plead guilt or innocence to the crime that he was accused of. Courts were put in a quandry if suspects refused to plead; if a prisoner pleaded guilty the law stepped in, confiscated their estates and meted out punishment – frequently the death penalty. If they pleaded innocence a trial would ensue, if found guilty the convict would be punished and again all possessions were forfeited to the crown. Defendants who decided to remain mute under old laws would stay unconvicted as it was not until 1827 that silence by a defendant was construed as a 'not guilty' plea, before that time their goods could not be touched and although the accused may be incarcerated, families of the accused enjoyed a degree of protection. This was a powerful incentive for many not to plead – pressing became the laws' equally persuasive method of forcing a plea. Sometimes, like in the case of Samuel Hawes in 1711 he may suffer his 'thumbs squeezed' in thumb screws first, others like Spiggott were immediately spreadeagled on the floor, minimal sustenance given, and over the course of three days weights were piled up leaving the prisoner with the agonising choice of plead or die. *Newgate Calendar* states that Spigott bore the

Pressing for a plea at Newgate.

weight of 350lb. for half and hour on his naked breast, and it was only when an additional 50lb. was added that he broke down and pled his case. Spigott ended up being hanged at Tyburn, others took the pressing and succumbed to the torture. If a woman failed to plead she could be whipped to force an answer, in one case from 1721 Mary Andrews 'proved so obstinate three whipcords were broken before she would plead.'

DO YOU RECOGNISE THIS MAN?

In March 1726 a watchman discovered a human head floating in the water at the wharf near the Horse Ferry, Westminster. No idea of identity was ascertained so to not waste time printing a description of the head the Magistrates ordered the head be placed atop a pole in the churchyard of St Margaret's to see if anyone could put a name to the face. Hundreds came to view the eerie relic but no name was forthcoming. In the meantime friends of John Hayes who had not seen or heard from him for a while made enquiries where he had gone. His wife, Katherine told them he had left London for a few days. But he did not return and when two of his close friends pressed Katherine she claimed John had gone into hiding after killing a man.

The head displayed for identification in the churchyard of St Margaret's, 1726.

The friends were not happy with this answer and having heard about the head on display at St Margaret's they sought out a magistrate. Very soon warrants were issued, Mrs Hayes and two conspirator named Wood and Billings were in custody and stood trial. Mrs Hayes denied the crime but Wood and Billings pleaded guilty. The story emerged that she had tired of her husband and offered them shares in his fortune if they assisted her in his murder. They murdered John Hayes with a hatchet as he slept and decided the best way to dispose of the body was to decapitate it, throw the body parts in the pond on Marylebone Fields and dump the head in the wharf – assuming the tide would carry it away. All three were found guilty and were sentenced to death, Wood died of gaol fever before he faced the hangman. Hayes and Billing were both taken to Tyburn on 9 May 1726. Billings was hanged but Mrs Hayes had committed petty treason in murdering her husband and was burnt at the stake. It was custom to strangle those being burnt before the flames reached them but in the case of Hayes the fire scorched the hands of the executioner as he attempted to tighten the rope about her neck. She was burnt alive, it was recorded it took three hours for her body to be reduced to ashes.

RIOT AT THE PILLORY

The Weekly Journal: or, The British Gazetteer for May 1727 reported 'Last Tuesday Mr Hitchen was erected on the Pillory (after being found guilty of 'an unnatural act' – an eighteenth- and nineteenth-century term usually used for homosexuality) over-against Catherine-street in the Strand. His friends had so barricadoed the Avenues leading to him with Coaches and Carts, as almost render'd the Approaches of the Mob inaccessible: However, the Artillery used in these Occasions, play'd incessantly from all Corners, and a Battery in Catherine-street, conducted by a great Number of Drury-lane Ladies play'd with good Success for Half an Hour. Mr Curll's Windows suffer'd pretty much by it; and the Constables, endeavouring by a Sally to level that Work, were drove back to the Pillory by a strong Body of the Mob, tho' not without some Blood spilt on both Sides. All Means used by the Peace Officers and Mr Hitchen's Friends and Brethren to repel the Fury of the Populace proving ineffectual, the Criminal met with the Reward due to his Demerits. He was taken down at the usual Time, and carried back to Newgate, almost ready to expire, with the Fatigue he had undergone in the Rostrum, his Night-Gown and Breeches being torn in Pieces from his body.'

SCOFFING AT AN EXECUTION

Colonel Francis Townley, George Fletcher and seven other Jacobites were hanged, drawn, beheaded and quartered on Kennington Common for their part in the 1745 rebellion. When their hearts were tossed into the fire one of the bystanders snatched one of the organs out of the brazier and ate it as a demonstration of his loyalty.

PILLORY AND PENSION

Dr John Shebbeare, a trained surgeon, decided that his real métier was to be a man of letters. He felt he had much to articulate on topical matters but in doing so he freely stated he would 'write himself into a pension or the pillory.' His works such as *Letters to the People of England* were satirical and incisive, some said even virulent, but above all they were galling to the King and his Ministry. Letters saw Shebbeare brought before the King's Bench and a libel was found against him. Shebbeare was fined £5, ordered to a stand at the pillory for one hour and to be imprisoned in the Marshalsea for three years and provide sureties thereafter. The under-sheriff at the time was a Mr Beardmore and he shared Shebbeare's views and out of sympathy took Shebbeare to the pillory on 5 December 1758 in a city state-coach and allowed him to literally stand at the pillory for an hour (but without his head and hands through the holes. It was raining and Shebbeare's servant was even allowed to stand beside him in full livery holding an umbrella over his master. Beardmore was taken to court for this favour but he argued that Shebbeare had stood at the pillory as per the sentence. Judge was not amused and ordered he pay a fine of £50 and suffer two months imprisonment. Shebbeare did serve his sentence but when released the ministers had changed, Lord Bute was already an unpopular man and thought it better to befriend Shebbeare than offend him so Shebbeare was accordingly granted a pension.

PICNIC ON THE PILLORY

As Daniel Defoe found out (see p. 129), not all who stood in the pillory were subject to a hail of rotten fruit, stones and excrement. If you were popular the crowd could well be merciful. Often women were shown more mercy and Sarah Thomas was certainly doubly fortunate as she was not only a very finely proportioned women but she was well-known for running a well-patronised brothel. The *St James's Chronicle* for 29–31 October 1761 recorded: 'Yesterday at Noon Sarah Thomas stood in the Pillory in the Old Bailey, opposite to Fleet-Lane, for keeping a disorderly house, pursuant to her sentence at the last quarter session in Guildhall. The mob behaved to her with great humanity, she standing on the pillory all the time drinking wine, hot-pot, &c. It was diversion to her rather than a punishment.'

STONED TO DEATH

Annual Register for 16 April 1771 records 'Yesterday, between four and five o'clock a mob assembled in a field near Bethnal Green consisting of upwards of two thousand, when they set upon one Clark, a pattern drawer, who was the principal evidence against the two cutters that were executed at Bethnal Green sometime since; they continued pelting him with brick-bats for three hours which laid his skull entirely open. Never did any poor mortal suffer more than he did; he begged of them several times to shoot him; but they kept stoning him till he died in the greatest agonies. Six or seven are said to be taken into custody on this account.'

THE GROOM WAS NOT ALL SHE SEEMED

One of the most unusual crimes to land the guilty party in the pillory was that of Ann Marrow who was pilloried at Charing Cross on 22 July, 1777, for marrying three women. Convicted at the Quarter Sessions for the city and liberty of Westminster, on the 5 July 1777, of going in men's clothes and personating a man in marriage, with three different women and defrauding them of their money and effects. She was sentenced to be imprisoned three months, and during that time to stand once in and upon the pillory. 'Agreeably to the pillorying part of her sentence, she was placed within; and so great was the resentment of the spectators, particularly the female part, that they pelted her to such a degree that she lost the sight of both her eyes.'

THE LAST BURNING AT THE STAKE IN ENGLAND

It is a little known fact that far more women were burnt in England for offences described as 'Petty Treason' rather than witchcraft (almost without exception every witch in England was in fact hanged). Petty Treason could be applied to such as the murder of a husband, betrayal of their master and household by breaking the sacred bond of trust between master and servant by such actions as unbolting a door to knowingly allow in burglars or even counterfeiting, especially coining – all of which, for ladies, meant burning at the stake. The very last woman to be formally burnt at the stake in England was Catherine Murphy who was executed outside Newgate Prison on 18 March 1789 for the crime of coining. Her husband and eight others convicted of the same offence were all hanged before she was brought out passing the dangling legs of those she knew twitching on the gallows. In a separate area she was made to stand on a platform of about a foot in height in front of the stake to which she was secured with an iron ring. A noose was hanging from a ringle on the top of the well-secured stake, this was fastened around her neck. When she finished her prayers the platform was removed and she was left to hang as the faggots were piled about her. By the time the flames reached her she was probably already dead; she deserved some small mercy at least.

THE LAST MAN TO STAND IN THE PILLORY

The ignominious 'hounour' of being the last person to be sentenced and stood in the pillory was Peter James Bossy (aged thirty-one) who had pleaded guilty to perjury at the Old Bailey. His full sentence was to be incarcerated for six months, ordered to stand in the pillory for one hour on 22 June 1830 and then to be transported for seven years. The pillory was finally abolished from the statutes in 1837.

BLACK MEGGIE

When the congestion caused by crowds of thousands observing executions at Tyburn became too much of a headache in 1783, public executions

'Half-Hanged Smith' – having been strung up for fifteen minutes, a reprieve came for him. He was cut down and revived.

were moved to the open area directly in front of Newgate. The night before the execution the scaffold and gallows known as 'Black Meggie' would be assembled in front of the debtor's door in the north wing for the ultimate letter of the law to be enacted and allowed a good view of the proceedings for the massive crowds drawn to these public executions. Also known as the 'New Drop' this scaffold consisted of a wooden platform, formed of two flaps, level with the ground, beneath which was a

'Black Meggie' or the 'New Drop' in action in front of Newgate in 1783.

10ft drop. Two sturdy uprights supported a massive beam, long enough to allow as many as twenty felons to be hanged at the same time. Multiple executions were a regular feature in the early nineteenth century. The year 1810 saw the unprecedented number of 220 offences which carried the death penalty on the statute books, a selection of the capital crimes included: arson, piracy, sodomy, forgery, bankrupts hiding assets, highway robbery, burglary, pickpocketing above the value of 1*s*, shoplifting goods above the value of 5*s*, stealing above 40*s*, pulling down buildings, destroying a pond containing fish, cutting down trees, hops or vegetation on river or sea embankments, returning from transportation, stabbing an unarmed victim who dies within six months, sending threatening letters, sacrilege, riot by twelve or more people who have not dispersed an hour after the magistrate's proclamation and impersonating a Chelsea Pensioner. By 1861 the number of capitol offences had been reduced to four – murder, treason, arson in a Royal dockyard and piracy.

TWELVE

GAOL DELIVERY

INFAMOUS NEWGATE

The most notorious of all the London prisons outside the Tower was Newgate. It had acquired its notoriety over almost 900 years, not only for its harsh regime, overcrowding and unsanitary conditions but because it was from here generations of felons, infamous and obscure, were carted to Tyburn for execution. Indeed the infamous 'Newgate Calendar' of executions became the standard reference work to find the most notorious criminals who had been brought to justice in England. A late nineteenth-century account from Hare's *Walks in London* records a visit: 'Passing through low massive doors and a gloomy narrow passage, visitors are still shown the Pinioning Room, where malfactors were pinioned before being led to execution. Here, in two large cupboards, are preserved the leg-irons worn by prisoners, with the anvil upon which they were riveted on arrival . . . and the axe with which many of the condemned were beheaded after being hanged. Also shown are the cells for refractory prisoners, in which an American visitor has described the darkness as 'something to lean against;' the gallows; the whipping horse and the open air passage called

Newgate Prison, 1888.

'Birdcage Walk' from the open iron cross-bars with which it is covered, used as a cemetery for the condemned, and where letters cut in the wall record their last resting places. The coffins are filled with quick lime and covered with ordinary paving stones. In a lumber shed stands the whipping post, used for robbers with violence.'

Condemned as a prison in 1882, in its last years Newgate was only used for prisoners awaiting trial or those under sentence of death until it finally closed in 1902 and was demolished. The Central Criminal Court in Old Bailey now stands on the site.

TO SPEAK WELL OF CRESSWELL

During the reign of Charles II, Mrs Cresswell was one of the more notorious inmates of the Bridewell. When she died she left a bequest of £10 for her funeral sermon – on the condition the preacher said nothing but good things about her. Earning this generous legacy was not easy for a man of God who had sworn to uphold morals and truth; he extricated himself by concluding his sermon thus: 'By the will of the deceased it is expected that I should mention her, and say nothing but what was well of her, therefore, is this. She was born well, she lived well, and she died well; for she was born with the name of Cresswell, she lived in Clerkenwell and died in Bridewell.'

FOR WHOM THE BELL TOLLS

One of the oldest traditions of the London prisons was the 'Newgate Bell' which was tolled, twelve times with double strokes as any condemned prisoner left Newgate on their final journey to the gallows at Tyburn. This tradition was maintained through the endowment of Robert Dow, a London merchant, who, in 1604, bequeathed £1 6s 8d a year for the sexton or bell-man of St Sepulchre's Church (opposite Newgate) to toll the bell accordingly. Originally the sexton was also required to ring a hand bell outside the prison at midnight and exhort a standard tract to implore all within to search their souls and repent their sins;

> All you that in the condemned hold do lie,
> Prepare you, for to-morrow you shall die:
> Watch all and pray, the hour is drawing near
> That you before the Almighty must appear:
> Examine well yourselves, in time repent,
> That you may not to eternal flames be sent:
> And when St Sepulchre's bell to-morrow tolls,
> The Lord above have mercy on your souls!

The hand bell and exhortation tradition did not endure but the tolling bell did. Even after executions were removed behind prison walls in 1868, the bell began to strike at the appointed hour when the condemned prisoner left his cell to proceed to the execution shed. In September 1888 Robert Dowe's Charity was recognised by the Charity Commissioners and was noted for its benevolence towards providing clothing for juvenile offenders and aiding prisoners discharged from the Central Criminal Court district. After strict observance for 286 years a request was made to the vicar of St Sepulchre's that the bell be not tolled for the execution of Mary Pearcey in 1890 on account of a guest at the nearby Viaduct Hotel being seriously ill. The bell was not tolled and never rang for another execution.

The debtors' gate of the Fleet Prison.

THE WORST GAOLER OF LONDON

Bambridge, the gaoler of the Fleet prison was one of the cruellest and most devious men ever to occupy his office. His methods led to him being put on trial in 1729 and only then were some of his nightmare-like horrors revealed to the public. Bambridge was found to have beguiled unwary and innocent people to come to the prison gatehouse where he would suddenly seize and manacle them without authority or official reason. Locking these unfortunate people in a cell, Bambridge would only release then on payment of a fine (or ransom more like). In several cases his prisoners were tortured, some he ordered to be stabbed with the guards' cutlasses and they died from their undressed, festering wounds; while others left for days without food and 'died from inanition.'

FLEET MARRIAGES

After the introduction of marriage licenses a clandestine or forbidden union could still be obtained by a 'Fleet Marriage.' Such marriages seem to have originated with the incumbents of Trinity Minories and St James's, Duke's Palace, who claimed to be exempt from the jurisdiction of the Bishop of London and performed marriages without banns or license until 1616 when the Reverend Elliot, Rector of St James was suspended. The 'trade' in marriages was then taken up by the prisoners from the clergy who were imprisoned as debtors in the Fleet prison; having neither cash, character nor liberty these men of God became 'the ready instruments of vice, greed, extravagance and libertinism.' There were about eighty-nine, most infamous of their number was John Gayman (also spelt Gainham) described as a 'lusty, jolly man, vain of his learning he was known as "The Bishop of Hell".' The *Weekly Journal* of 29 June 1723 reported

> From an inspection into the several register for marriages kept at the several alehouses, brandy shops etc. within the Rules of the Fleet Prison, we find no less than thirty-two couples joined together from Monday to Thursday last without licenses, contrary to an express act of parliament against clandestine marriages, that lays a severe fine of £200 on the minister so offending and £100 each on the persons offending . . . Several of the above-named brandy-men and victuallers keep clergymen in their houses at 20s per week, hit or miss but it is reported that one there will stoop to no such low conditions, but makes at least £500 per annum, of divinity jobs after that manner.

A 'Fleet Marriage' between a 'brisk young sailor and his landlady's daughter', 1747.

AT THEIR MAJESTYS' PLEASURE

In 1736 Major John Bernardi died in Newgate Prison aged eighty-two. Imprisoned for his alleged involvement with the plot to assassinate William III, eight of the plotters were convicted and sent to the gallows but there was not enough evidence to convict him and five other alleged conspirators. By special Acts of Parliament they were detained 'at His Majesty's pleasure.' Successive monarchs released another two then another two leaving the last of them, Bernardi, to rot in the gaol. When Bernardi died not only was he one of the oldest prisoners in Newgate but one who had served the longest sentence on record, having been incarcerated there for forty years.

HE PREACHED HIS OWN FUNERAL SERMON

In 1777 Dr Dodd was under sentence of death in Newgate for forgery. Even in this situation he was not lost for words and even preached his own funeral sermon (on Acts xvi. 23) before he went to the gallows.

THE BLACK PEW

In the chapel of Newgate prison there was a 'condemned bench' – a horse hair chair, only used by prisoners under sentence of death. Until 1817 they had sat in a black pew, which had a table in the centre with a coffin upon it. In the early nineteenth century when there were over 200 hanging offences as many as twenty-one people were recorded as having been seen sat together on the condemned pew.

THE RISE AND FALL OF 'PLUMB' POPE

Benjamin Pope began life as a tanner in Southwark, he worked hard and made a considerable fortune which he used to give up his old trade and became a money-lender and mortgagee. It was said his fortune was some £100,000, a fantastical sum in its day and he was known as 'Plumb Pope.' He was, however, greedy, his run of good luck in investments waned and his money grasping methods became more and more cut-throat; this saw him brought before the courts on a number of occasions on charges of usury. One case saw him fined £10,000 damages, he bitterly complained about the sentence, he even went to France with property and effects but returned to England in 1782 and voluntarily to prison rather than pay the damages. A gesture was made for him to only pay £1,000 and the matter would be considered settled but Pope turned it down flat as 'this would acknowledge the justice of the debt, which I would die sooner than do.' From the prison he carried on his money-lender business but became miserly in his habits. A pint of small-beer lasted him two days and he always checked the fullness of the measure before he paid for it and the fourpenny-plate meals he bought in from the cook shop served him for lunch and dinner. Pope died in August 1794, he had spent the last 12 years of his life in the debtors prison – well, he did say he would rather die than pay the debt!

DAILY LIFE IN A TYPICAL VICTORIAN LONDON PRISON

Pentonville Prison on Caledonian Road, Islington was built (1841–2) as a 'model prison' on American lines but still maintaining the British 'separate and silent system.' The prisoners even wore blinker masks to prevent communication and only allowed the wearer to see the floor immediately beneath him. Originally intended as a processing prison for convicts due for transportation, if you behaved there you might

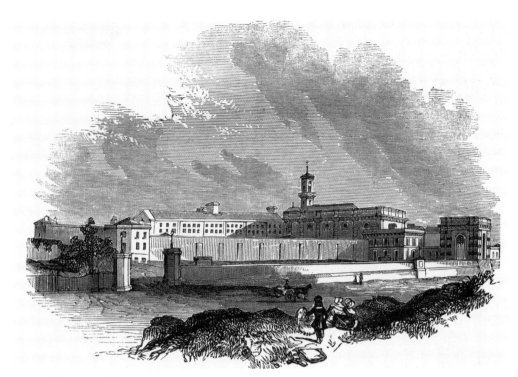

Pentonville Prison, 1844.

earn a ticket of leave that would allow freedom to seek employment in the New World. If you did not toe the line you could well end up working on a chain gang in the blistering sun. The new prison caused quite some outcry because it was considered it was 'managed on the most extravagant footing, with a cost to the country for each prisoner of £50 annually.'

In 1844 Dr Luke Roden recorded his observations of a visit to this new Model Prison at Pentonville for *The Illuminated Magazine.* The following excerpts examine the living conditions and daily routine at the 'ville.

> The five hundred men here collected are in the prime of life, from the age of eighteen to thirty five; they are the most desperate, reckless, and abandoned of human beings and they have been sentenced to long periods of transportation as a punishment for serious crimes; that they come into the prison generally utterly ignorant, and without even the rudiments of education, diseased in mind and body from effects of long-continued vice and debauchery, and they are placed in this correctional prison not merely as a punishment but as means for reformation.
>
> On entering an unoccupied cell, the inmate being at work in a distant part of the prison, I was surprised at the number of its accommodations. A hammock hung up at the side, with hair mattress, pillow, two sheets, two blankets, and a rug; a wash-hand-stand and bason, fixed; two cocks for the supply of water, of which each prisoner is allowed six gallons daily; a table, stool, pint mug, plate, knife, spoon, soap, towel and duster; there is also a large carpenter's bench at the side (or other device for the trade they were learning be it a weaving loom or

The cell of a typical Pentonville inmate in 1844.

equipment for tailors, rug or mat maker); a gas light burning until nine o'clock; school books and slate, Bible, prayer book, hymn book; one religious book, and one secular. I noticed the *Penny Magazine, Saturday Magazine*, and *Chamber's Journal*. The ventilation is entirely artificial, and is most perfect. The air enters over the door through a perforated plate and passes out on a level with the floor under the window, into a flue connected with a central chimney, where a fire secures a constant current.

The prison day was described thus:

5.30 a.m. The first bell is rung as a signal of preparation for the warders to assemble and the prisoners to rise.

Male convict at Pentonville and female convict at Millbank, 1862.

6 a.m. Warders unlock and (in winter) light the gas, and deliver the prisoners their tools and utensils which had been removed for security from the prisoners when they had been locked up the previous night. At the same time two pump parties of 16 prisoners march in file at intervals of five yards, are conducted to the pumps, where they remain an hour, one fourth of the number always resting alternately, so that the entire body only works three quarters of an hour. Other prisoners are turned out to clean the corridors, distributed at intervals of ten yards, cleaning only one side of the corridors at a time, while the warders are placed in the best positions for commanding a complete inspection, and preventing communication. The cleaning is completed in an hour. During the whole of that hour the bedding, which had been unfolded and shaken at rising, is left open and exposed for the purpose of being aired.

7 a.m. All pump parties are withdrawn and the warders have breakfast. The senior warders take charge of the prison and prepare their reports for the governor. The prisoners who had been employed cleaning the corridors, now roll hammocks, arrange their cells, and wash.

7.30 a.m. Principal warders have breakfast and the warders serve breakfast to the prisoners.

8 a.m. Pump parties turn out again. Exercise parties representing about half the prison population, moving in single file, at intervals of fifteen feet (officers were positioned along the line to prevent communication) proceed to their exercise yards for the duration of one hour.

8.05 am Chapel bell rings and the other half of the inmates attend divine service in the chapel. Conducted in single file to the chapel the prisoners are locked and bolted in separate stalls, where everyone can see and be seen by the clergyman, but no one prisoner can see another. The prisoners remove their caps, and hang up their brass numbers so as to be seen by the inspecting officers.

8.45 am Chapel service over, the prisoners are signalled to leave their stalls 'by an ingenious contrivance. A large black board with two square holes in it, behind which are two discs, with letters and numbers – these being turned, present to the eyes of all, for example A, 5. The man thus designated rises, puts on his cap, draws the visor over his face, puts on his ticket, open his door and marches out, and so in succession each row. All prisoners are now returned to their cells and locked up.

9 a.m. All warders assemble for parade, are inspected by and present their reports to the Governor or Assistant Governor. Immediately after this parade a new group of prisoners are set to the pumps.

10 a.m. One sixth of the inmates are returned to the chapel for school instruction. Another sixth are tutored in their cells by three assistant schoolmasters.

11 a.m. Pump and exercise parties are withdrawn and fresh ones sent out.

Noon. Prisoners at school are withdrawn, principal warders dine and the prisoners who attended schooling go for exercise.

1 p.m. Dinners for the prisoners are distributed. Warders then dine. All prisoners are returned to their cells. Governor and Deputy Governor make the daily inspection, taking notes of any complaints and requisitions. Each is accompanied by a principal warder, who unlocks and afterwards proves (examines) the doors. After they have dined, the prisoners are at liberty to read or write till two o'clock.

2 p.m. Warders return from their dinner and turn out the pump and exercise parties, more lessons are given in the chapel and cells, the remainder of the prisoners are employed in their respective trades.

3 p.m. Exercise and pump parties are exchanged.

4 p.m. All prisoners withdrawn to their cells.

4.30 p.m. Bell rings again for divine service. Those who were absent in the morning attend this service and return to their cells at 5.15 p.m.

5.30 p.m. Suppers are delivered and warders ensure the inmates have sufficient work to occupy them for the rest of the evening, prisoners are counted and cells are checked to be in proper order.

5.55 p.m. Signal is given for principal warders to make ready to go off duty. They assemble in the central hall and keys are handed back to the principal warder. Night warders come on duty.

8 p.m. Signal bell rings to cease work and sling hammocks. The ensuing hour is spent as the prisoners please, reading or writing.

9 p.m. Lights in the cells are extinguished and open fires checked to be safe. As the Principal Warder does his rounds he is followed by the warder responsible for each wing who then locks and proves all passage doors, locks and outlets ensuring all ladders are chained, all dangerous implements put away, and that every portion of the prison is secure for the night.

10 p.m. Principal Warder surrenders charge of the prison to the First Warder for the night watch and delivers the keys to the Deputy Governor and gives him a final report of prisoners locked up and having ensured all is right he goes off duty.

10 p.m. – 6 a.m. The night warders patrol the interior of the prison and pull the strings of the watch-clocks every quarter of an hour.

5.30 a.m. The fourth watch rings the signal bell for warders to assemble, and the prisoners to rise for another day.

MOTHERS, WITH THEIR CHILDREN, EXERCISING AT TOTHILL FIELDS PRISON.

The treadwheel at Brixton Prison.

THE FIRST TREADWHEEL

The treadwheel was devised in the early nineteenth century by Suffolk based engineer and iron founder, William Cubitt. The principal of the device was simple. Looking like an elongated mill wheel, each wheel contained twenty-four steps set 8in apart, so the circumference of the cylinder was 16ft. The wheel, under the power of the convicts walking up its 'steps' revolved twice in a minute with a mechanism set to ring a bell on every thirtieth revolution to announce the spell of work was finished. Every man put to labour at the wheel worked fifteen quarter hour sessions, climbing up to 18,000ft every day. The enterprising Justices of Surrey were to be Cubitt's first customer and paid £6,913 3s 6d for the treadwheel to be installed at the Brixton House of Correction. Coldbath Fields Prison was made infamous for its brutal regime; labour for prisoners here was specifically designed as a punishment rather than an educative or corrective activity. In this prison alone there were six treadwheel yards containing a total of twenty wheels. As the nineteenth century drew to a close a number of horrific accidents (limbs and heads torn off in accidents as prisoners missed footings or attempted to talk to one another) and wider penal reforms saw the treadwheel lose popularity and by 1895 there were only thirty-nine treadmills and twenty-nine cranks still in use in prisons across Britain. Treadmills were finally banned by an Act of Parliament in 1898.

THE TURNING OF THE SCREW

The Crank was a widely adopted means of occupying prisoners within the 'Separate System' within British prisons during the latter half of the nineteenth century. In certain London prisons like Wandsworth they were widely used instead of the treadwheel while in most prisons they were used to occupy refractory prisoners in their solitary cells. Operated by a single prisoner the Crank comprised a drum on a metal pillar or a handle set into a wall with a dial to register the number of times the crank handle had been turned – usually about twenty times a minute, a typical target being a total of 10,000 revolutions in eight and a half hours. If the target was not achieved in time the prisoner was given no food until the dial registered the required total. A legacy of the crank remains today; if the prisoner found this task too easy or proved refractory the prison warder would come and tighten the screw making the handle harder to turn hence the prison parlance for prison warder has, for generations, been 'the screw'.

HARD LABOUR — SHOT DRILL

Hard Labour was a familiar addition to sentences for crimes which carried short periods of incarceration but merited extra punishment; in the mid-nineteenth century such offences included: abduction, assaults unnatural (homosexual), on women and children or policemen, bestiality, concealing the birth of a child, frauds tried at Sessions, trespassing, illegal fishing, poaching, selling or exposing obscene prints, keeping brothels, unlawful collection of dust, disorderly prostitutes, fortune telling, indecent exposure of person and incorrigible rogues. Typical types of hard labour for women tended to be pounding and picking oakum, perhaps the Crank, if they proved troublesome but men would undoubtedly have been set to the Treadmill, Shot Drill and Stone Breaking. Shot Drill entailed a prisoner having to lift single cannonballs (weighing up to about 32lbs) up to chest height, carry it a set distance and make another pile, repeating the process until the set number of cannonballs had been moved in like manner. In the larger prisons up to fifty convicts could be engaged in 'Shot Drill;' they would be formed into three sides of a square and standing three deep and three yards distant from each other. Each end of the open square would have a neat pile of cannon balls which would be picked up one at a time and then passed from man to man and from one end to the other. The exercise would be repeated for a standard hour and a quarter.

THE LAST PUBLIC EXECUTION

The last time an execution was carried out in public in England was in front of Newgate Prison on 26 May 1868. The condemned was Michael Barrett, the man convicted of blowing up Clerkenwell Prison in an attempt to free two Fenians imprisoned there. One hundred and fifty people had been killed or injured in the blast. After this public hanging all executions were removed to 'behind prison walls.' Newgate became the main place for execution in London. Executions were carried out in the shed beside the prison yard, the crowd outside were notified of the enactment of the sentence by tolling bell (until 1890), hoisting of a black flag and posting of notices on the prison doors. The 'Newgate Hangman' was also the main executioner for London and the man most likely to be hired in by provincial counties to carry out their executions; a job carried out between 1829 and 1874 by our county's longest serving hangman, William Calcraft.

FIRST PRIVATE EXECUTION OF A WOMAN AT NEWGATE

The first private execution of a woman at Newgate after Parliamentary Act banned public executions was carried out on Frances 'Fanny' Stewart (aged forty-three) on 29 July 1874 at Newgate for the murder of her infant grandson. Mrs Stewart was a widow who lived with her daughter and son-in-law and their twelve-month-old child in Chelsea. On 27 April Mrs Stewart had a trifling quarrel with her son-in-law, in the evening she and the child were found to be missing. Fanny Stewart wrote to her son in law stating she would make his heart ache as hers did, threatening suicide for babe and herself. The second letter to the daughter confessed the murder of the child and begged her to meet and give her over to the police, this was done. The body of the child was recovered from the river off Millwall on 7 May. After sentence was passed she 'accepted her fate with earnestness' and wrote a letter full of penitence to her daughter. Fanny Stewart went to the gallows with 'remarkable courage,' in contrast to the usual efficiency of sober executioner William Marwood, her struggles after the drop fell 'were momentarily prolonged by some unfortunate twisting of the rope.'

'BIRCHING'S TOO GOOD FOR THEM'

Cries of 'bring back the birch' may still be heard after particular instances of street crime, this punishment was reserved mostly as a corporal punishment for wayward boys'; adult males who took the wayward path to crimes against the person, such as robbery with violence, especially garrotting would receive 'the lash.' *The Illustrated Police News* related the following after witnessing this punishment at Newgate in 1871. 'The effects on his skin were horrible, the diagonal pink lines glowing scarlet and running into one another till there was a broad scarlet band which quivered and flushed and changed colour, but there was no blood. Twenty-four, twenty-five lashes and then came a loud voice 'Stop' and the prisoner was cut loose to walk quietly away from the post.

A flogging at Newgate.

MONEY FOR OLD ROPE

Oakum-picking was a common occupation set for prisoners during the nineteenth century. The process could be carried out in solitary confinement cells or with other prisoners (in silence) in workrooms or oakum sheds. It involved the prisoner being given a weighed amount of old ships' rope, often black with tar and deeply engrained with salt and cut into lengths. After separating the rope into its corkscrewed coils these would then be unrolled by sliding them back and forth on the knee with the palm of the hand until the meshes were loosened, the strands were then separated and cleaned of the salt and tar on them. This 'stuff' was used for caulking the seams in the sides and decks of wooden ships. Men, women and children prisoners all picked oakum; it was very hard on the fingers, rope cuts were common as were blisters which proved very painful until the skin on the hands hardened to the work. Prisoners were expected to produce between 3lbs and 4lbs every two hours; shifts of oakum picking could last up to twelve hours. At Tothill Fields the boys (all under seventeen) could earn up to 17s a year for their oakum pickings – literally money for old rope!

THE ONLY METROPOLITAN POLICE OFFICER TO BE HANGED

When PC George Samuel Cooke met Maud Merton (aka Smith, Crowcher or Locksley) in about 1891, she was a prostitute. Apparently they looked good together and Cooke desperately tried to reform but she continued to walk the streets. After quarrels and rent arrear issues with their landlady, Cooke threatened to leave Merton. She just turned nasty and made a chain of allegations to the notice of Cookes' superior officer. His seniors did not believe the stories but because Cooke was being indiscreet with 'an unfortunate' he was disciplined and transferred. He moved on, formed a new attachment with a ladies' maid and their engagement was soon announced. Maud could not bear this and traced Cooke down to his beat patrolling the common near Wormwood Scrubs. Their argument resulted in Cooke seeing red, he drew his truncheon, he felled Maud with it, smashed her skull and stamped on her neck. Her body was discovered by a shepherd the following day. Cooke soon confessed to the crime, his uniform was bloodstained and he had been noticed attempting to dispose of a truncheon and blood stained whistle. At his trial a number of the jury wished to bring a verdict of manslaughter but Justice Hawkins ended up putting on the black cap and Cooke was hanged on 25 July 1893.

THE LAST TRIO ON THE GALLOWS TRAP

The last triple execution at Newgate took place on 26 February 1896, those who succumbed to the executioner were namely, Seaman, Milsom and Fowler all petty criminals who had resorted to murder. William Seaman was convicted of the 'Turner Street Murders' in Whitechapel. While attempting a robbery at the home of John Goodman Levy (aged seventy-seven) Seaman was disturbed by the old man who he stabbed and battered. The body of the housekeeper, Mrs Gale, was found murdered in the bedroom. The intruder had been observed entering and the police were summoned. A large crowd had assembled outside but no-one had seen the intruder leave. Detective Sergeant Wensley saw the hole in the bedroom ceiling and spotted another in the roof – Seaman was on the tiles! Realising the game was up Seaman cursed the jews and threw himself off the roof at the crowd below. It was a 40ft drop and he broke both thighs. He was joined on the gallows by Harry Fowler and Albert

Milsom who had killed the elderly Mr Henry Smith while attempting to burgle his Muswell Hill home. Both burglars had intended to turn King's Evidence on each other and intense animosity was apparent between them to the extent that Fowler violently attacked Milsom in the court while the jury were making their deliberations. James Billington was appointed executioner and was assisted by William Warbrick. Seaman was put between the two, as he took his place in the drop he exclaimed 'First time I've ever been a bloody peacemaker.' No doubt relieved to have the three men on the drop without incident, Billington released the trap but did not see that Warbrick had not cleared and he shot head first into the pit. Warbrick held on to the legs of the man he was nearest to and swung into the pit, thus avoiding a nasty accident.

THE PRISON BUILT BY PRISONERS

Wormwood Scrubs was built by convict labour and completed in 1890. Truly a product of British prisons in every way, Wormwood Scrubs was raised from bricks made from clay on the site, stone came from Dartmoor and Portland prison quarries; Portland also provided iron castings while carpenters, joiners and blacksmiths were found amongst the prisoners of Millbank and Chatham. Over 7,030 prisoners assisted in the construction, they stayed in wooden barrack huts with the perimeter of the site guarded by ex-soldier civilians armed with rifles; only one prisoner escaped during the construction work.

PURE COINCIDENCE?

Frederick Preston (aged twenty-two), a French polisher was executed by James Billington on 3 October 1899 at Newgate for the murder of his girlfriend, Eliza James Mears. After going out together for some time Eliza's mother had suggested she give him up because of the way he treated her. Eliza explained the situation to Preston and he beat her to death in a drunken frenzy with a blunt instrument. Almost a year to the day later, on 2 October 1900 John Charles Parr (aged nineteen) was also executed by James Billington at Newgate, he had shot his girlfriend near Bethnal Green Police station after she had left him; he had claimed to be a French polisher.

A WOMAN WAS FIRST TO BE EXECUTED IN THE TWENTIETH CENTURY

After seeing in the new year, and indeed a new century, within the walls of the condemned cell on 9 January 1900 Louisa Masset (aged thirty-three) had the ignominious distinction of being the first person to be executed in Britain during the twentieth century courtesy of the public executioner James Billington at Newgate prison. Louisa claimed she had handed over some £12 and placed her son, Manfred, in the care of a Mrs Browning who had just started a 'children's home' (Browning was almost certainly a baby farmer). Manfred was found later the same day in the ladies' waiting room of platform three on Dalston Junction station, wrapped in a black shawl. He had been battered with a brick and suffocated. The shawl was traced to Masset and a witness stated they had seen her on London Bridge Station at a time consistent with her committing the crime. Masset said she was in Brighton at the time of the murder and the witness must have been mistaken. A waiter came forward stating he could identify Masset as having a meal at his Brighton restaurant at the time in question. The jury decided she was guilty beyond reasonable doubt and she was sentenced to death, there was no reprieve. It is said as the hour of execution approached Louisa agreed her sentence was just – it could be argued this was not a confession to the murder but the concurrence of a penitent mother who had unwittingly sent her beloved son to his doom.

FIRST MAN HANGED IN BRITAIN IN THE TWENTIETH CENTURY — FOR THE SAKE OF A SHILLING

Henry Grove (aged twenty-six) was one of a number of local hawkers who used his neighbour, Henry Smith's yard and stables in Enfield for 6*d* a week. Behind with two weeks rent Smith (aged thirty-four) told Grove he could not use the stabling again until he had settled his arrears. Grove returned to the yard later that night, he was very drunk and was told where to go by Smith. A row developed and Grove ended up punching Smith but that was not the end of it. Smith went back into the yard and picked up two rusty scythes and took them to his own garden. Returning a few minutes later Grove found Smith in the yard and battered to death's door with the shaft and flat of the blade of scythe. Mrs Smith tried to intervene but was fought off with a number of blows by Grove. Removed to hospital, Smith was later able to give a statement to a magistrate in the presence of Henry Grove. Smith died of his injuries a few weeks later. At his trial Grove swore he used no weapons, that he did not throw the first punch and was acting in self-defence. The jury were not impressed and returned a verdict of 'Guilty'. Henry Grove has the infamous distinction to be the first man hanged in the twentieth century; he was executed on 22 May 1900 by James Billington at Newgate.

THIRTEEN

THE DREGS OF THE ABYSS

LONDON'S DESCENT

When Jack London visited 'The Abyss' that was the East End of London in 1902 he wanted to walk the street unnoticed, bought suitable old clothes, lived the day-to-day life and recorded what he saw around him. In the opening pages of his book *The People of the Abyss* he wrote this evocative introduction to the area: 'Nowhere in the streets of London may one escape the sight of abject poverty, while five minutes walk from almost any point will bring one to a slum; but the region my hansom was entering was one unending slum. The streets were filled with a new and different race of people, short of stature, and of wretched or beer-sodden appearance. We rolled along through miles of bricks and squalor, and from each cross-street and alley flashed long vistas of bricks and misery. Here and there lurched a drunken man or woman, and the air was oscene with sounds of jangling and squabbling. At a market, tottery old men and women were searching in the garbage thrown in the mud for rotten potatoes, beans and vegetables, while little children clustered like flies around a festering mass of fruit, thrusting their arms to the shoulders into the liquid corruption, and drawing forth morsels but partially decayed, which they devoured on the spot'.

BABY FARMING AT BRIXTON

On 11 October 1870 Margaret Walters (aged thirty-four) was executed at Horsemonger Lane for the murder of John Walter Cowen, an illegitimate child she had assumed the charge of for a consideration of money at her baby-farming establishment at 4 Frederick Terrace, Brixton. When first brought before the courts Walters appeared with her sister, Sarah Ellis (aged twenty-three) on the same indictment. The case looked even worse when the bodies of emaciated babies were discovered near the trail of different addresses Walters and Ellis left behind them. The evidence against Ellis apparently failed to support the capital charge so she was acquitted. Ellis did, however, confess under her own volition to obtaining money by false pretences in connection with baby-farming and was sentenced to eighteen months hard labour. The full letter of the law was enacted against Walters. Protesting her innocence of intention to murder to the last, Margaret Walters went to the gallows unaided and without resistance uttering 'a most touching and fervent prayer for forgiveness as the white cap and noose were adjusted . . . with the words still on her lips the bolt was drawn and she soon ceased to live.'

A BUNCH OF TOSHERS

One of the people to be given a wide berth on the street was the Tosher. Whole families followed the Tosher trade of descent into the gloom of the sprawling sewerage network of London and spent their day sieving excrement and effluvia for

FLUSHING THE SEWERS

the likes of coins, jewellery and silver cutlery which may have been flushed away or lost when a sink was emptied. The foul smell of the effluent in which they worked clung to their clothes and their houses often stunk too. Marriage into a Tosher family was looked down on in the East End. The one real benefit of being a Tosher was the constant exposure to vile substances from early age gave them a far greater immunity, than that enjoyed by their cleaner neighbours, to the diseases of the time.

A DESTITUTE MOTHER

On 6 February 1888 Mary Ann Minty, a destitute widow of Whitechapel appeared at Lambeth Police Court charged with begging on Walworth Road. Found by Joseph Bosley the Mendicity Officer, she had been found standing in the gutter with her children aged seven and ten. Approaching the pathetic group and explaining to them it was probably best that they came with him to the police station. Widow Minty became loud and abusive but Bosley insisted she should go and he escorted them to the station. A group of 'roughs' had assembled at the scene and followed shouting abuse and throwing stones at Bosley. Once at the station the children were given a bath, they were discovered to be covered in vermin, which in some places, had eaten into their flesh. Court decided 'it was monsterous the mother had deliberately dragged the children about the streets in order to incite the sympathy of those who were stupid enough to believe they were acting in a charitable manner.' Mary Minty was sentenced to one month hard labour and her children were removed to the workhouse.

A NIGHT IN THE WORKHOUSE

Jack London sought admission to the casual ward of the Whitechapel Workhouse, known on the street as 'The Spike.' After being turned away due to it being full on several occasions, London got there early and queued for hours to gain admission for a bed for the night. Upon entry all were questioned if they carried knives, matches and tobacco. All said no, most lied on all three counts. Given a brick of bread, the men (the sexes, even married couples were separated in the workhouse) sat at dirty tables where they dipped the hard bread into the piles of salt scatted over the surfaces. Water was available and a three quarters of a pint pannikin of skilly, a mixture of Indian corn and hot water. London described it as 'course of texture, unseasoned, gross and bitter. This bitterness which lingered in the mouth after the skilly had passed on, I found particularly repulsive. The worst of the evening was yet to come for after the meal the men were to bathe before they went to 'bed.' The bathroom was communal; '. . . two by two, we entered the bathroom. There were two ordinary tubs, and this I know: the two men preceding had washed in that water, we washed in the same water, and it was not changed for the two men that followed us . . . twenty-two of us washed in the same water . . . I did no more than make a show of splashing some of this dubious liquid at myself, while I hastily brushed it off with a towel wet from the bodies of other men. My equanimity was not restored by seeing the back of one poor wretch a mass of blood from attacks of vermin and retaliatory scratching.' He then retired to bed, it was many hours before he could sleep children noisily played in the street outside until midnight. Jack was in a room shared with many others coughing, wheezing, grunting, groaning and snoring punctuated by occasional shrieks and yells caused by nightmares, the heady blend of body odour filled the air to the degree London could only describe it as both 'frightful and sickening.' He concludes his night in the workhouse thus 'Toward morning I was awakened by a rat on my breast. In the quick transition from sleep to waking, before I was completely myself, I raised a shout to wake the dead. At any rate, I woke the living, and they cursed me roundly for my lack of manners.'

PITY THE POOR BEGGAR

Physical disability was a very visible fact of life accepted as much a feature of life on the streets of Victorian London as fallen leaves in the winter. One would encounter men and women bent double with malformed spines, rickety-legged beggars on crutches, all manner of deformities, amputees blind, deaf, dumb or combinations of the aforementioned were all to be found on the streets of London. A number of beggars who were on the streets for many years became well known 'characters' and folks did look out for them – if they were not at their usual pitch at least the question why would be asked. One such character had been a shunter at Bricklayer's Arms goods yard in the Old Kent Road who had lost both his legs when run over by a goods train. When he was out begging he displayed with him a crude painting of the incident complete with blood not only painted spurting out onto the rails in the painting but over the frame too! Another tragic fellow was Arthur Abbott who suffered for years from the injuries he received as a result of the Clerkenwell bombing of 1868. He went completely blind as a direct result in 1892 and was a known character in High Holborn seen begging with a notice recalling the catastrophe beside him. All told, he was reduced to begging on the streets for over forty years.

MATCH GIRLS

Working conditions for many in late nineteenth-century London were absolutely horrendous, workers would be crammed into sweat shops cobbling boots, making clothes, rubber, soap and fashioning metalware. One of the most horrible places to work was in a match factory where much of their labour force were women and children. Many were made sick by the chemicals they were exposed to which caused loss of breath. One condition was particularly nasty, known as 'Phossy Jaw' the ingested phosphorous caused gums to rot and teeth fell out until it ate into live bone when actual pieces of jaw could be easily pulled out. The homeward paths of the workers could always be traced by the luminous vomit which gathered in the gutters along the way. In 1888 social reformer Annie Besant led the Bryant & May's Match Girls to down tools on 5 July 1888 and they successfully went on strike for better working conditions and wages.

DR BARNARDO AND THE RIPPER VICTIM

During the month of October 1888 the Victorian philanthropist Dr Thomas John Barnardo was to become involved in the story of Jack the Ripper. Writing an impassioned letter about the suffering of the children in common lodging houses to *The Times*, published on 9 October, he revealed 'Only four days before the recent murders I visited no. 32 Flower and Dean Street, the house in which the unhappy woman Stride occasionally lodged . . . In the kitchen of No 32 there were many persons, some of them being girls and women of the same unhappy class that to which poor Elizabeth Stride belonged. The company soon recognised me, and the conversation turned upon the previous murders. The female inmates of the kitchen seemed thoroughly frightened at the dangers to which they were presumably exposed . . . One poor creature, who had evidently been drinking, exclaimed somewhat bitterly to the following effect: 'We're all up to no good, and no one cares what becomes of us. Perhaps some of us will be killed next!' Barnardo continued 'I have since visited the mortuary in which were lying the remains of the poor woman Stride, and I at once recognised her as one of those who stood around me in the kitchen of the common lodging-house on the occasion of my visit last Wednesday week.'

THE MOST NOTORIOUS BABY FARMER

On 10 June 1896 Mrs Amelia Dyer (aged fifty-seven), a baby farmer and one of the most infamous and callous women of the nineteenth century was executed at Newgate. Although executed in London, Dyer, like most baby farmers had operated at several locations across Britain and in her case had done so quite successfully for about fifteen years. Living at 45 Kensington Road, Reading at the time of her capture, she was traced there after a baby wrapped in brown paper was pulled out of the water by a bargeman at Caversham Lock. The infant had been strangled by a piece of fabric tape tied under its left ear. Dyer had made a fatal mistake, she had wrapped the baby in paper from a parcel sent to her at her old address of 20 Pigott's (spelt Wigott's on the parcel) Road, Caversham. She had also been spotted before the horrible discovery by a witness waddling up the Caversham tow path with a parcel under her arm. By the time the police came knocking at her door a total of seven babies had been recovered from the Thames, Lord knows how many were never found. Shortly after Dyer's arrest her daughter and son in law – Arthur and Polly Palmer were arrested at their Willesden home. More baby clothes were found there; their complicity in Dyers' horrible trade was clear but there was no clear evidence to link them to any crime, and young Polly was hardly backwards in coming forward to deflect any blame and condemnation onto her mother, the Palmers were acquitted but Mrs Dyer went to the gallows. Chillingly, when Mrs Dyer was asked about the identification of the babies she replied, 'You'll know mine by the tape around their necks.' The ice-cold glower of Mrs Dyer frightened generations of visitors to Madame Tussaud's Waxworks.

HOUSE OF ILL-REPUTE

Amy Hopkins was brought before West London Police Court on 15 August 1899 for permitting her house at 86 Finborough Road, Kensington to be used as a brothel. Her husband John, a supervisor at the Earl's Court Exhibition also appeared on charges of living off immoral earnings. Inspector Seabright of F Division in describing the character of the house stated 'On a recent occasion I saw one of the South African natives enter the house with a woman . . . ' After a stream of convincing incidents were related the couple were found guilty and sentenced to six week imprisonment or £15 fine for Amy and three months' hard labour for John. Three young children, all girls, were rescued from the house; they were ordered by the magistrate to be taken to the workhouse with a view of sending them to industrial schools.

THE LITTLE PARCEL FOUND AT BATTERSEA

On 6 March 1900 Ada Chard Williams (aged twenty-four) was executed at Newgate for the murder of Selina Ellen Jones, a child which had been placed in her care. Williams was baby farmer and was exposed after the body of a baby wrapped up in a parcel was washed up on the banks of the Thames at Battersea and identified by her mother as twenty-one-month-old Selina Jones. This baby had been placed in the hands of Chard Williams who, for a fee, had agreed to find the babe a new home. Chard Williams saw the report in the press and having moved she did not wait to be traced, she wrote a letter admitting she was baby farming but denied any knowledge of the child's murder. Chard Williams and her husband were both arrested; he was considered more an accomplice than a murderer and charges were not pursued. Chard Williams was found guilty and sentenced to death. Although she was found guilty of this one horrible death other bundles of unrelated baby clothes were discovered as police searched the house, all had been tied with the same knot as the parcel poor little Selina had been wrapped in . . .

CARRYING THE BANNER

If there was no room in the casual ward of the workhouse the homeless of East London would have to 'Carry the Banner,' that is stay awake all night, walking the streets for a discreet hide hole to sleep in. The law was clear, no person was allowed to be found asleep on the street, if they were found by a passing policeman they would be shaken awake and sent on their way. It was widely known among those who 'Carried the Banner' that Green Park was one of the earliest to open its gates so rain or shine the homeless would pour in and soon every available bench would become a day bed for one who had been up all night, if no bench was found the tired vagrants would simply lay on the wet, dewy grass. During the daytime the Spitalfields Garden was another haunt of the homeless and dispossessed of the East End. Situated in the shadow of Christ's Church here could be found whole families who were, 'little more than rag sacks of humanity' huddled together and asleep on the benches. Many of the vagrants here were filthy dirty and heavily infested with lice and sores, it was little wonder the Spitalfield's Garden was known locally as 'Itchy Park'.

LIFE IN THE TENEMENTS

Tenement housing was cramped, dirty, unsanitary and inhumane. For a weekly rent of about 4s families of five, six and seven people crammed themselves into these filthy rooms furnished only by a rough, worn table, broken down bedstead, or more likely a contrivance of wooden boards resting on old wooden crates or bricks with an unwashed, flea-infested straw mattress on top and rags for a blanket. Andrew Mearns in *The Bitter Cry of Outcast London* stated these examples among many: 'In one cellar a sanitary inspector reports finding a father, mother, three children and four pigs! In another room a missionary found a man ill with smallpox, his wife just recovering from her eighth confinement, and the children running around half naked and covered with dirt. Here are seven people living in one underground kitchen, and a little dead child in the same room. Elsewhere is a poor widow, her three children, and a child who had been dead thirteen days. Her husband, who was a cabman, had shortly before committed suicide.'

FOURTEEN

A SHORT CATALOGUE
OF DISASTERS

THE GREAT FIRE OF LONDON

The Great Fire of London began in Farriner's Bake House on Pudding Lane on the night of 2 September 1666. Those in the bake-house panicked, the winds caught the blaze and it began to spread through the old timber framed buildings. After an hour the fire caused such concern Sir Thomas Bloodworth the Lord Mayor was woken from his slumbers and informed of the situation which he dismissed with the word 'Pish – a woman could piss it out' and went back to bed. On 3 September the diarist, John Evelyn recorded: 'The fire having continu'd all this night (if I may call that night which was light as day for ten miles round about, after a dreadful manner) when conspiring with a fierce easten wind in a very drie season.' From Bankside in Southwark he observed 'the whole South part of ye Citty burning from Cheapside to ye Thames and all along Cornehill (for it kindl'd back against ye wind as well as forward), Tower Streete, Fenchurch Streete, Gracious Streete, and so along to

The Great Fire of London, 1666.

Bainard's Castle, and was now taking hold of St Paule's Church, to which the scaffolds contributed exceedingly. The conflagration was so universal, and the people so astonish'd that from the beginning, I know not by what despondency or fate, they hardly stirr'd to quench it . . . God grant my eyes may never behold the like, now seeing above 10,000 houses all in one flame; the noise and cracking and thunder of the impetuous flames, ye shrieking of women and children, the hurry of people, the fall of Towers, Houses and Churches, was like an hideous storm . . . The clouds of smoke were dismall, and reach'd upon computation neer fifty miles in length. Thus I left it this afternoone burning, a resemblance of Sodom, or the last day. London was, but is no more!' The fire blazed for a total of five days, only after streets of houses were torn down to stop it spreading and the wind died down did the fire, at last die out. There were surprisingly few human casualties of the fire, most of those were too old, infirm or sick to join the exodus of thousands who fled the city. One of the fatalities was recorded by Taswell as being found near the east walls of St Paul's 'a human body . . . parched up as it were with flames, whole as to skin, meagre as to flesh, yellow as to colour. This was an old decrepit woman who fled here for safety, imagining the flames would not have reached her there. Her clothes were burnt, and every limb reduced to a coal.' Over 13,000 houses had been destroyed along with eighty-nine parish churches, forty-four Halls of City Livery Companies and countless hundreds of other buildings were destroyed in The Great Fire of London.

THE PLOT BACKFIRED

The *Annual Register* for February 1767 records an incident where a man lodging in Earl Street, Seven Dials, returned home expecting his dinner ready but found his wife much the worse for drink and insensible on the bed. Enraged by his wife's behaviour he resolved to blow her out of bed with gunpowder. Pouring a pool of powder under the bed and trailing the powder to a 'safe' distance he set fire to it only for the flame to return upon him and flare up the dusty powder upon his clothes causing him near fatal burns. His wife remained unharmed and surprised to find out what had happened when she came out of her stupor.

LONDON TOWN IS FALLING DOWN

Throughout the history of London, before the days of modern building techniques or materials, there are numerous accounts of buildings simply collapsing – often without warning. One such disaster occurred on 22 May 1811 when a dilapidated old timber framed building belonging to Mr Hastings, rented out to a variety of tenants, on the corner of White Lion Street and Great St Andrew's Street, Seven Dials, collapsed without warning. A contemporary account recorded 'The screams and cries of the inhabitants were dreadful as most of them were buried under the ruins. In a short time 500 persons surrounded the spot, many of who set about digging the unfortunate person from their perilous situation. An old man, with an infant in his arms, dead, was the first shocking spectacle that presented itself. (During the digging out) the most horrid groans were heard in the ruins, but in consequence of some timber stopping up the way, the bodies could not be got at for some time after. A young man unfortunately received the spade on his skull; he with four others, in a dreadfully mangled state, were taken to hospital. An old woman named Toogood who lodged in the second floor, being appraised of her danger, threw herself out of the window, by which she was so much hurt as to leave little hope of recovery.'

77. *Contending for a Seat.*

'Thump-ups' at the theatres were common occurrences in early nineteenth-century London.

Another tragic fire, the burning of Covent Garden Theatre, 1856.

TRAGEDY AT THE THEATRE

On 3 February 1794 the Haymarket Theatre was presenting a bill including 'My Grandmother,' 'No Song No Supper,' and 'The Prize.' A great crowd was entering the playhouse and descending the steps to take their places in the pit when one of the audience tripped and fell, so vast was the crowd behind that the momentum could not stop and people were forced to step over the audience member. The long evening gowns and corsetry of the ladies did not make stepping over a body an easy process and more people began to tumble over. The unabated momentum of the crowd caused a terrible pile of bodies whereby many were injured by trampling and crushing. Only when the horror became apparent was some order was restored and rescues were made from the tumbled and crushed heap of humanity in the theatre. The insensible bodies were removed to Mr Wynch's druggist shop and other local shops and the rest removed to St Martin's Bone House. 'Everything was done to restore animation, if it was only suspended . . . but success attended the process in one case only.' Fifteen were killed in the Haymarket Theatre Tragedy.

WHEN WESTMINSTER BURNED

On 16 October 1834 the House of Lords was found to be 'unbearably hot.' Concerns raised by Mrs Wright the Deputy House Keeper were answered that men were burning a large number of the old exchequer tallies in the stove of the heating apparatus. She was assured there was no danger. A 6 p.m. the House of Lords was found to be on fire, by 7 p.m. the Palace of Westminster was a raging mass of flame.

Despite the attendance of every fire appliance in London and many volunteers the Palace was doomed by its warren of passageways and rooms, the winds that fanned the flames and the difficulties caused to the fire pumps by the Thames being at its lowest ebb. Many brave rescues of historic treasures were made, none less than the Deputy Sergeant at Arms who against strong warnings climbed a ladder and retrieved the Mace and The Earl of Munster who remained in the Library of the House of Commons directing the removal of the most important books until he was pulled out by the collar by a workman – just before the ceiling collapsed. Vast numbers of people came to see the blaze, Peelers and the Guards had to be called to manage the crowds who gave one unruly cheer as the great roof fell in.

THE LAST CHIMES OF THE BURNING EXCHANGE

The first Royal Exchange was destroyed during the Great Fire of London in 1666. The rebuilt second exchange did not stand for 200 years at it too succumbed to flames on 10 January 1838. As the fire reached the clock tower a tale circulated that the chimes bravely sounded out first 'Life let us cherish,' then, 'God Save the Queen,' and finally 'There's nae luck aboot the Hoose.'

TRAGEDY ON PEACE DAY

St Mary's on The Strand was the scene of a tragedy when it should have been a day of celebration. A proclamation was to be made for what was to prove a short peace with France in 1802 and a large crowd had gathered to hear the announcement. Just as the heralds came abreast on Somerset House one of the crowd on the roof of St Mary's pushed too hard against one of the stone urns and sent the 200lb ornament and part of its cornice plummeting onto the crowd below. Three persons were killed as a result of this – one on the spot, the second on his way to hospital and the third lingered on for two more days, then expired. Several others were seriously injured. The unfortunate man who had caused the urn to fall, fell back on the roof and fainted. He was discharged of blame, the urn having been 'fastened by a wooden spike instead of being clamped with iron' but the man was said to have 'never been the same again.'

FIRE AT THE TOWER

On 30 October 1841 the great armoury and adjoining Bowyer Tower in the Tower of London were discovered ablaze in a fire found eventually to have been caused by the overheated flue of a stove. 150,000 stand of firearms were said to have been destroyed by the fire and a total of £200,000 of damage was caused. The fire was localised but it was a near run thing, at one point The White Tower and the Jewel House appeared under imminent danger. Superintendent Pierse of the Metropolitan Police, accompanied by Mr Swifte the keeper of the Jewel House, constables and tower warders effected a brave evacuation of the jewels. Pierse had to get into the house via a barred grating which they forced open with crow bars. Despite cries warning of the ever approaching flames Pierse kept on passing out the jewels and regalia that were carried to safety by warders, police and firemen to the Governor's House. The heat of the fire was such that many of the garments worn by those involved in the rescue of the jewels were reduced to a charred state. Chambers' *Book of Days* (1879) stated 'Some public reward to Mr Pierse, who had thus so gallantly imperilled himself to save the Regalia of the United Kingdom, would, we should imagine, have been a fitting tribute to his bravery. But no such response was ever bestowed.'

THE TRAGIC HEROINE

Fire broke out at 8 Lincoln Court, off Great Wild Street on 28 August 1873. Ellen Donovan (aged thirty-seven), a neighbour at No. 10 knew children to be at No. 8 and she had not seen them evacuate the building. Rushing inside she ran upstairs amid a house full of flame and smoke. The tragedy was that this selfless act was unnecessary, the children were all out of the building and Ellen's escape route was blocked as the stairs erupted into a mass of flames. Her remains were only recovered after the fire had been extinguished.

THE PRINCESS ALICE DISASTER

The *Princess Alice* was one of the most popular pleasure steamers on the Thames, returning from Sheerness on the evening of 3 September 1878 she was loaded to the gunnels (overloaded by about 200 passengers for its official capacity of 500) with day tripping Londoners. At Woolwich the iron clad collier *Bywell Castle* (a vessel five times the weight of the *Princess Alice*) was en route to Newcastle to take coals on for Alexandria. For some reason Captain Grinstead of the *Princess Alice* suddenly changed course and the *Bywell Castle* could not manoeuvre away in time and loomed out of the darkness ploughing its bows just forward of the starboard paddle box almost cutting *Princess Alice* in two. The *Princess* sank in less than four minutes, over 640 drowned, many bodies were never recovered. In the days afterwards the waters around Woolwich were filled with any small vessel the enterprising could get their hands on – recovered bodies earned their finder 12*s* a cadaver, many unseemly struggles and fights to recover the dead ensued.

Recovering bodies from the river and wreck of the Princess Alice, *as reported in the* Illustrated London News, *September 1878.*

THESE TOYS ARE DANGEROUS

On 3 August 1888 an explosion occurred at the works of Mr H.J. Cadwell, toy firework maker, South Fields, Merton Road, Wandsworth. When the three buildings affected by the blast were examined there was hardly a portion of each structure left that was more than a foot in length. Luckily most of the factory hands (who were predominantly female) were at dinner when the explosion occurred. Tragically there were two fatalities, both of them women, who were standing in the doorway of one of the sheds, their death made all the more heartrending when it was realised that the girls were sisters – Lizzie and Eliza Thornton aged twenty-one and nineteen respectively. Another girl, Lucy Harwood, was so badly injured her arm had to be amputated, she died a few days later in the Wandsworth & Clapham Union infirmary.

THE HANDY HANSOM

Fire broke out shortly after 3 a.m. on 18 January 1888 at the Duke of York Tavern, Ormond Yard on York Street, Jermyn Street, Piccadilly. Living above the pub was Mr Dale, his wife, a niece and the pub potman. Awoken by the crackling and burning of the fire they all left their rooms and descended the stairs to escape but found their exits blocked by smoke and fire. Only able to reach their upstairs drawing room and having no means of getting down the final storey they opened the windows and shouted for help. Fortunately, in the nick of time, the quickwitted driver of an empty Hansom cab ran his cab alongside the flaming building. A brave policeman clambered up and effected the rescue of the trapped people, to the cheers and applause of the gathering crowd.

WHEN THE SKY AND STREETS TURNED BLOOD RED

Fire broke out at the Shadwell Dry Dock on 30 August 1888, it spreads rapidly to become one massive conflagration and is not brought under control until the following morning. Fires always drew hundreds of spectators especially from the nearby East End. On this night the sky was stained red by the raging fire and many folks scuttled along the back alleys and roads to watch as the steam fire engines with their shiny brass boilers and streams of hoses struggled to contain and quench the conflagration. It was not only the sky that was to be stained blood red that night. Policemen were thus distracted from their normal beats by the pressing duties of crowd control. It just so happened in the early hours of the 31 August the body of Polly Nicholls the first widely accepted victim of Jack the Ripper was discovered on Buck's Row. Many subsequent witnesses at the inquests into the Jack the Ripper murders would remember their whereabouts by recalling where they were on the night of the great Shadwell dock fire.

THEY ALL ASSUMED

On 19 November 1897 flames and smoke were observed flicking out on the first floor of a warehouse on Hamsell Street. Soon a crowd gathered to watch the fire, everyone assumed the fire brigade had been summoned and stood watching in anticipation of hearing the hooves of the horse drawn appliance thundering along the streets, brass steamer billowing smoke and attendant fire crew resplendent in their polished brass helmets. Nobody had sent word and it was only when concern was expressed of where the fire engine was that the brigade had any knowledge of the fire. By the time the first steamer fire engine arrived the fire had taken hold and had spread to adjoining buildings. Fanned by high winds it spread yet further to Jewin Street, Jewin Crescent and the back of Well Street. It took no less than sixty fire appliances and three hundred firemen and an estimated 15,000,000 gallons of water to get the blaze under control. The fire left the majority of Hamsell Street as 'nothing else than a heterogeneous pile of masonry, twisted ironwork and burnt goods.' A total of over 100 warehouses covering 100,000 square yards were totally destroyed. Though initially to have been caused by a gas explosion – at the City of London inquiry it was decided the fire had been caused by an arsonist.

FIFTEEN

GASTRONAUGHTS

HE ATE THE HEART OF A KING

William Buckland (1784–1856) was a notable academic, geologist and palaeontologist, with a sense of adventure and keen eye for the anomalous, one account tells of how when visiting a cathedral at which spots of saints' blood were said to be always fresh on the floor, never evaporating or vanishing, Dr Buckland, with the use of his tongue, determined that the 'blood' was in fact bats' urine. He was also known for his eccentricities. His passion for scientific observation and experiment extended to his home life and his home was filled with a bewildering array of fossils, flora and fauna.

He claimed he had eaten his way through most of the animal kingdom and he proudly shared accounts of these gastronomic experiences with others, advising them the most distasteful of all he had eaten were mole and bluebottle. His dinner guests would also be treated to what he considered the more savoury treats of the likes of crocodile, panther and mouse.

Shortly before Buckland's appointment as Dean of St Paul's in 1845 the writer and raconteur Augustus Hare recorded what has become Buckland's most infamous incident. 'Talk of strange relics led to mention of the heart of a French King (Louis XVI) preserved at Nuneham in a silver casket. Dr Buckland, while looking at it, exclaimed, 'I have eaten many strange things, but have never eaten the heart of a king before,' and, before anyone could hinder him, he had gobbled it up, and the precious relic was lost for ever.'

DINING AT HIGH TABLE

In 1820 a group of builders involved with repair work on St Paul's had a luncheon 365ft above the ground inside the new cross and orb they had erected on the top of the dome of the cathedral.

WHILE AWAITING NELSON...

In 1843, after erecting the column for Nelson in Trafalgar Square and while the plinth was vacant, awaiting the arrival of the great maritime hero, fourteen men sat down for a steak dinner – 166ft above ground.

DINNER IN A DINOSAUR

On new year's eve 1853 a number of eminent scientists attended a dinner inside an iguanodon! The beast was in fact one of the twenty-nine life-sized dinosaurs and prehistoric creatures created by Mr Benjamin Waterhouse Hawkins who hosted the party within the massive belly of the plaster-covered, brick and iron-framed monster at Crystal Palace.

DINING WITH A DIFFERENCE

George A. Kessler was a rich man with a penchant for unusual ways to entertain friends to dinner. His parties included dinner in an airship hovering over the Atlantic and a tramps' dinner where guests attended in worn out old clothes and they ate out of cans. He hosted his most extravagant dinners at the Savoy Hotel. For his birthday on 30 June 1905 he took Venice as his theme; magnificent backdrops were painted, the scene illuminated with 400 Venetian lamps and the courtyard of the hotel was flooded and the water dyed blue to make a 'canal.' Surrounded by 12,000 carnations and a vast quantity of roses his twenty-four guests sat boarded a massive gondola which drifted on the water as they ate food prepared by fifteen master chefs, served by waiters dressed as gondoliers.

SIXTEEN

ECCENTRICS, ODDBALLS & HOAXERS

MUGGLETONIANS

About 1651 two tailors, one Ludovick Muggleton and the other named Reeves began to announce themselves as 'the two last witnesses of God that would ever be appointed on earth.' Even going so far as to claim they had been invested with the gift of prophesy and an exclusive power over the gates of heaven and hell they did draw a number of followers. After the death of Reeves, Muggleton carried on and built up his cult of followers by preaching and 'raving' in print. Muggletonians grew to quite a size, predominantly women joining their number, but public authorities were concerned by Muggleton's 'incomprehensible rhapsodies' and the growing number of followers he was attracting so they resolved to put him down. Brought up at the Old Bailey on 17 January 1677 his trial ended with him being sentenced to a stand in the pillory for three days on three parts of London, and being ordered to pay a £500 fine or gaol on failure of payment. His books and papers were also ordered to be burnt in public.

OLD PARR'S TRIP TO LONDON

Thomas Parr of Shropshire became famous as Britain's oldest inhabitant. It was alleged he lived through a total of ten reigns, married his first wife when in his eighties and his second at the age of 122. His fame saw him made great offers of money for him to come to London and be put on public show. The temptation was great and eventually 'Old Parr' came up to the city in 1635 with Lord Arundel to make the acquaintance of Charles I but only survived a few weeks – the city life and, the Lord's fine food and the excitement was all too much for him and he died. Buried in Westminister Abbey the age ascribed to Old Parr was that he died at 152 years old!

FLAMING ECCENTRIC

In 1665 Solomon Eccles was sent to Bridewell House of Correction for striding through Smithfield Market stark naked while carrying a pan of blazing sulphur on his head while prophesising doom, destruction and the end of the world. Although the end was not quite nigh the Great Fire of London did follow on the very next year. If only someone had listened to him . . .

THEY DIDN'T SEE THE FUNNY SIDE!

A performance of unique appeal was advertised for the evening of 16 January 1749 at the Haymarket Theatre where a versatile conjuror would; 'play on a common walking cane the music of every instrument now used, to surprising perfection; that he would, on stage, get into a tavern quart bottle, without equivocation, and while there, sing several songs, and suffer any spectator to handle the bottle; that if any spectator came masked, he would, if requested declare who they were; and that in a private room he would produced the representation of any person dead, with which the person requesting it should converse some minutes as if alive'. The prices proposed for the show were gallery 2*s*, pit 3*s*, boxes 5*s*, stage 7*s* 6*d*. The Haymarket was packed for this fantastic show but no conjuror appeared. The crowd grew restless and after a few shouts it was soon apparent the audience had been duped by a hoaxer and boiled over to rioting that threatened to tear the theatre down. The manager of the theatre said he had reserved all the monies taken and would have gladly refunded them – if they had only asked.

THE FORTUNE OF A BEGGAR

In August 1765 the death of John Cornwall was recorded in *Annual Register*. Cornwall, aged ninety-one, was living at the time on Kent Street, Southwark and was known as 'the cripple of Kent', a familiar beggar upon the streets around London for more than sixty years. The woman he called his wife was in for a surprise (as were any who knew Cornwall) when he left her upward of 400 guineas in gold and a considerable sum in silver.

SHE WAS A HE

In April 1772 many residents of Streatham mourned the passing of one of their great local characters, the noted 'infallable Doctoress and fine sempstress' Elizabeth Russell in her 108th year. It was even noted that Dr Johnson had found Elizabeth a 'shrewd and sensible person, with a good memory, and was very fond of conversing with her.' When Elizabeth died suddenly 'her' true sex, that of a male, was discovered 'to the extreme surprise of all the neighbourhood.'

BAD OR MAD?

On 9 July 1787, one of the literati of his day, one Dr Elliott, fired two pistols in the direction of a lady and gentleman while walking on Prince's Street. Neither were injured but both were deeply shocked and the lady's dress singed from the discharge of the shots. Elliott was arrested, taken to Newgate and brought up on charges of attempted murder. Friends of Elliott had feared the worst and had already set about establishing a plea for insanity to save the eccentric doctor from the gallows. Dr Simmons of St Luke's hospital for lunatics presented evidence from a paper Elliott was going to put before the Royal Society where Elliott argued his case that the sun was not a 'body of fire as alleged by astronomers . . . its light proceeds from a dense and universal aurora, which my afford ample light to the inhabitants of the surface (of the sun) beneath, and yet be at such a distance aloft as not to annoy them'.

The Recorder objected to this being any proof of insanity 'If any such extravagant hypothesis were to be considered a proof of lunacy many learned and perfectly sane astronomers might be stigmatised as madmen. Elliott was however acquitted on a technical point – there was no proof the pistols had actually been loaded with ball or shot. Tragically he was never to enjoy his freedom, he died on the 22nd after he died of starvation having resolutely refused all food offered to him since his arrest.

THE TALE OF DIRTY DICK

One of the great characters of Bishopgate Without in the eighteenth century was Nathaniel Bentley known to all as 'Dirty Dick.' He had been born of a good family and inherited a prosperous business from his father in 1761.

Bentley had a sweetheart and they were due to marry, all preparations were made and even a magnificent feast prepared in the upper rooms of his ale house and shop but on that day which was to have been the beginning of the happy union news was brought that his intended had died. Bentley was inconsolable and he ordered that the dining room, feast and all, be shut up and left to the rats and mice, never to be opened again in his lifetime. It was from that day Bentley descended into a solitary life wearing clothes many times mended by his own hands, living on 'only the commonest and cheapest eatables' that despite having plenty of money for servants he cooked for himself. His personal cleanliness that above all led to his *nom de plume* was the subject his friends expressed most concern about, to which he answered 'It's of no use; if I wash my hands to-day, they will be dirty again tomorrow.' After the death of 'Dirty Dick' in 1809 the rooms that were sealed for about fifty years were entered, and there, just as they were left were the utensils, glasses, plates, pictures and furniture, just as they had been left but now scarcely recognisable under the think layer of dust that covered them all, some say these rooms were one of Dickens's inspirations for the situation of Miss Haversham. The dead and mummified cats, rats, mice, items of clothing and household effects that could be salvaged were used to decorate the walls of Dirty Dick's pub for generations after – until health and safety regulations ordered they be taken down.

'Dirty Dick'.

WHEN THIRTEEN WAS LUCKY

When John Hatfield died at his home in Glasshouse Yard Aldersgate on 18 June 1770 at the age of 102 his next of kin took pains to record the truth of a story relating to the dear departed that had become a London legend. In his youth, during the reign of William and Mary, Hatfield had been a soldier and had been brought up on a charge of having fallen asleep when on duty on the terrace at Windsor. He vehemently denied the allegation and solemnly declared as proof that he had been awake at the time he had heard the clock of St Paul's Cathedral strike thirteen. This claim was dismissed and poor John was condemned to death for his misdemeanour. While awaiting his fate a number of persons of note heard of the soldier's plight and swore affidavits that they too had heard the thirteen strikes instead of twelve on the night in question. In the light of this the court could not stand by their judgement and Hatfield received His Majesty's pardon.

MORE ON THIRTEEN AND FORTUNE?

The *Public Advertiser* of 28 September 1769 recorded, 'Died a few days ago at Chelsea, aged 90, Mr Henry Tropp, formerly a coach master and stable keeper, worth £12,000. The Deceased had married thirteen wives, the last of whom died five months ago in the 46th year of her age.'

HE COUNTED THE PENNIES BUT FORGOT THE POUNDS

John Elwes was the son of a successful brewer in Southwark and had inherited a considerable fortune but even from an early age he always seemed to be a spendthrift. He would do things like sit in wet clothes for hours rather than light a fire or eat meat so near putrification the butcher could only charge the minimum amount for it. But like so many misers his penny pinching cost him dearly as for want of a few repairs his country mansion fell into rack and ruin; he preferred to occupy any of the properties he owned and rented out in London that happened to be without tenant at the time. As age caught up with him he became increasingly paranoid about being attacked and robbed so he took to sleeping in his clothes with his hat on and staff in his hand. As he declined his dreams were haunted with such images he was heard to cry 'I will keep my money! I will! Don't rob me! Oh, Don't.' When he died on 26 November 1789 he had been too indolent to maintain regular accounts and as a consequence some £150,000 in bad debts were owed to him. His physician said frankly that if Elwes had worried less about not spending his own money he could have happily enjoyed another twenty years of life.

KING OF THE MISERS

Daniel Dancer was the seventeenth-century king of the misers, he prided himself on it and carried on a family tradition of both his Grandfather and his Father and even inherited their paranoid fear of being robbed so he regularly barricaded himself into his home and hid money in all sort of unusual places inside and out of the house – even under dung heaps! He had inherited a reasonable tract of land in London and with it an annual income that should have kept him, and his family, very comfortably – instead he chose to live frugally, to say the least. He bought one shirt once a year and wore it until it disintegrated, the rest of his clothes were little more than threadbare rags supplemented by bundles of straw in the colder weather. If offered a pinch of snuff he would take one, but rather than sniff it he would put it in a box. When the box was full he would trade its contents for candles, when he could not barter for candles he chose to sit in the dark and retire early to his bed where he slept in a sack. When his sister was dying in 1766 he obstinately refused to call a doctor justifying his stance by saying 'Why should I waste money in wickedly endeavouring to counteract the will of Providence?' Dancer's sister had been cared for by Lady Tempest, to whom she had intended to leave her fortune but died before making out a will so Daniel Dancer made his claim for thirty years' back rent for her accommodation and food and received two thirds of her estate. When Dancer himself died in 1794 Lady Tempest inherited his estate but she was not to enjoy it for long because within four months she too was dead.

WASHING THE LIONS

Dawk's News-Letter of 2 April 1698 stated 'Yesterday being 1st April several persons were sent to the Tower of London to watch the annual lion-washing ceremony.' This fictitious annual event was reported for over 150 years even up to 1856 when a number of tickets were sold to those gullible enough to wish to reserve the best views. Clearly they had not realised the significance of the date and were unaware that the menageries in the Tower had been removed to the London Zoological Gardens twenty-one years earlier.

DON'T PRETEND . . .

In the British Museum there is a curious tract entitled *The True History of the Life and sudden Death of old John Overs, the Rich ferryman of London*. The tale, said to have dated from before the Norman Conquest is quite probably apocryphal but deserves to be included because it was given credence for so many years, and it is a good tale too. It relates how John Overs was a mean and greedy man who died through his own frugality. His most ambitious scheme was to save spending out on a day's food for his household by pretending to be dead, in the vain expectation his servants would, out of propriety, fast until after his funeral. The pretence made, Overs was put into a sheet and stretched out in his chamber with, as per tradition of the day, a taper left burning at his head and his feet. But his servants did not mourn the passing of their miserly master; they broke into the larder and feasted instead. Upon hearing the merriment Overs was filled with such indignation he could not keep up the pretence any longer so 'stirring and struggling in his sheet, like a ghost with a candle in each hand, he purported to rise up, and rate 'em for their sauciness and boldness.'

The rising figure was spotted by an apprentice and mistaken for a ghost. The terrified apprentice caught hold of the nearest blunt object, the butt-end of a broken oar and 'struck out the brains' of the figure with a single blow thus killing Overs on the spot! The apprentice was acquitted of any crime and Overs declared an accessory and cause of his own death. A curious postscript to the tale states the Ferryman's daughter, although made a wealthy woman by his death was embarrassed by the grasping and miserly behaviour of her father and paid for the construction of a bridge across the Thames were her father used to ply his trade – the first London Bridge and sought to save her family's soul by building the church of St Mary Overs in Southwark.

THE GHOST OF MARSHAM STREET

In 1761 a white apparition appeared in the cloisters of Westminster Abbey, in St John's churchyard, Millbank and Marsham Street. Many 'credulous inhabitants' from those districts were struck with terror, but a few kept their heads about them and entered into a subscription which raised a reward of five guineas to any person who would seize the 'ghost' 'in order to remove the superstitious error adopted by their weak-minded neighbours.' A brave buck took the ghost by surprise and revealed him to be a servant of 'one of the gentlemen who belonged to the Abbey', the spook having affected his diguise with the aid of a large white sheet with the corners 'hanging over his head in imitation of feathers.' It is not recorded if or how the 'ghost' was punished.

THE END OF THE WORLD IS NIGH

Two minor earthquake tremors, twenty-eight days apart, were felt in London in 1761. Ex-soldier William Bell was convinced these were precursors to the end of the world, or at least there would be a flood of Biblical proportions in another twenty-eight days after the last tremor. People were reported as taking his warnings so seriously a number fled the capital and one man was said to have purchased a boat and had begun to collect a menagerie of animals upon it. The predicted day of judgement came, and went, without even the slightest hint of another tremor.

MORE EARTHQUAKE TERROR

In May 1761 the terror of earthquakes permeated London. One afternoon, a little after two, people in the Royal Arcade were panicked by the appearance of a cow which had, in fact, escaped from Smithfield. The appearance of the poor beast at the south gate led to an alarm which was rapidly misconstrued and escalated into the belief another earthquake was coming causing terror and confusion across the Exchange; 'some losing hats and wigs, and some their shoes, while others lay upon the ground in heaps with their limbs bruised, and during the alarm, a rumour of an earthquake prevailing, some threw themselves upon the ground expecting to be swallowed up.' In the meantime the cow a frightened by the hullabaloo took off down Sweeting's Alley and was only secured after being knocked down by a carman in Gracechurch Street.

THE MAN FROM FORMOSA . . . OR WAS HE?

In the early eighteenth century a man calling himself George Psalmanazar wowed the fashionable London social scene with stories of how he had been raised in the distant and obscure homeland of Formosa. Captured by crusading Jesuits he had been taken to France and even though he was tortured he resisted conversion to Catholicism. He escaped to Holland and met a Protestant minister, Reverend William Innes who was stationed in the country with a Scottish Regiment. Armed with a letter of introduction from Innes to the Bishop of London, Psalmanazar came to city and was taken in by society, or should I say society was taken in by him. His tales told of roads, temples and buildings decorated with gold, strange religious rites, customs and extreme longevity of Formosans. In 1704 Psalmanazar's accounts of his exotic homeland were published in *An Historical and Geographical Description of Formosa*,

An Island Subject to the Emperor of Japan. The book included illustrations of national dress, the Formosan alphabet and even the translations of the likes of the Lord's Prayer and Ten Commandments. The book became a best seller but he was not without his critics. Formosa was in fact a province of China, not Japan, his descriptions did not fit with anything else known about the area. Despite Psalmanazar dismissing his critics as liars scepticism of his stories remained unabated and he was soon scorned as a fraud. He had enjoyed twenty years of good living on his tales but after a serious illness in 1728 the pressure to tell the truth had mounted to the degree he dismissed his past. Psalmanazar died on 3 May 1763 aged about eighty-four. He had written an account to be published after his death where he confessed he had invented it all but George Psalmanazar still remains an enigma because the secret of who he really was and where he came from went to the grave with him.

THE PROPHETESS

Joanna Southcott, a woman of humble origins, came to prominence in London during the early 1800s with her pretensions as a prophetess, declaring herself to be the woman mentioned in the twelfth chapter of the book of Revelation. She claimed that she had 'received a divine appointment to be the mother of the Messiah.' Despite being of an age way beyond child bearing she was subject to a condition that gave an appearance of pregnancy and gave credence to her proclamations among her hundreds (some said thousands) of followers. A magnificent crib was prepared for the arrival of the miracle child but on the 27 December 1814 she died. Her most ardent followers would not believe she was dead they kept her body unburied until 'the most active signs of decomposition appeared.' At the post-mortem the tumour in her stomach was revealed but her followers were unperturbed and despite burying her in the burial ground attached to the chapel in St John's Wood they believed she would rise again and the men vowed not to shave their beards till her resurrection. Her staunch supporters grew their beards to fantastic lengths and were still to be found in the late nineteenth century but they all were to go their graves unshorn.

Joanna Southcott.

SPIRIT PHOTOGRAPHY

In the Victorian age death was an everyday fact of life. Most families would have some cabinet portraits to fill their elegant albums and to decorate their mantle piece but the 'new wonder' of photography was not just limited to living subjects and many examples survive of photos of the dear departed in all their funeral finery. It was only one small step for some enterprising photographers, inspired by the late Victorian fascination in spiritualism to capture the dearly departed revisiting their living relatives from the spirit world. The bereaved family would have to supply a photograph of the

One of the early Boursnell 'spirit photographs'.

deceased and before they knew it, with just one sitting the translucent or misty figure of their dead relative would appear on the print, often surrounded with suitable clouds of ectoplasm. In London the most famous exponent of 'the art' was Richard Boursnell (1832–1909). Working with a professional photographer on Fleet Street, 'psychic markings' were found on his photographs as early as the 1850s. Boursnell's business partner was far from impressed and said he had not cleaned his photographic plates properly. Boursnell said he wanting nothing more to do with the photographic side of the business. Years later W.T. Stead persuaded Boursnell to take photographs again and the spirits did not let them down. Stead and Sir Arthur Conan Doyle were both committed spiritualists and were convinced, as were many of his sitters, and the Spiritualists of London presented him with a purse of gold and a testimonial. That was, of course in the days before many people understood the principals of double exposure photographs.

SEVENTEEN

WHAT A WAY TO GO

THE TOWER OF DOOM

Stowe records that the tower of St Mary-le-Bow church was the scene of two tragedies. William Fitzobert – known as' Longbeard' and 'the champion of the wrongs of people' protested against the taxation levied upon the people for the rescue of Richard I and incurred the wrath of the king. Fitzobert took refuge in St Mary's church tower after being pursued there by the monarch's assassins in 1196. He was forced out after they set fire to the tower, and was dragged 'at the tail of a horse' to the Tower and was later hanged at Smithfield. Laurence Ducket was slain in the same church tower in 1284 after he attempted to find sanctuary there following an incident where he wounded Ralph Crepin. Numerous heavy fines were levied by the church, sixteen people were hanged, and a woman burnt, for their involvement in the slaying of Ducket.

A KNIGHT TO REMEMBER

One of the eight knights whose figures eerily decorate the floor of the Temple church is said to be that of Gilbert Marshal, one of the sons of Protector Pembroke, Earl Marshal and last of his line. His family were said to be brought to an abrupt end due to a curse put on them by the Abbot of Fernes from whom the Protector robbed lands. Poor Gilbert, like the others is shown in armour and chain mail, but the sword he is seen drawing he was never able to bear to the crusades; Gilbert was killed in 1241 at a tournament, not upon the tilting field, but upon collision with a runaway horse as he was about to start.

LITERALLY PLASTERED

In 1381 the rebels of the Peasant's Revolt stormed the Duke of Lancaster's house of the Savoy. Many just pillaged the property and left with their trophies but some found his cellars stocked with barrels of fine wine and about thirty-two of them drank themselves into stupors. While in this state they were walled in and left to die. Stow recorded that the voices of the unfortunates walled in 'were heard crying and calling seven dais after, but none came to help them out till they were dead.'

OH, DEER!

Among the tombs recorded as once being in the monastery of the Grey Friars that stood on what became Newgate Street was one for Thomas Burdett who was beheaded in 1477 after 'having too vigorously lamented a favourite buck of his which had been killed by Edward IV.'

DEAD LETTER

Northumberland House, which had an entrance from The Strand, was crowned by the inscription Algernon Somerset Princeps Northumbriae. At the funeral of Anne of

Denmark in 1619 a crowd was gathered beneath when unfortunately a large letter 'S' fell from the inscription onto the crowd below killing a young man named Appleyard.

VENGEANCE ON THE MAN WHO ARRESTED GUY FAWKES

One man who rose to celebrity for one notable deed was Peter Heiwood – the man who arrested Guy Fawkes as he was setting his charges and barrels and gunpowder to blow up the Houses of Parliament in 1605. Thirty-five years later, John James a Dominican friar, still fired up about the foiling of the gunpowder plot, tracked Heiwood down to Westminster Hall and stabbed him to death.

THE EXPERIMENT THAT BACKFIRED

Lord Bacon, the philosopher and long serving Chancellor of Gray's Inn was pondering his latest research into the 'conservation and induration of bodies' during his ride from Holborn to Highgate one bright and snowy morning in March 1626. Seized by the idea of an experiment using snow to preserve flesh from putrefaction his lordship purchased a fowl and proceeded to stuff its crop with snow. The results of his experiment could have proved fascinating and useful for mankind but sadly Lord Bacon caught a chill in the process, his sickness rapidly progressed until he recorded 'in troth my fingers are so disjointed by this fit of sickness that I cannot steadily hold a pen'. And, in troth he never held a pen again and died on Easter Sunday, 9 April 1626.

AN ALCHOHOL-RELATED DEATH

Nat Lee, the poet and dramatist, described as 'stout, handsome and red faced' was well known for heavy drinking, Oldys said of him 'He drank himself into Bedlam where he wrote a play in twenty-five acts.' The Earl of Pembroke was his chief patron. On one visit to the Earl's house it was said the butler had feared that Lee would empty the cellar! Lee was staggering home after a heavy wine drinking session at the Bear and Harrow in Butcher Row one night in 1692. His journey, fogged by his alcohol intake was made even more difficult by a severe blizzard as he staggered through the deep, settled snow through the lanes of Clare Market. Unfortunately the hour was unsociable and there was no-one around to help him up when he fell and due to his intoxicated state he could not get himself up again and eventually suffocated in the snow. He was just thirty-five when he died.

A TOAST TO THE 'LITTLE MEN IN BLACK VELVET'

On 8 March 1702 William III's horse stumbled on a mole hill while riding in the grounds of Hampton Court. The king sustained fatal injuries as a result of his tumble and died a short while later. In honour of moles and their role in the demise of King William Jacobites regularly toasted 'the little gentlemen in black velvet.'

NO REST FOR THE WICKED

In 1732 Sarah Malcolm (aged twenty-two) was a fine looking young woman of good breeding reduced to the trade of washerwoman due to the spendthrift habits of her father. She worked around the Temple for a number of families but one day it appears she committed a robbery during the course of which she murdered the elderly mistress of the house – Mrs Duncomb, her companion Elizabeth Harrison

Sarah Malcolm, drawn from life by William Hogarth, in the condemned cell two days before her execution.

and her maid Anne Price were all strangled. Sarah Malcolm was found to have bloodstained clothes, and a silver tankard belonging to Mrs Duncomb was found in the rooms of one of Sarah's employers at Tanfield Court. After being searched at Newgate £53 was found hidden in her hair. Sarah tried to mitigate her circumstances and swore she did not act alone and implicated another woman and two brothers in the crime. Only Sarah was to stand trial she was found guilty and sentenced to death. Her looks did not escape public notice and she sat for a sketch 'dressed up in scarlet and sate' for Hogarth two days before she went to the gallows. Executed opposite the scene of her crime (Mitre Court) on Fleet Street she was buried, without sanction, in St Sepulchre's churchyard. Unceremoniously dug up again and removed to the surgeons, her skeleton was exhibited for many years at the Botanic Garden in Cambridge.

KILLED BY A SNIFF OF BEER

In May 1752 a cooper and a chairman in the employ of Mrs Hucks descended to work in a store cellar under Pall Mall. They were both overcome and eventually suffocated by the steam from forty butts of unstopped beer – and neither got the chance to taste a drop!

DEATH IN THE DITCH

In *Annual Register* for January 1763 it was recorded a man was found in the Fleet Ditch standing upright and frozen to death. It appeared he had wandered into the mud of the watercourse and being the worse for drink he was unable to extricate himself.

THE RETURN OF MARGARET CARPENTER

In February 1767 Mrs Margaret Carpenter, a journeywoman to Mr Smith, a livery lace maker in Little Queen Street, Lincoln's Inn Fields was pronounced dead and properly laid out in preparation for interment. That very night however movement was heard in the room where she lay and eerie footsteps were heard to cross the floor and descend the stairs. Her family drew back in horror as she stood before them stark naked and quite alive. Placed in a warm bed and given refreshment she kept saying she was 'bitter cold' and although declared dead had in fact 'only been in a trance.' It was said the shock of the whole affair was too much for her and within a couple of days she was dead for real.

A GRAVE END FOR THE GRAVEDIGGER

In September 1769 the gravedigger of St Catherine Cree in Leadenhall Street, was employed to open a grave to receive the body of the lately deceased Mrs Osborne, and laid a wager he could dig the grave 10ft deep. With victory and his winnings within sight the sides of the grave caved in and caught him up to the middle before he could scramble out. Several onlookers attempted to extricate him but in vain 'for the rottenness of the ground not being able to bear so much weight, the earth gave way a second time and the poor man was smothered.' A similar incident took place at Newington in Surrey in October 1804. John Ricketts, the sexton, had dug a grave for the remains of a lady from Kent Road. He was standing by the grave as the coffin and pall bearers entered the church yard when the grave collapsed and buried Ricketts to a depth of some 6ft. Within seconds horrified mourners had run to the grave to try to dig him out but more and more people came to look causing as much earth to fall again where it had been dug out by his would-be rescuers. It was over an hour before the body was recovered. All attempts of revival failed and Rickett's lifeless body was carried away on a shutter 'amidst the cries and complaints of a disconsolate wife and five children who were witnesses of the affecting scene.'

THE TRAGIC, FREEZING COLD FEBRUARY OF 1771

In February 1771 a poor boy with nowhere else to go, and driven to distraction by the bitter cold, sought out some warmth in the only place available to him – a dung heap in a stable yard in Holborn. Burying himself deep inside the steaming heap it was undoubtedly warm but the tragic lad was overcome by the fumes and suffocated, his body was discovered the following morning by an ostler. The February of 1770 was truly bitter, and another tragedy was discovered at Rag Fair where a huddled bundle of rags revealed a woman, a child at her breast and another of about three years old lying by her side – all of them dead from the cold.

PREMATURE BURIAL

The *Annual Register* of 23 July 1776 records the burial of a coachman who had died suddenly at Fulham. '. . . When the funeral was over, a person insisting that during the performance of the service he heard a rumbling and struggling in the coffin, the earth was removed, and the coffin taken out of the grave; when, on opening it there appeared evident proofs that the unhappy man, though then absolutely dead, had come to himself as his body was very much bruised in several places some of which were still bleeding, and there appeared besides a quantity of blood in the coffin.'

SHE DIED LAUGHING

The *Gentleman's Magazine* for 19 April 1782 carried the story of Mrs Fitzherbert of Northamptonshire who came with a party of friends one evening to London's famous Drury Lane Theatre to see *The Beggar's Opera*. A certain Mr Bannister was playing Polly. So amusing was his performance the auditorium rocked with laughter. From the first entrance of Bannister, Mrs Fitzherbert was seized with such paroxysms of laughter she lost all sense of control and was respectfully asked to leave the theatre. The poor lady could not banish the image of Bannister's performance from her thoughts and her hysterics continued without intermission until two days later when she expired.

CRISPY BACON

William Bacon, Clerk to the Salt Office met a sudden and awful end in July 1787. He was drinking tea with his wife when a terrible storm blew up outside. He walked to the open window with a view to shutting it when a bolt of lightening struck the gun he kept on the window ledge in case of burglars and the 'electrical fire' blasted out of the barrel of the gun and struck Bacon with such force 'it tore out his intestines, and made his body a most shocking spectacle.' Poor Mrs Bacon was so shocked at the sight she was subject to fits and 'great doubts were entertained whether she would ever recover.' The mangled remains of William Bacon were interred in Lambeth Parish Church and a memorial to his horrible end was erected in the porch.

THE FATE OF THE HEADSMAN

Giuseppe Ceracchi was one of the most notable 'headsmen' of his day. He carved some of the heads of the river gods for the keys stones of the Strand front of Somerset House. He taught a few lucky children of gentlefolk wealthy enough to pay for his tutorage in sculpture and acquire such a reputation he executed the only bust in marble that Sir Joshua Reynolds ever sat for. Sadly, Ceracchi was not so lucky with his own head. Imprisoned for his involvement in a plot against Napoleon he went mad in prison and eventually, dressed in the garb of a Roman emperor his own head ended up in the basket of the guillotine in 1801.

TO KILL AN ELEPHANT

In 1810 Chunee the elephant was brought to London and displayed by Mr Cross and 'The Royal Menagerie' at Exeter 'Change where Burleigh Street now stands. The area, described as a 'little crowded nest of shops and wild beasts' was frequented by many visitors, but horses left nearby were often disturbed by the growls and whoops of the exotic animals from within. In March 1826 poor Chunee suffered the worst bout of a recurrent 'paroxysm' aggravated by inflammation of the large pulp of one of his tusks and the poor elephant, driven wild with pain that did not respond to veterinary treatments, became aggressive and dangerous and it was decided to put it out of its misery. His keeper first threw in buns steeped in prussic acid; but they produced no effect. A drastic measure was called for and a company of soldiers was sent for and the tragic beast was finally felled in a hail of 100 bullets. It was recorded 'In the midst of the shower of lead, the poor docile animal knelt down at the well-known voice of his keeper, to turn a vulnerable point to the soldiers. The massive skeleton of Chunee was later wired together and exhibited for many years afterwards at the College of Surgeons in Lincoln's Inn Fields.

THE END OF THE FIRST MRS SHELLEY

In 1816 the body of Harriet Westbrook, pregnant and deserted by her husband, Percy Bysshe Shelley, was found drowned in the Serpentine. Much conjecture surrounds her death to this day, did she fall, was it suicide or was she pushed?

Another popular dropping-off point for suicides was the Monument, until this fatal leap by a maidservant in 1842 led to the gallery being enclosed with a cage.

Advertisement for the two trades of Joseph Waller, c. 1740.

DEATH OF A CLIMBING BOY

One of the most notorious practices of the early nineteenth century was the employment of children, especially boys to act as 'climbing boys' for chimney sweeps. One case in January 1811 recalls how the boy shinned up a chimney in Orchard Street, Westminster, and having completed his job climbed out on the roof for a breather. Ready to get back down the chimney, sadly the boy was disorientated and climbed back down a different one to that he had just cleaned and found to his horror a fire was lit at the bottom of this one! The boy panicked, got stuck clambering up to escape and was suffocated before help arrived.

THE WATERY END OF ILLUSTRATED LONDON NEWS FOUNDER

Herbert Ingram was an industrous man who made newspapers his life. He began as a humble newspaper vendor who was known to run five miles to deliver a paper to oblige a good customer. In 1842 he founded the *Illustrated London News* which, within a few years had a multi-million circulation and dominated news stands for over 100 years. Ingram eventually obtained a seat in Parliament but drowned in a steam collision on Lake Michigan.

THE MECCA OF SUICIDES

Of all the places in London to end your days more suicides choose Cleopatra's Needle than any other. It has been suggested the ancient Needle, fashioned before Christ walked the earth, carries a curse with it. On its journey from Egypt the 'needle' was placed in a specially built ship casement named Cleopatra. The steam ship Olga that was towing Cleopatra faced such a storm in the Bay of Biscay the tow ropes had to be cut and six men drowned during the incident. Cleopatra was found again and towed into Ferrol Harbour and eventually towed back to England where the needle was erected on the Embankment in 1878. The two bronze sphinxes, cast at the Ecclestone Iron Works in Pimlico were added in 1881.

THE UNWANTED CHILD

The head of a child was recovered from the Thames on 19 May 1880. Over the following days further remains were recovered and an inquest was held by Mr G.H. Hull at the Star and Garter, Battersea. Dr William Henry Kempster stated he had examined the remains and concluded the head, when it was found, had not been in the water twenty-four hours and that death had occurred about three days previously and the body 'had been cut up in an unscientific manner.' Inquest was adjourned to enable the police to obtain some clue to the identification of the remains.

A NOT SO FUNNY THING HAPPENED AT THE FORUM

On 6 August 1888 John M'Carthy was one of three charioteers taking part in a display in the grand arena of the Italian Exhibition. M'Carthy was driving a chariot pulled by two magnificent black horses, in turning the corner near the Emperor's box the chariot tilted and then righted itself, throwing M'Carthy onto the ground. Mr Knowles who was following close behind in the second chariot, pulled the reigns to the off side so hard he broke the splinter bar of the chariot and he was also thrown to the ground. The near wheel of Knowles's uncontrolled chariot passed over the right side of M'Carthy's body. Despite being rapidly removed to the West London Hospital he was pronounced dead on arrival.

HUMAN JIGSAW

Throughout late May and June 1889 newspapers detailed body parts being washed up on the shore or picked up on the Thames. The body was identified by means of old scars as that of Elizabeth Jackson. The only possible clue to the identity of the murderer was that some of the body parts had been wrapped in clothing bearing the name tape of 'L.E. Fisher.' Nobody was ever brought to justice for this foul deed.

Dead Peculiar

On 17 January 1889 an inquest was held at Marylebone Mortuary into the death of Charles Dubery Foskett. The young man had been brought home in an insensible condition suffering from injuries to the head and shoulders allegedly caused by a horse and cart running over him. Despite recovering consciousness before he died he could not explain how the accident happened. Dr O'Brien was called to the inquiry and stated he knew the family who had 'the peculiarity that if any one of them received the slightest scratch he would almost bleed to death.' The doctor stated he had known as many as three of the family at one time had been laid out apparently dead but were found to only be exhausted through loss of blood. A verdict of 'Accidental death' was returned. (The 'peculiarity' suffered by the Foskett family would be recognised by later medical authorities as haemophilia).

Death of 'Champagne Charlie'

One of the most popular songs of late Victorian England was 'Champagne Charlie,' a song popularised by George Leybourne who trod the boards of London Music Halls immaculately turned out in tails and top hat evening wear and sporting a monocle, he was the archetypal 'tipsy gent.'

The tragedy is that must of the time he was not acting. Having squandered all his money on drink he died lonely and penniless on 15 August 1884 at his Islington home. He is buried in Abney Park, Stoke Newington under the epitaph 'God's finger touched him and he slept.'

Acrobat Takes a Tumble

The killing of acrobat and trick cyclist George Gorin, better known as George Letine (aged thirty-six), leader of 'The Wonderful Letines' hit the headlines in July 1889. Gorin was entering the Canterbury Theatre of Varieties on Westminister Bridge Road when Nathaniel Curragh (aged fifty-three) stepped up beside him and plunged a blade into his abdomen.

Before the passers by could understand why Gorin was slumping towards the floor Curragh had crossed to the other side of the road, put a pistol in his mouth and pulled the trigger. The shot did not kill him, the bullet lodged in the roof of his mouth and his life was saved at St Thomas's Hospital. It emerged that Curraghs daughter had been a member of the Letines but left about a year previous, she died shortly after and Curragh believed the death was in some way due to he training at the hands of Gorin. Curragh was found 'unsound of mind' and was ordered to be detained at Her Majesty's pleasure.

Fatal Ice-Cream

An inquest held at St Pancras Coroner's Court on 27 August 1888 into the death of Louisa Minnie Fairservice (3½), whose parents resided at 25 Marsden Street, Kentish Town. Following the attestation of the surgeon and medical officer it was concluded the little girl had died 'from exhaustion following enteric fever, probably caused by eating ices purchased in the street.' A strong recommendation was made that the sanitary authorities should be called upon to purchase ices from street vendors with a view to their being submitted for analysis to ascertain whether they contained anything injurious to health or not. In a previous analysis of 'Street ices' or 'Penny licks' otherwise known as 'Hokey-Pokey' in 1881 one sample was found to not only contain milk and water but an array of cotton fibres, straw, human and cat hairs, fleas, lice and bed bugs – delicious!

END OF A COACHMAN

Noted coachman James William Selby (1843–88) died of exposure on 16 December 1888. Piloting his coach *Old Times*, his exploits and speed were renowned. In the year of his death Selby won a bet for covering the 108-mile journey from London to Brighton in seven hours and fifty minutes. His demise was hardly surprising to those who knew him well, he was out in all weathers, rain, wind and snow would not deter this brave coachman but there are only so many times you can get so cold your hat freezes to your head and has to be steamed off!

THE STRANGE CASE OF ELEANOR MARX

Eleanor Marx, favourite daughter of Karl Marx, the father of Communism followed proudly in her father's footsteps and championed the socialist cause with a passion and was widely known for her work across the East End. After Karl's death in 1883 Eleanor became involved with Dr Edward Aveling, a man described by Engel's biographer as a man with 'the thieving instincts of a jackdaw and the morals of a tom-cat' but Eleanor would not be turned from him and although not married to him she was 'devoted to the point of slavery' and adopted his surname with her own. Her death is surrounded with some mystery. On the morning of 31 March a note was taken by a woman claiming to be Aveling's maid to a Sydenham chemist stating 'Please give the bearer chloroform and a small quanitity of prussic acid for the dog.' Dr Aveling's card was enclosed. Curiously the chemist's poison book was initialled E.M.A. Later that same morning, dressed all in white Eleanor was found dead on her bed. At the inquest Aveling's answers were 'evasive' but the verdict of suicide was delivered. A twist to the tale came a few years later, it was rumoured Aveling had deceived Eleanor into a suicide pact but after she took the prussic acid he did not keep his side of the bargain. We will probably never know the truth.

WHEN A MAGIC TRICK GOES WRONG

American magician William Ellsworth Robinson was one of the most popular illusionists in his day but few would have known him by that name for his stage persona of Chinese magician Chung Ling Soo was how he was know on both sides of the Atlantic. So committed was Robinson to his role that he affected the full garb of a Chinese mandarin, he never spoke on stage and even used an interpreter when he spoke to journalists. He perfected many great illusions but will be remembered for just one – the bullet catch. The trick consisted of Soo facing a firing squad of his assistants dressed as Boxers (Chinese nationalists who had rebelled against foreign rule in 1900). He would invite two members of the audience to inspect a pair of old muzzle loader rifles that were to be used as his wife Suee Seen took two lead bullets into the audience for two people to scratch their initials onto them. The marked bullets were placed into a cup and brought back to Soo on stage who supervised their loading into the rifles. The two voluntary observers then shook hands with Soo and then resumed their seats in the auditorium. Soo would then face the firing squad with only a willow pattern plate held over his chest. When the squad fired it would appear the bullets were caught on the plate and the enraptured audience would burst into applause as the bullets were examined and the initials marked by the audience members were found thereon. This trick saw Soo fill many theatres but even Harry Houdini was moved to warn Soo; 'Be careful with your bullet catching trick as your method is certainly daring.' The trick was based on subterfuge and trick guns, Soo would palm the bullets ready to drop them on the plate when the shots rang out. The rifles were made with a special mechanism whereby they could be loaded with powder and bullet but when fired the guns would only discharge a harmless flash of powder from the ramrod tube beneath the barrel. On the fateful night of 23 March 1918 at Wood Green Theatre the trick was all set as normal but when the rifles fired this time the plate fell to the floor and smashed as Soo doubled over in agony and collapsed with a bullet wound to his chest. Soo died in hospital the next day. Rumours soon spread that someone had tampered with the guns or that Soo had affected his own death after financial concerns caught up with him. Robert Churchill, the respected gunsmith, was called in to investigate and discovered the truth was far more prosaic. He found out the way the illusion worked and how due to part of the trick mechanism in the rifle being worn that the detonating spark had reached the main barrel and the lethal charge had been fired at Soo. The bullet catch trick in various forms have been performed by successive generations of magicians, its danger remains and at least ten others have been subsequently seriously wounded or killed by this illusion.

EIGHTEEN

THE DEAD . . .
& BEYOND

JUST IN CASE

Francis Bancroft, city magistrate and founder of the Mile End Almshouses left a codicil and bequest in his will that for a hundred years a loaf of bread and a bottle of wine might be placed in his grave at St Helen's Bishopgate every year on the anniversary of his death because he was convinced 'that before that time he should awake from his death sleep and require it.' Before the removal of the tomb in 1892, just to make sure Bancroft was dead, upon the appointment of each new Master of the Draper's Co. the tomb would be entered, the lid of the coffin turned back and respects would be paid to the skeleton of Francis Bancroft.

KEPT HANGING AROUND

Geoffrey de Magnaville is one of the knights whose reclining figure adorns the floor of the Temple Church. The story attached to him is that he was driven to desperation by injustices inflicted upon him by King Stephen (1135–54). Mortally wounded during his attack upon Burwell Castle in Cambridgeshire he died while excommunicated. His body was soldered up in lead and hung up by the Templars on a tree in their orchard, till he received absolution upon it being proved he expressed repentance in his last moments.

TO KISS A QUEEN

The tomb of Queen Catherine de Valois, who died in 1437, was removed from her original chapel of rest after Henry VIII demolished it to make room for his own chapel and her coffin was left by the side of her husband's tomb – for the next 300 years. Among the many who were shown her remains was Samuel Pepys who recorded the event in his diary 'I had the upper part of her body in my hands, and I did kiss her mouth, reflecting upon it that I did kiss a Queene.'

Samuel Pepys.

THE MIRACULOUS HEAD OF THE BISHOP OF ROCHESTER

John Fisher, Bishop of Rochester was beheaded on Tower Hill in 1535 for denying Henry VIII was supreme head of the English church. The decapitated head was parboiled, impaled on a pole and displayed on London Bridge. For the next twelve days it was said that the Bishop's head grew fresher and ruddier to the degree it appeared the head was in a more healthy state than when attached to the body. People began to talk of miracles, potentially very embarrassing for Henry. So he ordered the head be taken down at night and cast into the river.

MORE ON MORE

After his execution on Tower Green in 1535 the body of Sir Thomas More was first interred in St Peter ad Vincula church within the walls of the Tower but his head was impaled on a pole and displayed on London Bridge, where it remained for fourteen days. More's eldest daughter, Margaret Roper, resolved to end the ignominy inflicted on her father and sought to obtain the head. According to Aubrey she implored God in prayer 'That head has lain many a time in my lap, would to God it would fall into my lap as I pass under!' Her wish was granted and miraculously the head did fall into her lap. News of the incident reached the authorities; they believed she had bribed the bridge keeper to obtain the head. Brought before council she said her father's head would 'not be food for the fishes.' She was imprisoned but soon was liberated and allowed to keep her father's head, which she had enclosed in a leaden box and preserved it with tender devotion. When she died in 1544 she asked her father's head be buried with her.

OFFAL AT THE SAVOY

George, third Earl of Cumberland, a great admiral in his day, died in the Duchy House in the Savoy on 3 October 1605 but curiously only his bowels were buried in the Savoy Chapel, the rest of his body was buried at Skipton.

THE HEAD OF SIR WALTER RALEIGH

After his execution in Old Palace Yard on 29 October 1618 the decapitated head of Sir Walter Raleigh was shown on either side of the scaffold then the head, according to historian Arthur Cayley, '. . . was put into a leather bag, over which Sir Walter's gown was thrown, and the whole conveyed away in a mourning coach by Lady Raleigh.' Her ladyship kept the head in the bag with her for the rest of her life, some twenty-nine years. The tradition was equally observed by their loyal son Carew, with whom the head was believed to be buried with upon his death.

DONNE WAS DONE PROUD

As John Donne, poet and Dean of St Paul's was approaching death in 1631 his friend Isaak Walton recorded; 'he caused to be made a wooden urn, and a board just the height of his body. Several charcoal fires being made in his large study he brought with him into that place his winding sheet, and having put off all his cloathes, had this sheet put upon him and his hands placed so as dead bodies are usually fitted to be placed into their coffins. Upon this urn he stood with his eyes shut and with so much of the sheet turned aside as to show his lean, place and death-like face . . . In this posture he was drawn. And when the picture was fully finished he caused it to be set by his bedside till his death, and then given to his dearest friend and executor, Dr Henry King, who caused him to be thus carved in one piece of marble.' This carving was set up in St Paul's as a memorial to Donne.

THE LITTLE WHITE-BREASTED BIRD OF DOOM

In one of his *Familiar Letters*, dated 3 July 1632, James Howel records his account of a tombstone he had seen being prepared in a stone-cutters' shop on Fleet Street. Upon the stone were the names of four members of the Oxenham family who had all been visited by a white-breasted bird which fluttered over their heads on the bed where they lay shortly before each of them died. A similar bird is also recorded as having visited Thomas, second Lord Lyttelton at Pit Place shortly before his death in 1779.

AN UPRIGHT MAN

Ben Jonson, dramatist and scholar, described as one of the wittiest and most learned men of his time, was being railed by the Dean of Westminster about being buried in Poets' Corner; always mindful of his lack of finances the poet is said to have replied 'I am too poor for that and no one will lay out funeral charges upon me. No, sir, six feet long by two feet wide is too much for me: two feet by two feet will do for all I want'. 'You shall have it', said the Dean. So Jonson, who died on 6 August 1637, has the unique distinction of being the only person to be buried standing on his feet in Westminster Abbey (Jonson is not actually buried in Poets' Corner but rather nearby only his memorial, erected some years later is actually in Poets' Corner.) The simple inscription 'O Rare Ben Jonson', was said to have been done at the expense of Jack Young an almost forgotten poet and contemporary of Jonson who was walking by when the grave was covered and gave the mason eighteen pence to cut it into the stone. In 1849, Jonson's grave was disturbed by an excavation in preparation for a burial nearby and the clerk of works saw the two leg bones of Jonson fixed upright in the sand. Jonson's skull with some red hair still attached to it came rolling down from a position above the leg bones into the newly made grave.

ROBBING THE DEAD

The horrors of bubonic plague in London between 1664 and 1665 did not deter corpse-robbers who would not only pick over corpses in the pits for jewellery but even stole their winding sheets. Over 1,000 of these shrouds were found in the possession of just one night thief who had been brought to justice after the plague.

NO WAY TO TREAT AN ARCHBISHOP

During the Civil War Lambeth Palace was turned into a prison for Royalists. The roundheads also demolished the Great Hall and desecrated the chapel. The tomb of Archbishop Parker caused particular offence to the Puritans and one Hardinge was charged with its removal. Opening the lead coffin and removing the cerecloths the body of the archbishop was found to be 'very fresh.' Unceremoniously stripped the corpse was removed to an outhouse and 'buried among the offal.' Upon the Restoration, Hardinge was ordered to recover the body and it was honourably re-interred near the steps of the altar.

A HEAD OF HISTORY, OR HISTORY OF A HEAD

Oliver Cromwell, England's Lord Protector after the bloody Civil War died on 3 September 1658. After laying in state at Somerset House he was finally buried in Westminister Abbey near his old compatriots Henry Ireton and John Bradshaw. And so they rested in peace until after the restoration when Charles II wreaked terrible revenge on the cadavers of those who committed treason against his father. On 30 January 1661 (the twelfth anniversary of his fathers' execution) the bodies of Cromwell, Ireton and Bradshaw were unceremoniously disinterred, drawn on a sledge to Tyburn, hanged until sun down when they were beheaded. Parboiled and covered in pitch the decapitated heads were impaled on spikes at Westminister Hall on the anniversary of Charles I's funeral. Cromwell's head remained atop the hall for several years until it was brought down in a gale and was picked up by a sentry. The head passed through a number of hands for various amounts of money, including museum proprietor Herr du Puy who informed visitors in 1710 he could command sixty guineas for it. At one time there were two shows that claimed to display the head of Cromwell – when compared one was found to been considerably smaller that the other to which the quick thinking showman replied that his skull was the one Cromwell had when he was a young man. Having been exhibited in a number of curiosity shows the head was given by the niece of the last show proprietor to her family doctor, Dr Josiah Henry Wilkinson, for safe keeping. She eventually sold it to him and down this family line it was passed to Canon Horace Wilkinson of Woodbridge, Suffolk. During the 1930s, while in the hands of Canon Wilkinson, the head, still on its iron spike and fragment of wooden pole, was scientifically examined by Dr Karl Pearson and Dr G.M. Morant as well as Mr A. Dickson-Wright, surgeon who noted the evidence of the eight axe blows used to remove Cromwell's head, his 'reddish hair' and even 'the historical wart which Cromwell insisted on his portrait painters putting in, and there in the proper place was the depression from which it had been chipped.' The nose had been flattened during the beheading, almost all the teeth were gone and the lips broken to fragments but all the tests and comparisons proved this was the head of Oliver Cromwell. Canon Wilkinson eventually saw to it that Cromwell's head was given a fitting final resting place when he presented it to Cromwell's old edifice of learning, Sidney Sussex College at Cambridge. The head resides there to this day in a secret location known only to a few staff.

RESTING IN PEACE?

John Milton, the author of *Paradise Lost* was laid to rest in the church of St Giles, Cripplegate after his death from consumption in 1674. A story handed down since the late eighteenth century tells of how in 1790 Milton's bones were scurrilously disinterred 'his hair torn off, and his teeth knocked out and carried off by the churchwardens' and for many years afterwards. Elizabeth Grant the female gravedigger used to 'keep a candle' and would, for the consideration of threepence a head take visitors into the undercroft to see the mutilated skeleton.

GUARANTEED TO KEEP FRESH

Advertisement from 1679: 'At the sign of the "Golden Pall and Coffin", a coffin maker's shop, at the upper end of the Old Change, near Cheapside, there are ready made to be sold, very fashionable, laced and plain dressings for the dead of all sizes, with very fashionable coffins, that will secure any corps above ground without any ill scent or other annoyance as long as shall be required.'

MURDERERS REVEALED IN DREAMS

A Grub Street victualler named Stockden was murdered on 23 December 1695. Investigations drew blanks and it looked like the perpetrators of this heinous deed were going to escape justice when a Mrs Greenwood of Thames Street had three visionary dreams. In the first, Stockden showed her the house on Thames Street where his killer lived. In the next dream Stockden showed her the likeness of Maynard, his assailant. With no other suspects in the offing Maynard was brought to Newgate where he confessed to the deed and named three accomplices. Mrs Greenwood's final dream also identified one of the three named by Maynard as an accomplice. Three of the four suspects in this case stood trial and were sent to the gallows.

THE DEATHBELL OF ST PAUL'S

The Great Bell of St Paul's which hangs in the south tower bears the inscription 'Richard Phelps made me.' It is only tolled on the death and funerals of members of the royal family, Archbishops of Canterbury, Bishops of London, Deans of St Paul's and Lord Mayors who die in their mayoralty.

HEADS UP ON TEMPLE BAR

Body parts, particularly the heads of the executed were displayed on poles or spikes at a number of locations around London, most notably upon London Bridge and upon the centre gate at Temple Bar. Horace Walpole wrote in 1746; 'Passed under the new heads (those of Jacobite rebels Townley and Fletcher, who joined the old head of Colonel Henry Oxburgh who died for the same cause in 1716) on Temple Bar, where people make a trade of letting spy-glasses at a halfpenny a look.' A rare booklet had these lines of this topic;

> Three heads here I spy,
> Which the glass did draw nigh,
> The better to have a good sight;
> Triangle they're placed,
> Old, bald, and barefaced,
> Not one of them e'er was upright.

THE UNDERTAKER'S JOLLY

In the last quarter of the eighteenth century a pub by the name of The Falcon flourished on the corner of the lane leading from Wandsworth Road to Battersea Bridge. It was kept by a man named Mr Death, however, his hale, hearty and jolly demeanor certainly meant he did not live up to his name but many a witty jibe and wordplay was made at the expense of his surname. One which has travelled down the years is based around a cartoon by John Nixon who observed a group of undertakers having buried a 'rich nabob' at a nearby cemetery and having been richly paid for their troubles the undertakers took their first opportunity to drink, smoke, carouse and make merry at Death's door. Nixon recorded that Sable, the foreman of the men in black sang the following to the tune of 'I've kissed and I've prattled with fifty fair maids':

The Undertaker's Jolly – At Death's Door.

Dukes, lords have I buried, and squires of fame,
And people of every degree;
But of all the fine jobs that came in my way,
A fun'ral like this for me.
This is the job
That fills the fob,
O! the burying a nabob for me!

Unfeather the hearse, put the pall in the bag,
Give the horses some oats and some hay;
Drink our next merry meeting and quackery's increase,
With three times three and huzza.

THE DUCHESS'S CONSTANT GUEST

The Duchess of Marlborough, was so bereft after the death of William Congreve (1670–1729); a man who was once her lover that she still wanted to see his face every day. Thus she had a lifelike wax image of him made and placed upon her toilette table and as Theophilus Cibber claimed in his *Lives of the Poets of Great Britain and Ireland*, 'To this she would talk as to the living Congreve, with all the freedom of the most polite and unreserved conversation.'

GONE, LOST, BUT NOT FORGOTTEN

John Weever the author of *Antient Funeral Monuments* was buried in the church of St James, Clerkenwell in 1632. His monument eulogised his work including the lines:

> Weaver, who laboured in a learned strain
> To make men long since dead live again,
> And with the expense of oyle and ink, did watch
> From the worm's mouth the sleeping corse to snatch,
> Hath, by his industry, begot a way
> Death, who insidiates all things to betray,
> Redeeming freely, by his care and cost,
> Many a sad herse, which time gave long since lost . . .

Unlike those he immortalised in writing, Weavers' monument is now lost.

THE REPORT OF MY DEATH . . .

In 1708 Jonathan Swift had, like many in his literary circle, tired of Mr Partridge the cobbler who had an active line as an 'impudent sham-almanac maker' who had made much of his prediction of the death of the King of France. To silence and perhaps provoke an exposé of this 'noisy charlatan and his hap-hazard predictions' Swift, under the name of Bickerstaff, reported and soulfully lamented the death of Partridge in the *Tatler*. Partridge was so incensed by the report when an unsuspecting hawker passed his stall crying the account of his death in the papers he was selling, Partridge ran out and knocked the poor man to the ground. This act of aggression along with the many who believed the original account brought about the ruin of Partridge's almanac. Poor old Partridge eventually died, for real, in 1715.

GRAVEDIGGER TURNED GRAVEROBBER

Gravedigger John Loftas was committed to gaol in May 1732 after his arrest and trial for the robbery of a corpse. At the hearing he admitted to the plunder of over fifty bodies, not only taking their coffins and burial clothes but also 'their fat, where bodies afforded any, which he retailed at high price to certain people, who, it is believed, will be called upon to account thereof.' After the horrific discovery several recently bereaved families were so concerned they had their nearest and dearest exhumed to find the bodies 'quite naked, and some mangled in so horrible a manner as could scarcely be supposed to be done by a human creature.'

BODYSNATCHERS — SNATCHED!

Annual Register carried the following account of 24 March 1794. 'This evening a set of resurrectionists were apprehended at a house near the turnpike, Mile End. That morning a coach was observed to stop at the house, and ill-looking fellow came out of it with a sack containing, as was supposed, a body which he carried into the house and returned immediately with a large hamper – they then drove off to a neighbouring public house when, after a short stay, the took up some others, and were traced to a launch at Deptford. In the meantime the Parish Officers were informed of the circumstances and at six in the evening the coach returned with a similar lading which was deposited in the house. Some Constables, accompanied by a number of people, surrounded the house, and forcing an entrance, they found two men and a woman drinking tea on a bench; at one end of which lay the bodies of two children. They were secured, and one entering an adjoining room the bodies of six adults were discovered unmutilated, besides which the floor was strewed with limbs too shocking for public description.'

A NOBLE GESTURE TURNED SOUR

In 1739 three highwaymen and a housebreaker were executed at Kennington Common. The surgeons fixed on one of the hanged men to take for anatomisation but he was by trade a cobbler, and many of those being from his craft having watched the execution, were not going to have one of their number taken by the surgeons and wrestled the body from them and took it back to the cobbler's wife. She had 'withdrawn herself' and the cobblers were left with a body on their hands. Frustrated by this they determined to sell the body themselves and took it to apothecaries from Horsley down to Rotherhithe.

No purchaser was found so in a final act of desperation they buried the body in St George's Fields.

DEAD . . . BUT NOT BURIED

Martin van Butchell was a true London eccentric. After studying surgery and anatomy he turned to dentistry in the 1760s. Always keen to draw trade and cut a dash he went so far as to paint the white pony he rode with different coloured spots for each day of the week. His most notorious gimmick was after the death of his wife in January 1775 when rather than bury the poor woman he consulted Dr William Hunter and Dr William Cruikshank about preserving her body to look as lifelike as possible.

This they did, to the best of their ability, including the use of a pair of 'nicely matched glass eyes' and injection of the body with preservatives that contained colouring to give Mary's cheeks a fine rosy glow. She was then put on display within a glass-topped coffin with curtains.

Butchell's trade boomed as people came from far and wide to see the body at the house where he practiced. When van Butchell remarried it was hardly surprising that his new wife was not so keen living with the ex-wife so the preserved body was given to Dr Hunter's brother John for his museum and there she stayed, although becoming quite repugnant as the years passed. She was finally cremated when firebombs fell on the museum in 1941.

THE HEAD SHY

On 20 January 1766 a man was taken up in the early hours of the morning for discharging musket bullets from a steel crossbow at the heads on top of Temple Bar. On being examined he 'affected a disorder in his senses' and gave the reason for his actions being from 'his strong attachment to the present government, and that he thought it was not sufficient that a traitor should merely suffer death.' When the man was searched about fifty musket bullets were found wrapped up in a paper with the motto *Eripuit ille vitam* – 'his life was snatched away'.

BODYSNATCHERS

The *St James's Chronicle* of November 1767 records: 'The Burying-Ground in Oxford Road, belonging to the Parish of St George's, Hanover Square, having been lately robbed of several dead bodies, a Watch was placed there, attended by a large mastiff dog, notwithstanding which on Sunday last some villains found means to steal out another dead body and carried off the very dog.'

A GRAVES' BEQUEST

St Anne's churchyard in Soho had a most unusual memorial erected in the 1760s for Stephen Theodore, Baron von Neuhoff. He offered the people of Corsica protection in 1736 but embarrassingly did not have funds to pay his army and was forced to seek money in London where he was arrested for debt. After imprisonment he was released but died penniless a few days later;

> Near this place is interred Theodore,
> King of Corsica, who died in this parish,
> December 11th 1766, immediately after
> leaving the King's Bench Prison by the
> benefit of the Act of Insolvency; in con-
> sequence of which he registered his Kingdom
> of Corsica for the benefit of his creditors.
> The grave great teacher, to a level brings
> Heroes and beggars, galley slaves and kings,
> But Theodore this moral learn'd ere dead;
> Fate pour'd its lesson on his living head –
> Bestow'd a Kingdom and denied him bread.

St Anne's, Soho, 1840.

THE FIRST CREMATION?

The first British cremation of modern times is often accredited to Dr William Price who cremated the body of his son in his garden at Llantrisant, Wales, in 1883. This act, once declared legal by law, led to the opening of the first crematorium, but looking through earlier records a certain Mrs Pratt, a woman of good breeding and many gentry connections was concerned 'the vapours arising from the graves in the churchyard in populous cities will prove hurtful to the inhabitants' ordered in her will that her body be burned 'in hopes that others would follow her example.' Accordingly, as recorded in the *St James's Chronicle* for September 1769, 'The corpse of the late Mrs Pratt, which was buried in the new ground near Paddington (near Bayswater Road) was burnt to ashes in the grave by means of un-slacked Lime, agreeable to her will.'

THE ANATOMISTS WERE NOT TO HAVE HIM

In February 1770 eleven convicted were executed at Tyburn. Among them was a former soldier named Dunk. When the hearse arrived to take his body away some of his former comrades mistook it for the surgeons wagon and determined to save his corpse from the anatomist's table. They knocked down the undertaker, beat his men and wrestled the body away from them and carried it off along the New Road followed by a cheering crowd. When the men and the body came to the end of Gray's Inn Lane where they buried the corpse after first breaking its legs and arms then throwing a vast quantity of unslacked lime into the coffin and the grave.

THE GIFT THAT KEEPS ON GIVING

In 1770 Stephen Swain of the parish of St Olave, Southwark left provision in his will for John Abbot and his wife Mary the sum of 6*d* each to buy them 'halters' (two hangman's nooses) 'for fear the sheriff's should not be provided.'

THE TWO HEADS OF COUNCILLOR LAYER

In 1772 another head from Temple Bar, thought to be that of Councillor Christopher Layer who had been executed at Tyburn for High Treason in May 1723, was blown off its spike during a violent storm. The shrivelled and blackened head was picked up by an attorney named John Pearce who proudly showed his trophy to friends at a local pub, under the floor of which it was buried. News of the head travelled quickly and soon Pearce was traced by the Jacobite historian Dr Rawlinson who begged for the relic but 'was imposed on with another.' The poor doctor took his belief in the authenticity of the head to the grave with him, literally, as he stipulated the head be placed in his right hand when he died and was to thus be buried with him!

THE EPITAPH THAT SHOULD HAVE BEEN

In the churchyard of the Temple Church lies Oliver Goldsmith, the poet and author best known for *The Vicar of Wakefield* who died on 4 April 1774, aged forty-four. Despite warnings from his doctor, he had taken too many of 'James's Powders' and his kidneys failed. Goldsmith was financially inept and had only narrowly missed being thrown into debtors' prison but when he was in money he never forgot to make kind gestures to the poor of the parish. His tombstone said simply 'Here lies Oliver

Goldsmith,' if only it had gone on to include simple tribute to him by his dear friend Dr Johnson: 'Let not his faults be remembered; he was a very great man.'

NO REST FOR THE SMUGGLER

In 1775 William Hunter had espied a particularly good specimen of a man due for execution at Tyburn after being convicted of smuggling. Hunter thought this man would make such a good model for the students at the Royal Academy of Arts he acquired the body while it was still warm and before rigor mortis had set in posed the cadaver in a position to best show off its muscle tone. After allowing the body to stiffen he then flayed it of skin and made a mould of the corpse. Used by generations of art students, the college still has one of the casts of the body known simply as 'Smugglerius.'

THE HUNTER GETS HIS MAN, WHATEVER THE COST

Charles O'Brien (also known as Byrne) was a giant of a man standing a massive 7ft 8in tall. He earned a living by exhibiting himself at shows but certainly did not fancy that as an eternal fate for his bones. Often men of great height have short lives;

John Hunter. So proud was he of the giant's skeleton, that the foot of it can be seen in the top right of his portrait.

O'Brien did not help himself with excessive drinking and became grievously ill when he was still in his early twenties. The scouts for John Hunter the anatomist were circling like vultures but O'Brien was determined his bones would rest in peace and left strict instructions that after his death his body be watched day and night until his coffin of lead was made and his body taken out to the Downs for burial in 20 fathoms of water. O'Brien died aged twenty-two in 1783 while staying at Cockspur Street, Charing Cross. Hunter was not to be dissuaded and met with those charged to watch over the giant's body and carry out his last wishes to see if they could 'reach an understanding.' As the drink flowed the deal was discussed, the cost was high, some accounts state £500 (other as much as £700) was paid out to secure the body. The coffin of O'Brien was buried in the waters with due ceremony but the massive frame of O'Brien was already in the hands of Hunter who lost no time taking the body to his house in Earl's Court, boiled off the flesh of the O'Brien in a massive vat in his basement and the anonymous skeleton of a giant was soon on display in Hunter's museum, later in the Royal College of Surgeons. After seeing the skeleton of O'Brien in 1886 Oliver Wendell Holmes said wittily 'His hand was the only one I took, either in England and Scotland, which had not a warm and hearty welcome in it.'

MOMENTO MORI

In the last will and testament of John Aylett Stow in 1781 he directed his executors 'to lay out five guineas in the purchase of a picture of a viper biting the benevolent hand of the person who saved him from perishing in the snow, if the same can be bought for that money; and that they do, in memory of me present it to (name withheld), a member of King's Counsel, whereby he may have frequent opportunities of contemplating on it and by a comparison between that and his own virtue, be able to form a certain judgement which is best and most profitable, a grateful remembrance of past friendship and almost parental regard, or ingratitude and insolence. This I direct to present to him in lieu of a legacy of £3,000, which I had, by a former will, now revoked and burnt, left him.'

THE LAST DRINK'S ON ME

In 1788 David Davis of Clapham in Surrey stated in his will that he '. . . do give and bequeath to Mary Davis, daughter of Peter Delaport, the sum of 5s. which is sufficient to enable her to get drunk for the last time at my expense.'

SHAKE — FOR OLD TIME'S SAKE

In 1793 Philip Thicknesse, formerly of London but then residing in Bologna, left direction in his will that after his death his right hand be cut off and sent to his son, Lord Audley, 'in hopes that such a sight may remind him of his duty to God, after having so long abandoned the duty he owed to a father who once affectionately loved him.'

BEFORE CATS' HOMES . . .

Catherine Williams of Lambeth wanted to make sure her beloved pets were well provided for after her death, so in her will of 1796 she left Mrs Elizabeth Paxton £10 and £5 a year paid in weekly instalments by her husband to take care of her cats and dogs for the rest of the animals' lives. To her servant boy George Smith she left £10 'and my jackass, to get his living with, as he is fond of traffic.'

The Company of Undertakers – Hogarth's satire on London quackery. The characters in the upper portion are, from left to right, John Taylor, oculist; Mrs Mapp, bone-setter and Joshua 'Spot' Ward, doctor.

THE LAST WORD

Charles Parker, a bookseller on New Bond Street left this last bequest in 1785 to his nearest and dearest 'to Elizabeth Parker, the sum of £50, whom, through my foolish fondness, I made my wife, without regard to family, fame or fortune; and who, in return, has not spared, most unjustly, to accuse me of every crime regarding human nature, save highway-robbery.'

SAVE ME FROM THE SURGEONS!

In 1750 William Smith, an Irish forger due for execution at Tyburn, published a plea from the condemned cell for a subscription to save his body from the anatomists: 'As to my corporeal frame, it is unworthy of material notice; but for the sake of that reputable family from which I am descended, I cannot refrain from anxiety when I think how easily this poor body, in my friendless and necessitous condition, may fall into the possession of the surgeons, and perpetuate my disgrace beyond the severity of the law . . . The depravation of life is a sufficient punishment for my crimes . . . Those who compassionate my deplorable situation are desired to send their humane contributions to Mrs Browning's next door to the Golden Acorn, in Little Wild Street.'

BODY OF TRISTRAM SHANDY AUTHOR, STOLEN BY BODYSNATCHERS

The Revd Laurence Sterne, the author of *Tristram Shandy*, a man described by Thackeray as a 'great jester, not a great humourist' died in a 'mean lodging' on 18 March 1768 and was buried in a cemetery near Hyde Park which belonged to St George's, Hanover Square. In Sir James Prior's *Life of Edmund Malone* (1860) it was quoted; 'having been marked by some of the resurrection men, (Sterne's body) was taken up soon afterwards, and carried to an anatomy professor in Cambridge. A gentleman who was present at the dissection told me (Malone) he recognised Sterne's face the moment he saw the body.'

RICHARD II'S JAWBONE

In 1766 the tomb of Richard II in Westminster Abbey had fallen into such a state of disrepair a local lad stuck his hand through a crack and pulled out the King's jawbone.

The final phase of 'A Harlot's Progress', the wake of young prostitute Moll Hackabout, by William Hogarth, c. 1731.

One of his older companions told the boy off and confiscated the bone. It remained in his family until 1906 when one of his descendants returned it to the Dean and the bone was restored to the tomb.

THE REAL SWEENEY TODD?

In July 1787 the story of an unnamed journeyman barber who lived on Hamilton Street near Hyde Park Corner appeared in a number of London broadsheets and papers. This man was said to have become paranoid about the 'secret life' of his wife, whom he believed had been performing 'certain services' for other men behind his back but he could never prove his suspicions. A young man came to his shop, worse for drink but full of the joys of having received the favours of a woman the night before. Sat in the barbers' chair the man enlarged upon his experiences with the woman as the barber lathered his face. His manly banter even described the woman in detail, and he even escorted her to her door on Hamilton Street. The barber was left in no doubt that the man was referring to his wife, seized with the frenzy his blade did not falter as he cut the young man's throat from ear to ear.

NELSON'S COFFIN

Most people know the story of how the body of Admiral Nelson was brought back to Britain in a barrel of spirits after his tragic death at the Battle of Trafalgar in 1805 (and that the sailors drank a toast to the great Admiral with the same liquor). But few know that when Nelson was buried at St Paul's his coffin was made from the mast of the ship *L'Orient* which had been presented to Nelson after the Battle of the Nile in 1801 by Ben Hallowell, captain of HMS *Swiftsure*, so that, when tired of life Nelson might 'be buried in one of his own trophies.'

NO REST FOR JOHN WILLIAMS

John Williams, the man imprisoned in Cold Bath Fields to await trial for the infamous Ratcliffe Highway murders of 1811 was found dead in his cell. It was assumed he had committed suicide. Irrespective of whether he had committed the murder or not his cadaver faced the same treatment of any suicide. Until the 1850s people who committed suicide could not be buried in consecrated ground but rather a separate, distant area in the north of the churchyard where the body would be laid face down facing west. Many believed the restless spirits of those who took their own lives would 'walk' to harass those they left behind so they would be buried away from the town or village at a four-way crossroads so the ghost would not know which path to take to return. To ensure the body and ghost stayed down it would be buried at a crossroads and 'pinned' with an oaken stake through the heart (a practice prohibited by Act of Parliament in 1823). Crowds would gather around the local sexton as he performed this duty at the crossroads grave, even children risked the wrath of their parents by creeping along and looking through the legs of those assembled at the grim rite. John Williams was buried, chained down and a stake driven through his heart at the cross roads where Cannon Street Road and Cable Street, in St George's-in-the-East crossed one another. It is thought that the body of Williams was the last in London to be subject to the full rigour of the old law. Others who were buried similarly until the 'rite' was outlawed were interred without the stake through the heart (the last crossroad burial in London was Abel Griffiths at the junction of Eaton Street, Grosvenor Place in 1823.) In 1886 John William's was still not allowed to rest, when works were carried out for The Commercial Gas Co. a trench was dug for pipe laying, at a depth of 6ft his skeletal remains were uncovered, the stake still clearly evident, driven between his ribs. His bones were then unceremoniously divided up to relic collectors and souvenir hunters around the area. I guess he may be able to find some solace; his skull was displayed in a pub near the crossroads where he was buried.

A DELIVERY FOR THE ANATOMISTS

One of the ignominies inflicted on the body of a felon after public execution was its removal to surgeon's hall and the anatomists. One of the most notorious murderers to receive this treatment was John Bellingham who had been hanged in front of the Debtor's Door of Newgate Prison for the murder of the Prime Minister, Spencer Perceval in May 1812. After being left to hang for an hour Bellingham was cut down and his body transported in an open cart accompanied by a rowdy crowd through the streets near Old Bailey, Newgate and St Martins-le Grand and finally to the beadle of the Company of Surgeons in St Bartholomew's Hospital. The college had hired a house in Cock Lane for the dissection. Sir William Blizard, attired in court dress, received the body from the hangman and 'made a small cut with a scalpel over the breast bone and bowed to the executioner. This was the formal recognition of the purpose for which the body had been delivered.' After a full dissection Bellingham's bones were boiled clean and prepared for future use by anatomical students. Bellingham's head disappeared a few years later and was only rediscovered in a box in the basement of the medical school. They had no problem identifying it, a helpful doctor had carefully written 'Bellingham' in ink across the forehead.

THE 'INJURED QUEEN OF ENGLAND'

Scarcely was the honeymoon over of the Prince of Wales (later George IV) and his bride, Caroline, daughter of the Duke of Brunswick before rumours began to circulate of serious arguments between the two. Scandalously at the end of a twelvemonth a formal and lasting separation took place. Stories soon came out about her 'filthy personal habits' and it was said Caroline was 'a woman of such coarseness of mind, and such vulgarity of tastes as would have disgusted many men of less refinement than the prince.' In later years she kindly adopted the child of one of the Deptford dockyard labourers, a kindly act twisted by malicious gossip and more rumours of infidelity and even bastardy that were checked by a Royal Commission that finally cleared her of any wrongdoing. The Princess of Wales quitted England in 1814 and resided mostly in Italy as her estranged husband carried on his debauched playboy lifestyle back home. She only returned for the coronation of her consort in August 1821 but she was refused admission to Westminster Abbey. Already a sick woman it was the 'vexation' after this final snub that many attributed her death just a few days later. Queen Caroline's remains were removed from Brandenburgh House on 14 August 1841 for what was planned by the palace authorities to be a discreet journey away from the City to Harwich for a boat and burial on the continent. Despite torrential rain a mob gathered at Hammersmith and demanded to be allowed to pay their respects, a phenomena that was echoed across London. Roads were blocked at Kensington, compelling the cortège to the City. At Kensington Gore Sir R. Baker head of the police force with a detachment of Life Guards attempted, in vain to get passage through the park gates, the crowd stayed firm shouting 'To the city – to the city.' At Hyde Park Corner the gates were also barricaded up so the cortège diverted up Park Lane, met with more obstructions it had to turn around, soldiers had cleared the gates and the procession then moved through Hyde Park. On reaching Cumberland Gate this was also found closed and a furious exchange broke out between soldier escorts and the mob. A park wall collapsed from the pressure of the mob and a number of insurgents began hurling stones from the broken walls at the troops. Many soldiers were injured and a resort to firearms was unavoidable. Two rioters were killed and several wounded. After clearing more obstructions and facing more mobs near Edgware and Tottenham Court Road they processed down Drury Lane through the Strand and the City. So resolute was the popular determination to compel the procession to traverse the city, that every street that could have provided a detour out, including Holborn, was blocked up and rendered impassable. Once out of London via Chelmsford and Colchester thence to Harwich the body of Queen Caroline was finally laid to rest in Brunswick at the ducal vault within the cathedral on the 25th. The plate desired for her coffin was also removed after objection by the British authorities – 'Here lies Caroline of Brunswick, the injured Queen of England.'

TURN AGAIN DICK WHITTINGTON

According to Stow, Richard 'Dick' Whittington, the hero of pantomime stories and Lord Mayor of London on four occasions has been buried almost as many times in the church of St Michael, Paternoster Row. The first time he was buried by his executors with due ceremony under a fine monument. During the reign of Edward VI the parson of St Michael's believed some great riches to be buried with the dead Mayor. The monument was moved and the grave opened, no treasure was found but the 'leaden sheet' Whittington had been wrapped in was removed and sold (possibly

to help pay for the replacement of the monument after no treasure was found) and Dick was laid to rest again. During the reign of Queen Mary, the story of the grasping actions of the old parson had not been forgotten so the parishioners clubbed together and paid for the monument to be removed again. Dick's body disinterred, he was again 'lapped in lead,' buried again with due formality and his monument, or one similar, replaced over the grave. Rest in Peace, Dick Whittington.

Richard Whittington and his cat.

KINGS OF BODYSNATCHING

London's most notorious resurrectionists or 'burkers' (named so after the notorious Scottish bodysnatchers Burke and Hare) operated out of no. 3 Nova Scotia Gardens, Bethnal Green in the early 1830s. John Bishop had worked with other resurrectionist gangs but set out in business on his own with his scam of disguising himself as a journeyman carpenter complete with his basket of tools. Keeping his ear to the ground he would identify lodging houses where a family had recently suffered a death. Taking rooms there he would soon identify where the body lay awaiting burial and then when all in the house were asleep he would make off with the body and sell it to the surgeons. He was soon joined by Thomas Head (alias Williams) and they carried off many a body from grave and house in mourning in the twilight hours but it seemed a little too much like hard work and rather like their notorious counterparts Burke and Hare from North of the border Head and Bishop began to acquire really fresh bodies by murdering transient and dispossessed people from the streets of London. Persuading the unsuspecting and vulnerable to join them for a drink liberally mixed with laudanum they removed their drugged victims to the back garden of their house at Nova Scotia Gardens and drowned them in a static water butt buried in the back garden. Immersed head first into this watery barrel of death Bishop and Head rarely had any trouble from their victims and all the burkers had to do was wait for all the movement and bubbles to stop and they had a body ready for sale. But of course they wanted to maximise their profit and regularly removed the long hair of female victims to sell to wig makers and worked the teeth out of the gums with a bradawl to sell to dentists for dentures.

They were joined later by James May, the man who was undoubtedly the brains of the outfit. The illegitimate son of a barrister and a laundress May, known on the street as 'Blaze Eye Jack' he was a keen negotiator and got better prices for the bodies but he was less discreet than his compatriots and prone to drinking and occasional outbursts of violence. One body led to their downfall. The posture of the body with its left arm raised over the head and bent with fist clenched did not imply the body had enjoyed a natural end, the teeth had been ripped particularly roughly from the jaws and by the time it had been hawked around a couple of hospitals some of the ribs were broken. William Hill the surgeons's porter from King's College dissecting rooms between Lincoln's Inn Fields and Clare Market was not keen but probably would have taken the body in if May had not argued so arrogantly about the price, it was not helped that he was worse for drink, and it was hard to reason with 'Blaze Eye Jack' with a few drinks in him. Hill spoke to his, Mr Partridge the Surgeon, who came to inspect the body for himself. His suspicions aroused he gave the pretence of going to get the money to buy the body but in fact he sent for the Bow Street Runners. Bishop didn't put up much of a fight but Jack flew into a rage and was eventually bundled into custody with his smock pulled over his head.

A search of 3 Nova Scotia Gardens and their out buildings soon revealed damning evidence of clothes, a woman's scalp and pieces of flesh. When brought to trial at the Old Bailey on 2 December 1831 the trial lasted just one day, the judge taking the lion's share of the proceeding with his summing up which last some three hours. The jury took just twenty minutes to find Bishop, Head and May guilty. Only May protested he was unjustly sentenced, as he was just the negotiator. In their condemned cells Bishop and Head had the decency to exonerate May and he was saved from the gallows and commuted to imprisonment where he died within the year

John Bishop

Thomas Head alias Williams   James May

Bishop, Head and May: the Bethnal Green bodysnatchers.

on a prison hulk. Both Bishop and Head paid the ultimate penalty with the Newgate noose around their necks before the vast crowd burst through the barriers trampling two men and a woman to death, and many more were seriously injured. Both Bishop and Head had made confessions before they died but one claim by Bishop remains a chilling thought, or was it perhaps bravado that led him to admit he had trafficked nearly 1,000 bodies during his career as a bodysnatcher?

THE FEMALE BURKER

Mrs Caroline Walsh was a tall and sturdy woman who, despite being in her eighties, earned her way selling tapes and threads from a basket around the streets of the East End. She kept in good health and was regularly visited by her married grandaughter, Ann Butin. In August 1831 Mrs Walsh was persuaded by her friend Eliza Cook (real name Elizabeth Ross, she had only assumed the name of the man she lived with) to go and live with her in the garret she shared with her husband and school-age son at Goodman's Yard, Whitechapel. Ann tried to dissuade her grandmother from this but on the 19 August the old lady had made up her mind and making her bed into a bundle, carried it and her few worldly goods to Goodman's Yard. When Ann made a visit to the garret shortly after, Eliza Cook told Mrs Walsh her grandmother had 'just left,' she did however notice the bundle containing her grandmothers night gown and cap, small mattress and bedding in the room. After a number of visits to the Cook's with no sign of her grandmother, Ann's concerns were raised; after checking at local poor-houses and hospital, all to no avail, she reported her concerns to the police.

Investigations revealed William Austin, a pawnbroker, had received a gown in the name of Welsh on 20 August, the Cooks were also seen by several witnesses offering articles of clothing identified as those belonging to Mrs Walsh at the nearby Rag-fair. Eliza Cook had also been seen carrying Mrs Walsh's distinctive basket from which she had sold her threads. The Cooks moved shortly afterwards to White Horse Court but the stalwart Mrs Butin found them and took Lea, the investigating officer from Lambeth Street to indentify and question Mrs Cook. When asked directly what she had done with Mrs Walsh, Cook replied 'If I have done anything with her, God burn my soul in hell's flames.' Edward 'Ned' Cook was later arrested from his place of employment at a tea warehouse on St Katherine's Dock, their son was also apprehended and the three confined in separate cells.

Young Edward cracked first and gave his statement, his parents both denied the story as lies but nonetheless the boy gave evidence against his parents in open court. He attended the Aldgate Charity School and having returned from school at about 5 p.m. on the 19 August he saw Mrs Walsh in their room drinking with his parents. The old lady laid on the bed and went to sleep, about half and hour later he 'saw his mother go towards the old woman and clap her hand on her mouth, and keep it there, perhaps half an hour. She put the other arm somewhere about the chest. Witness observed the woman's eyes rolling . . . he never saw the old woman speak or move after.' His father was also in the room, opened the window and stayed there looking out until the deed was apparently done. He then sat with Eliza by the bed for about a half hour until Eliza carried the old woman and down to the cellar 'like a baby in her arms.' The boy went to look in the cellar in the morning and saw a sack under the stairs with part of the head showing and some hair hanging out of the top. At 11 p.m. he saw his mother from their garret window, she was carrying a large sack across Goodman's Fields into the Minories. His mother later told him she was taking the body to the London Hospital.

The fate of the body of the old Mrs Walsh was never discovered but the damning evidence convinced the jury who after retiring for thirty minutes found Eliza Cook guilty of murder. Her husband was acquitted of murder but faced charges of accessory after the fact. Sentence of death was passed on Eliza and she was hanged in front of Newgate Prison on 9 January 1832, she was thirty-eight.

PRACTICAL USES FOR DEAD BODIES?

The eminent philosopher Jeremy Bentham had spent years contemplating the use of dead bodies for the good of society rather than simply burying them. When he died in June 1832 Bentham was preparing a pamphlet entitled *Auto-Icon; or Farther Uses of the Dead to the Living*. In the paper Bentham suggested people could be preserved to become their own memorials, exhibited in suitable places in family homes or varnished for protection against the elements in gardens to the extent 'if a country gentlemen had rows of trees leading to his dwelling, the Auto-Icons of his family might alternate with the trees.' Even the smallest house could have its Auto-Icons with just preserved heads exhibited in specially designed cabinets. Although Bentham's ideas did not catch on, his last wishes were carried out and his body was eventually placed on display in University College (the university he helped to found) in his own clothes with a few of his favourite objects although his head had been replaced with a fine wax likeness. His actual head was found wrapped in a tarred cloth and hidden within his rib cage in 1898. Attempts to preserve his real head had apparently failed and he soon appeared to look horrifyingly so like one of the undead with his face dark, leathery and decomposed. For some time the head was placed between the feet of the great man, with the glass eyes he chose in life for the icon, staring back out at all who passed.

A LONG WAY FROM HOME

In January 1835 Chief Little Boar and his entourage came to London for land negotiations. The English climate and filth of London did not agree with these noble outdoor living people of the Michigan tribe and two of their number went into rapid decline. Little Boar's squaw, twenty-six-year-old Diving Mouse succumbed first and was followed a few days later by a young Indian brave of similar age named Thunder and Lightning. Their funerals were conducted with great ceremony at St John's churchyard on the Waterloo Road. Each were baptised before burial in Christian ground but still the rites of the Indians were observed with elaborate shrouds, laid over their bodies that were dressed in full regalia completed with laurel leaves. Diving Mouse was also given a bouquet, her cheeks painted red and a splendid Indian shawl thrown over all with a small totem pole erected over her grave.

JIMMY GARLICK

In 1839 a group of workmen carrying out excavations under than chancel of the Church of St James, Garlickhythe in Upper Thames Street were shocked to discover the incredibly well preserved body of a man who had clearly been interred there centuries before. There was no clue as to who he was but it has been suggested he could well have been one of the six early Lord Mayors of London buried in St James's or even that of Richard Rothing the man who had built the original church on the site in 1326. For want of a positive identification the body was popularly known as 'Jimmy Garlick' and was preserved in a glass fronted coffin in the vestibule of the church with the old momento mori legend 'Stop stranger, stop as you pass by. As you are now, so once was I. As I am now, you soon will be, so pray prepare to follow me' displayed at his feet.

THE HEAD OF THE DUKE OF SUFFOLK

In 1849 a well-preserved head was found in the vaults of Holy Trinity Church which had been built on the site of the old Grey family chapel. Assessed by Dr Mouat, the head was, he concluded; 'belonging to a man past the prime of life, and that the head was removed by rapid decapitation during life admits no doubt. A large gaping gash, which had not divided the subcutaneous structures, shows that the first stroke of the axe was misdirected . . . The reaction of the skin, the violent convulsive action of the muscles, and the formation of a cup-like cavity with the body of the spinal bone at the base, prove that the severance was effected during life, and in cold weather.' Sir George Younghusband in *Tower of London* expanded; 'There was no shrinkage of the face, the eyes are wide open, and the eyeballs and pupils perfectly preserved, though of parchment colour. The skin all over is of the same yellowish hue, When first found, the hair of the head and beard were still on, but owing to its very brittle state and from being handled by several people, these broke off . . .' Examined by Sir George Scharf, Keeper of the National Portrait Gallery it was confirmed the features of the head corresponded to those in contemporary portraits of Henry Grey, Duke of Suffolk, who had been executed on Tower Hill eleven days after the execution of his daughter, the attempted usurper of the throne, Lady Jane Grey. It took two blows of the axe to decapitate the Duke on the cold morning of 20 February 1554.

DIVIDE AND BEQUEATH

The Victorian author, Harriet Martineau (1802–76) had suffered most of her life with deafness and ill-health. Having time to contemplate her fate, her will was very specific in respect of what should become of her mortal remains 'It is my desire from an interest in the progress of scientific investigation that my skull should be given to Henry George Atkinson of Upper Gloucester Place in London and also my brain if my death should take place within such distance of the said Henry George Atkinson's then present abode as to enable him to have it for the purposes of scientific observation.'

A SNACK FOR DEATH

During the reign of George IV (1820–30) the King and Queen of the Sandwich Islands paid a visit to London and stayed at Osborne's Hotel in John Street. They excited much curiosity and even a comic song was written in their honour. A few years later they both died of smallpox, upon which Theodore Hook produced the epigram 'one day Death, being hungry, called for "two sandwiches".'

THE LONDON NECROPOLIS

By the mid-nineteenth century the churchyards of London were many feet deep with centuries of burials. Increasing concerns and official enquiries into the health of the capital led to the creation of The London Necropolis and National Mausoleum

Another recipient of a one-way ticket to the London Necropolis.

Company, established by Act of Parliament in 1852. Two thousand acres of common land at Woking were purchased from Lord Onslow and laid out as Brookwood cemetery. The proud boast was the Necropolis was that it was 'large enough to contain all of London's dead for ever.' When Brookwood opened in 1854 it was the largest cemetery in the world. Because it was situated twenty-five miles outside of the city there was a direct rail link to this cemetery, The Necropolis Light Railway, with a private terminus near Waterloo station. At the cemetery there were two stations one for the nonconformist sections, the other for Anglicans. Class distinctions were also observed in death, and three classes of ticket and First, Second and Third, were available for both passengers and the dearly departed in their casket, although coffin tickets were only sold as singles.

DEATH AND THE MAIDEN . . . AND A BOOK OF POEMS

Elizabeth Rossetti, wife of Dante Gabriel Rossetti poet, painter and one of the founder members of the Pre-Raphaelite Brotherhood died from a overdose of laudanum in 1862. Overcome with grief for his darling wife, Rosetti buried her with the manuscript and sole copy of the poems he had written to her over the years, nestling it between her cheek and hair. In 1869 Rosetti regretted his emotional gesture and had her exhumed and the book removed from the wooden coffin, along with a long lock of her famous red-gold hair. After disinfection and cleaning the manuscript, entitled *Poems* was published in 1870.

YOU'LL NEVER GUESS WHAT I FOUND IN THE CELLAR . . .

On 9 May 1879 errand boy, William Strohman, sent to clear out the cellar of the Bastendorff residence in Euston Square discovers the decomposing body of a woman wrapped in cloth with a rope tied round her neck. The body was identified by Edmund Hacker who stated it was his unmarried sister Matilda, an eccentric woman who had been missing for some months. The previous occupant of the Euston Square residence, who had left without giving notice about six months previously, was a Miss Uish. Inquiries revealed Miss Uish's servant, Hannah Dobbs, was thought to be in possession of some of Miss Hacker's trinkets. Dobbs was traced, arrested and tried but was not convicted of any crime. She wrote a book on the affair attacking her former master, who, after brining an action for libel, was convicted of perjury. The murder of Miss Hacker and quite where Miss Uish disappeared to remain unsolved.

THE HARLEY STREET BARREL BODY MYSTERY

On 3 June 1880 a body was discovered crammed into an American barrel and covered in chloride of lime (no doubt in the mistaken belief this chemical would hasten decomposition) in the cellar of 139 Harley Street, London, the home of Jacob Quixona Henriques. Mr Henriques had lived at his Harley Street address for over 20 years and was astonished by the discovery and despite evidence presented by the three butlers he had engaged over the years no further light could be shed on how the barrel got there, how long it had been there or its occupant. The body discovered was that of a woman about forty years old, she was almost naked except for the remains of stockings and garters on her legs, the hair appeared to have been cut off. Dr Pepper of St Mary's Hospital stated the cause of death had been a stabbed in the chest 'by such as a table knife.' A verdict of murder by person or persons unknown was recorded. The mystery remains unsolved to this day.

HEARD THE ONE ABOUT THE BUSINESSMAN, THE ACTRESS AND THE DISMEMBERED MISTRESS?

On 11 August 1875 the dismembered body of a woman, wrapped in two parcels of American cloth was discovered in a hansom cab with an actress and respectable local businessman. The cab was occupied by pretty Whitechapel Pavilion chorus girl Violet Dash who had been offered a ride by philanthropic local businessman Henry Wainwright.

The cab was stopped in Borough High Street by a police officer who had been alerted by Alfred Stokes, a Wainwright employee, who had suspicions about the parcels when Wainwright had picked them up from his Vine Court warehouse. Offered £100 to just go away the policeman persisted to know what was in the parcels – the dismembered body of a woman was soon revealed and Miss Dash and Wainwright were taken into custody. Miss Dash was soon found to have no connection with the horrific discovery and was released but Wainwright was detained 'for further questioning.' Wainwright was seen by many as a respectable man, churchwarden, husband and father of four children. Enquiries soon revealed he had another family living between his home and brush making warehouse. Here he lived with Harriet Lane and their two children– as Mr and Mrs King.

Encountering financial difficulties he had to cut Harriet's allowance and move her to cheaper accommodation and sent the children to say with friends. Harriet went to the warehouse to complain but this became a row and Wainwright shot and battered her to death. Hiding the body down the drain in the warehouse, bankruptcy and the imminent sale of the warehouse forced it to be moved. Wainwright's brother Thomas assisted with the dismemberment but despite anxiously puffing away on a big cigar to cover the smell, Alfred Stokes, one of Wainwright's warehousemen, was suspicious about the packages and raised the alarm.

Wainwright's brother was given seven years hard labour for his complicity whereas Wainwright himself went to the gallows on 21 December. The case was a public sensation, over eighty 'guests' were invited to the behind doors execution at Newgate. A nasty piece to the end Wainwright discarded his cigar as he approached the gallows and called to those assembled 'Come to see a man die, have you, you curs?'

THE BEST POTS OF DRIPPING IN LONDON

Widow Mrs Julia Martha Thomas was known for her reputation as a tartar towards her servants and could never keep staff long but she certainly never expected to encounter a servant like Kate Webster. Webster was an Irish conwoman who took up a position as cook and general servant at Mrs Thomas's residence of 2 Mayfield Park Villas, Park Road, Richmond in January 1879. Thomas Although Webster was initially glad of honest work, or perhaps thought about working a long game scam the workload was heavy and her work was criticised by the mistress. Little more than a month later in the February, Webster was given notice to quit. Was it frustration and anger that after all the hard work she would not be able to rip off 'the black widow' or was it an argument gone bad which led to a fatal exchange between Webster and widow Thomas?

From the early hours one February morning washing and brushing were heard coming from the villa, a full complement of washing was hung out, all seemed normal except the unusual smell from something cooking in the kitchen. On 5 March a trunk full of human flesh was washed up by the Thames, a human foot was found in a dung hill and when Webster started appearing in and selling some of Mrs Thomas's clothes, effects and even her false teeth, stern questions about where Mrs Thomas was began to be asked. Webster fled to Killanne but was soon traced, brought to trial and found guilty of the foul murder. The Villa abounded with clues, poor Mrs Thomas had been felled with a blow from an axe, cut up, boiled and burnt on the kitchen and copper grates. Found guilty of the murder, Webster was executed at Wandsworth On 29 July 1879. The gentlefolks of London no doubt had a little shiver when reading this case but I wonder how those who had bought the gallipots of richly veined meat dripping hawked by Webster felt when they heard how she had dealt with her boss?

SHE'LL TELL YOU YOUR FORTUNE

The *East London Observer* in November 1888 carried an account of Sarah Tanner 'a middle aged woman' of Rowsell Street, St Paul's Road, Mile End Old Town who was brought before the magistrates on charges of obtaining money by pretending to tell persons their fortunes at 6*d* at time. The police were notified and upon apprehension Tanner immediately recanted and swore she would never do it again. From her abode police recovered a leaf torn from Napoleon's *Book of Fate* and two packs of cards. Tanner was sent down for one month's imprisonment with hard labour.

THE FINAL REST OF CHIEF LONG WOLF

On 13 June 1892 Sioux Indian Chief Long Wolf (aged fifty-nine) was buried at Brompton Cemetery. This great Indian Chief had died of bronchial pneumonia while appearing with Buffalo Bill's Wild West Show when appearing at Earl's Court during its European tour. Long Wolf's dying wish was to be returned home to native soil for burial but his wife feared he would be put over the side of the ship and buried at sea so Buffalo Bill Cody saw to it a respectful burial was made and a fine stone memorial was set up. The story did not end there.

Over 100 years later Elizabeth Knight, a Worcestershire housewife, was so moved to read Long Wolf's grave was laying overgrown and forgotten she set about tracing his living family and raising the money to have the great chief returned home. With due ceremony and reverence Long Wolf was exhumed and returned home for interment at the Oglala Sioux burial ground at the Pine Ridge Reservation in September 1997.

SIGN HERE AND WE ASSURE YOU ARE DEAD

In 1896 Arthur Lovell, an opportunist quack doctor established The London Society for the Prevention of Premature Burial. The service offered was a meticulous inspection of the declared dead body by their 'specially trained doctors' before funeral procedures were instigated. Those who signed up with the scheme were assured their wishes would be complied with because if the next of kin failed to notify the society or comply with the stringent terms laid out in the binding contract the entire estate of the deceased was forfeited to society.

RESTING IN PEACE OF MIND

In 1896 John Wilmer of Stoke Newington was so concerned about premature burial he arranged to have his remains interred in the garden of his house on Church Street. In his hand was a switch with a cable that led to an alarm bell in the house. In case of a system failure he even stipulated an examination of the equipment was to be carried out . . . annually!

Bunhill Fields in the nineteenth century.

SELECT BIBLIOGRAPHY

BOOKS

Adam, H.L., *Murder by Persons Unknown* (London, 1931)

'Aleph', *London Scenes and London People* (London, 1863)

——., *The Old City and its Highways and Byways* (London, 1865)

Andrews, William, *Bygone Punishments* (London, 1899)

Atholl, Justin, *Shadow of the Gallows*, (London, 1954)

——., *The Reluctant Hangman*, (London, 1956)

Ball, J. Moores, *Sack-'Em-Up-Men: The Story of the Resurrectionists* (London, 1928)

Barker, Felix & Silvester-Carr, Denise, *The Black Plaque Guide to London* (London, 1987)

Berry, James, *My Experiences as an Executioner*, (London, 1892)

Booth, Charles, *Life and Labour of the People of London* (London, 1903)

Brooks, J. A., *Ghosts of London* (Norwich, 1982)

Buckland, Frank, *Curiosities of Natural History* (London, 1866)

Burford, E.J. & Shulman, Sandra, *Of Bridles and Burnings: The Punishment of Women* (London, 1992)

——. & Wotton, Joy, *Private Vices – Public Virtues* (London, 1995)

Butler, Ivan, *Murderers' London* (London, 1973)

Chambers, R., *The Book of Days* (London, 1879)

Chesney, Kellow, *The Victorian Underworld* (Newton Abbot, 1971)

Culbertson, Judi & Randall, Tom, *Permanent Londoners* (London, 1991)

Curl, James Stevens, *The Victorian Celebration of Death* (Stroud, 2000)

Davenport-Hines & Gothic, Richard, *Four Hundred Years of Excess, Horror, Evil and Ruin*, (New York, 1999)

Egan, Pierce, *Life In London, Or the Day and Night Scenes of Jerry Hawthorn, Esq., and His Elegant Friend Cornithian Tom, Accompanied by Bob Logic, The Oxonian, in Their Rambles and Sprees Through the Metropolis* (London, 1821)

Engel, Howard, *Lord High Executioner* (London, 1997)

Evans, Hilary & Mary, *Hero on a Stolen Horse* (London, 1977)

Evans, Stewart P., *Executioner: The Chronicles of James Berry Victorian Hangman* (Stroud, 2004)

—— & Skinner, Keith, *Jack the Ripper – Letters from Hell* (Stroud, 2001)

Fielding, Steve, *The Hangman's Record (vol. I 1868–1899)* (Beckenham, 1994)

Frayling, Christopher, *Nightmare: The Birth of Horror* (London, 1996)

Gordon, Richard, *Ailments Through the Ages* (London, 1998)

Gosling, Ex-Det. Supt. John & Warner, Douglas, *The Shame of a City: An Inquiry into the Vice of London* (London, 1960)

Griffiths, Major Arthur, *Mysteries of Police and Crime* (London, 1920)

Haining, Peter, *Ghosts: The Illustrated History* (London, 1987)

——, *The Legend and Bizarre Crimes of Spring Heeled Jack* (London, 1977)

Hallam, Jack, *Ghosts of London* (London, 1975)

Hare, Augustus, *Walks in London* (London, 1901)

Harper, Charles G., *Highwaymen of England* (London, 1908)

Hooper, E. Eden, *History of Newgate and the Old Bailey: and a Survey of The Fleet and Other Old London Jails* (London, 1935)

Hopkins, R. Thurston, *Life and Death at the Old Bailey* (London, 1935)

Jackson,William, *The New and Complete Newgate Calendar or Malefactor's Universal Register* (London, 1818)

Lock, Joan, *Dreadful Deeds and Awful Murders: Scotland Yard's First Detectives 1829–1878* (Taunton, 1990)

——, *Tales From Bow Street* (London, 1982)

London, Jack, *The People of the Abyss* (London, 1903)

Low, Donald A., *The Regency Underworld*, (Stroud, 1999)

Mayhew, Henry, *London Labour and the London Poor* (London, 1851–62)

Mayhew, Henry and Binny, John, *The Criminal Prisons of London and Scenes of Prison Life* (London, 1862)

Meller, Hugh, *London Cemeteries* (Aldershot, 1999)

O'Donnell, Bernard, *The Old Bailey and its Trials* (London, 1950)

O' London, John (ed.), *London Stories* (London, 1911)

Pelham, Camden (ed.), *Chronicles of Crime* (London, 1886)

Pennant, Thomas, *Some Account of London* (London, 1791)

Quennell, Peter (ed.), *London's Underworld* (London, 1959)

Richardson, Ruth, *Death, Dissection and the Destitute* (London, 1988)

Rubenhold, Hallie, *Harris's List of Covent Garden Ladies: Sex in the City in Georgian Britain* (Stroud, 2005)

Rumbelow, Donald, *I Spy Blue: The Police and Crime in the City of London from Elizabeth I to Victoria* (London, 1971)

——, *The Triple Tree* (London, 1982)

Scott, George Ryley, *Ladies of Vice* (London, 1968)

Simons, G.L., *The Illustrated Book of Sexual Records* (London, 1982)

Sims, George R., *Living London: Its Work & Its Play, Its Humour & Its Pathos, Its Sights & Its Scenes* (London, 1903)

Storey, Neil R., *Jack the Ripper's London* (Stroud, 2004)

Stow, John, *Survey of London* (London, 1598)

Thornbury, Walter, *Haunted London* (London, 1880)

Timbs, John, *The Romance of London* (London, 1874)

Tobias, J.J., *Crime and Industrial Society in the 19th Century* (London, 1967)

Trench, Richard & Millman, Ellis, *London Under London* (London, 1985)

Walford, Edward, *Old and New London* (London, 1897–8)

Ward, Ned, *The London Spy* (London, 1927)

Weintraub, Ben & Hibbert, Christopher (eds), *The London Encyclopaedia* (London, 1983)

Wilkins, Robert, *The Fireside Book of Death* (London, 1990)

Wood, Clive & Suitters, Beryl, *The Fight for Acceptance: A History of Contraception* (Aylesbury, 1970)

NEWSPAPERS & PERIODICALS

Annual Register
Black & White Budget
Family Tree Magazine
Famous Crimes
Fraser's Magazine
Harmsworth Magazine
Punch, or the London Charivari
The Gentleman's Magazine
The Graphic
The Illuminated Magazine
The Illustrated London News
The Illustrated Police News
The Morning Chronicle
The Mirror
The Observer
The Penny Illustrated Paper
The Police Gazette
The Public Advertiser
The Quiver
The Sphere
The St James's Chronicle
The Strand Magazine
The Times

ACKNOWLEDGEMENTS

In my travels for this book it has been proved, yet again, that you can meet some of the nicest people when researching the grimmest tales. There are sadly too many to mention all by name but I wish to record specific thanks to: Stewart P. Evans, James Nice, Dr Stephen Cherry, Gordon Taylor, Archivist at the Salvation Army International Heritage Centre, the National Archives, the Museum of London, University of East Anglia Library, the National Maritime Museum, Greenwich, the London Dungeon, the Galleries of Justice, Nottingham, the Brookwood Cemetery Society, Peter Watson and Helen Tovey at *Family Tree Magazine*, Peter Cox, Robert 'Bookman' Wright, Elaine Abel, Clifford Elmer, Les Bolland, my wonderful students for their opinions and thoughts and the private police memorabilia and archive collections I have been given privileged access to.

Finally, but by no means least, I thank my family, especially my darling Molly and son Lawrence for their continuing love, support and interest in my research.

INDEX